BISON
BOOKS

D0882333

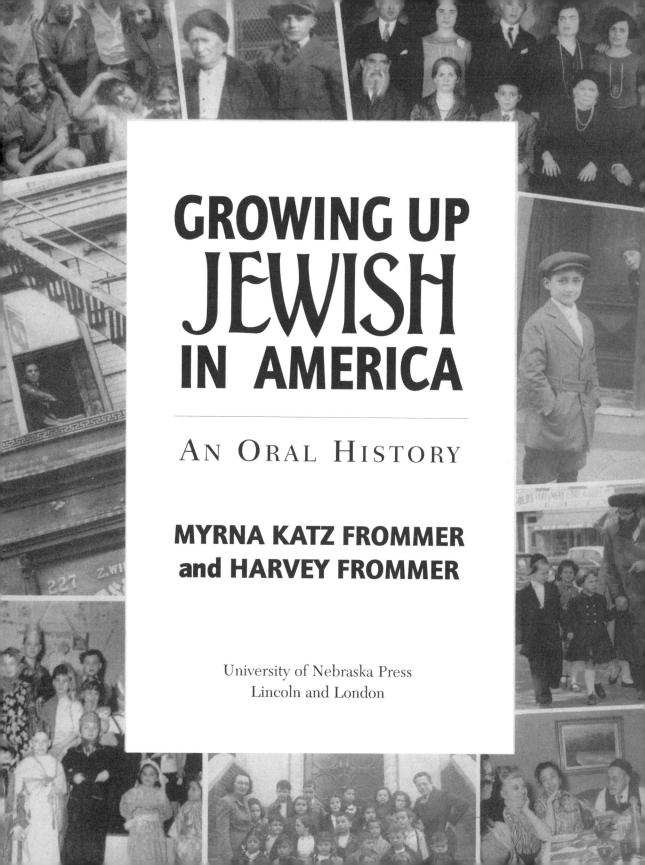

GROWING UP
JEWISH
IN AMERICA

AN ORAL HISTORY

MYRNA KATZ FROMMER
and HARVEY FROMMER

University of Nebraska Press
Lincoln and London

∞

First Bison Books printing: 1999
Most recent printing indicated by the last digit below:
10   9   8   7   6   5   4   3   2   1

Library of Congress Cataloging-in-Publication Data
Growing up Jewish in America: an oral history / [edited by] Myrna Katz Frommer and Harvey
Frommer.
p.   cm.
Originally published: 1st ed. New York: Harcourt Brace, c1995.
Includes bibliographical references and index.
ISBN 0-8032-6900-5 (pbk.: alk. paper)
1. Jewish children—United States Biography.   2. Jews—United States—Social conditions.
3. Judaism—United States.   4. Oral history.   5. United States—Ethnic relations.
I. Frommer, Myrna.   II. Frommer, Harvey.
[E184.37.A14   1999]
973′.04924′00922—dc21
[B]
99-34630   CIP

To our children:
Jennifer, Freddy, and Ian,
who—like their parents—were fortunate enough
to grow up Jewish in America.

CONTENTS

INTRODUCTION

We have cast our nets wide. Our subject is Jewish childhood across America over the course of this century. Some of its themes are common to most growing-up-in-America sagas: emigration at a point in the family's history and the accompanying process of settling in, learning a new language, surrendering old ways in the face of the new; and then movement into the larger culture, making a place for oneself while holding on to an ethnic identity. But other themes are unique to the Jewish-American experience, just as the four-thousand-year-old religion/culture/civilization that is Judaism is unique to history.

This is a work of memory, personal and particular. Nevertheless it touches on the monumental movements and events of the twentieth century, both in America and around the world: the Russian Revolution and the lure of left-wing politics, the Depression and two world wars, the tragedy of the Holocaust as encountered on this safe side of the Atlantic and the triumph of Israel, the civil rights movement, the counterculture rebellions, and postwar demographic changes.

At the same time, it lingers along the byways of intimate, intergenerational family life with its still-recalled but soon-to-be-forgotten European past. It dwells on the religion, constant in its cycles: the purity and sanctity of Shabbat preparations, the eager anticipation preceding the High Holy Days and Passover, the celebration of bar and bat mitzvah. It muses on the interaction with a gentile world: the anti-Semitism, both overt and implicit, but also the friendships and alliances with non-Jews that in a single generation erased centuries-old phobias of "the goyim" and made possible the move from the shtetl mentality to the vision of an open society.

Here are memories of how place stamped personality in landscapes as diverse as the tumultuous tenement neighborhood of the Lower East Side of Manhattan, the vital urban communities of Brooklyn and the Bronx, the scattered settlements in cities and towns across the nation, from Auburn, Maine, to Pueblo, Colorado; and the gilded suburban ghettos that girded old city neighborhoods whose names, such as Shaker Heights, so often incorporated the ascension they implied.

Here are accounts of what happened when energies pent up by centuries of repression were released in a free society, of how the leap from poverty to prosperity and from immigrant to American was accomplished. Here are expressions of the tension between the realms of the sacred and the profane, how the former provided stability and definition while the latter exerted a lure that was all but irresistible. And here are recollections of the compromises—which some saw as Faustian bargains—and the dilemmas: now that it was easy to be part of the whole, remaining apart from the whole had become the challenge.

Out of childhood memory comes Jewish-American twentieth-century life with all its vibrancy, complexity, and contradictions. There are the lox and bagels, the glitzy bar mitzvahs, the pungent Yiddish expressions spilling into American-English, the focused pursuit of "The American Dream," and also the tenacious idealism, the passion for scholarship, the elusive striving for *tikkun olam*—repair of the world.

There are people in this book whose ancestors fought in the Civil War. There are those who were born in Europe. They are as young as twenty-two and as old as ninety-nine. They are Orthodox, Conservative, Reform, non-aligned, assimilated; from affluent backgrounds and of working class origins. What all share is the singularity of their Jewishness, that and the contacts—be they powerful or peripheral, treasured or rejected, reinvented, revised or reformed—with the ethos, markers, and rituals of Jewish life that have joined the generations.

VOICES

Cal Abrams grew up in Philadelphia and Brooklyn. From 1949 to 1952, he was an outfielder for the Brooklyn Dodgers.

Artie Allen grew up in Montgomery, Alabama. He works in Jewish communal services in Wilmington, Delaware.

Marc Angel, rabbi of Congregation Shearith Israel—the Spanish and Portuguese synagogue in Manhattan—grew up in Seattle, Washington.

Manny Azenberg is a Broadway and off-Broadway theatrical producer who grew up in the Bronx.

Howard Baer is a businessman who grew up in Charleston, West Virginia.

Flora Berger is a retired teacher who was born in the Bronx and grew up in Brooklyn.

Mac Berger was born in St. Louis and spent most of his growing-up years in Schenectady, New York. He is a retired custom tailor.

Karl Bernstein grew up in Brooklyn. He is a former assistant principal.

Marnie Bernstein is the pseudonym of a writer who grew up in Brooklyn.

Henry Birnbrey, an attorney and accountant, grew up in Dortmund, Germany, and Atlanta, Georgia.

David Bisno is a retired ophthalmologist who grew up in St. Louis.

Sara Breibart grew up in Augusta, Georgia.

Sol Breibart is a local historian who has lived in Charleston, South Carolina, all his life.

Balfour Brickner, senior rabbi emeritus of the Stephen Wise Free Synagogue in Manhattan, grew up in Shaker Heights, Ohio.

Lucille Brody Noonan is a counselor for alcoholics in a veterans' hospital. She grew up in Brooklyn.

Arthur Cantor is a Broadway and off-Broadway theatrical producer who grew up in Dorchester, Massachusetts.

Marilyn Cohen is an artist who grew up in the Bronx and Queens.

Natalie Cohen Monteleone grew up in Baltimore. She is a flamenco dancer and law librarian.

Elliot Colchamiro, a professor at New York City Technical College, grew up in Brooklyn.

Dinah Crystal Kossoff, an office administrator, grew up in Duluth, Minnesota.

Is Crystal owns Crystal's International, a food emporium founded by his father. He grew up in Duluth.

Alicia Devora, *a costumer for theater and film, grew up in Miami and Los Angeles.*

Harriett Terry Drucker Rosin *grew up in Westminster, South Carolina, and Savannah, Georgia. Formerly a schoolteacher, she is now the office administrator of her husband's medical office in Jacksonville, Florida.*

Gail Eiseman Bernstein *is a teacher who grew up in Brooklyn.*

David Elcott, *program director for the National Jewish Center for Learning and Leadership, grew up in Los Angeles.*

Jason Freed *is the pseudonym of a journalist who grew up in Far Rockaway, New York, and on Long Island.*

Helen Fried Goldstein, *former president of Women's League of Conservative Judaism, grew up in Port Chester and Brooklyn, New York. She is a professor at Kingsborough Community College and the Jewish Theological Seminary.*

Addi Friedman *is a teacher, writer, and lecturer who grew up in Brooklyn and Manhattan.*

Morris Friedman *grew up in Brooklyn. He is rabbi of Temple Hillel of North Woodmere, New York, and past president of the New York Board of Rabbis.*

Ann Gold *is a marketing executive who grew up in Auburn, Maine.*

Marcia Lee Goldberg, *director of the performance department at MMB Music, Inc., grew up in St. Louis.*

Shalom Goldman *grew up in Hartford and Queens. He is a professor at Dartmouth College.*

Leonard Goldstein, *a retired rabbi and past vice president and dean of administration of the American College in Jerusalem, grew up in Trenton, New Jersey.*

Dorothy Gottsegen, *a longtime educator in the Boston area, grew up in Queens.*

Blu Greenberg *is a New York–based feminist Jewish writer and speaker. She grew up in Seattle.*

Irving (Yitz) Greenberg, *rabbi and teacher, is author of* The Jewish War *and president of the National Jewish Center for Learning and Leadership. He grew up in Brooklyn.*

Roger Harris, *a stamp dealer, grew up in upstate New York.*

Avrohom Hecht *is a member of the Rabbinical Board of Queens and works with Russian youth. He grew up in Burlington, Vermont, and Queens.*

Sidney Helfant, *who grew up in Brooklyn, is a professor at Kingsborough Community College.*

Herb Kalisman, *who has had a long career in publishing, grew up in Manhattan and the Bronx.*

Caroline Katz Mount, *director of Immigrant Services for UJA–Federation of Jewish Philanthropies of New York, grew up in Brooklyn.*

Linda Katz Ephraim, *a registered nurse, grew up in Quincy, Massachusetts.*

Marilyn Katz, *who grew up in New Haven, now makes her home in Jerusalem.*

Menachem Katz, *a retired businessman, grew up in Quincy and now lives in Jerusalem.*

Bel Kaufman, *a writer and lecturer, grew up in Russia and the Bronx. She is the granddaughter of Sholem Aleichem.*

Irv Kaze, *a radio talk show host and sports executive, spent most of his growing-up years in Jersey City, New Jersey.*

Morris Kerness, *a retired jack-of-all-trades, grew up in Duluth.*

Mary Klein, *a retired social worker, grew up in the Jewish Orphans' Home in Cleveland.*

Dan Kossoff *is a businessman who grew up in Duluth.*

Barbara Krause, *a high school librarian, grew up in Mitchell, South Dakota.*

Barbara Kreiger *is a writer who grew up in Shelton, Connecticut. She teaches at Dartmouth College.*

David Landau *is the pseudonym of a computer programmer of CD-ROMs at Sony Music Entertainment. He grew up in Far Rockaway and on Long Island.*

Mike Lecar, *an astrophysicist at the Harvard Smithsonian Center for Astrophysics and a lecturer at Harvard, grew up in Brooklyn.*

Robert Leiter, *news editor of* The Philadelphia Jewish Exponent, *grew up in Philadelphia.*

Alan Lelchuk *is a novelist and professor at Dartmouth College. He grew up in Brooklyn.*

Meyer Lesser *is a former auto parts executive and dismantler of businesses. He grew up "on the road."*

Susan Levin Schlechter, *a former English teacher and present teaching fellow at New York University, grew up in Birmingham.*

Al Lewis, *the television personality, grew up in upstate New York and Brooklyn.*

Mel Loewenstein, *the director of the Veiled Prophet Fair, grew up in St. Louis.*

Zipporah Marans *grew up in a variety of locales, including Raleigh and Savannah.*

Jacob Marcus *grew up in various towns in Pennsylvania and West Virginia. He is a highly esteemed figure in Reform Judaism and the oldest Reform rabbi in the United States.*

Miriam Mayers *grew up in Berwick, Louisiana.*

Doris Modell Tipograph, *the corporate archivist for Modell's Sporting Goods stores, grew up in Brooklyn.*

Daniel Musher, *grandson of the renowned theologian Mordecai Kaplan, grew up in New York City. He is a professor of medicine at the Baylor College of Medicine in Houston.*

Karol Musher *grew up in Laredo, Texas.*

Abraham Peck, *administrative director of the American Jewish Archives of the Hebrew Union College in Cincinnati, was born in a Detained Persons camp in Germany and grew up in Waterbury, Connecticut.*

Ruth Perlstein Marcus, *who grew up in Chicago, is managing editor of The Sentinel.*

Murray Polner, an author who grew up in Brooklyn, is editor of Shalom: The Jewish Peace Letter and coeditor of PS: The Intelligent Guide to Jewish Affairs.

Sam Popkin is a businessman who grew up in Toledo, Ohio.

Eric Portnoy is a designer who grew up in Barrington, Rhode Island.

Neil Postman, the media critic, author, and director of the Culture and Communications Program at New York University, grew up in Brooklyn.

Frank Rich is a columnist for The New York Times. He grew up in Washington, D.C.

Brenda Robinson Wolchok grew up in Savannah.

Alex Rosin is a gynecologist/obstetrician and an associate professor at the University of Florida Medical School. He grew up in Arcadia and Sarasota, Florida.

Jeff Rubin, editor of The B'nai B'rith International Jewish Monthly, grew up in the Dorchester-Mattapan area of Massachusetts and Randallstown, Maryland.

David Sager is a musician who grew up in Silver Springs, Maryland.

Irv Saposnik, the executive director of B'nai B'rith Hillel Foundation at the University of Wisconsin, grew up in Brooklyn.

Mitchell Serels is director of Sephardic Community Programs at Yeshiva University. He grew up in New York City.

Moe Skoler, a vice president at Prudential Securities, grew up in Quincy, Massachusetts.

Sylvia Skoler Portnoy, *the vice president of an employment agency, grew up in Quincy.*

Jim Sleeper, author and columnist at the <u>New York Daily News,</u> grew up in Springfield, Massachusetts.

Ansie Bernstein Sokoloff *grew up in Eldorado, Arkansas, and Cheyenne, Wyoming. Her entire adult life has been marked by active involvement in Jewish organizations and philanthropies, including the United Jewish Appeal and National Council of Jewish Women.*

Stephen Solender, executive vice president of the UJA–Federation of Jewish Philanthropies of New York, grew up in Cleveland, Ohio, and Mt. Vernon, New York.

Jeff Solomon grew up in New York City. He is the CEO of Program Services for the UJA–Federation of Jewish Philanthropies of New York.

Roz Starr, the celebrity sleuth, grew up in Brooklyn.

Marv Stein is a wholesale grocer who grew up and lives in Pueblo, Colorado.

Brooks Susman is rabbi of Temple Israel in Lawrence, New York. He grew up in the Squirrel Hill section of Pittsburgh.

Julie Sussman is the pseudonym of the director of CD-ROM production at Sony Music Entertainment. She grew up in Far Rockaway and on Long Island.

Nicki Tanner, an oral historian, directs the Oral History Project at UJA–Federation of Jewish Philanthropies of New York and is chair of the UJA–Federation Capital Development Fund. She grew up in Lake Forest, Illinois.

Phyllis Taylor works with people who have life-threatening diseases and is an active board member of Witness for Peace. She grew up on Long Island.

May Thaler Abrams grew up in Brooklyn. She is actively involved in Jewish philanthropies.

Norman Tipograph, a retired businessman, grew up in the Bronx and Brooklyn.

Leon Toubin is a businessman in Brenham, Texas, where he has lived all his life.

Max Wechsler is the pseudonym of a writer who grew up in Brooklyn.

Joshua Winer grew up in the suburbs of Boston. He is an artist specializing in architectural murals.

Robert Yaffe, who grew up in Omaha, works in Jewish communal services in Toledo.

May the children of the Stock of Abraham, who dwell in this land, continue to merit and enjoy the good will of the other inhabitants, while every one shall sit in safety under his own vine and fig-tree, and there shall be none to make them afraid.

—George Washington to the Jewish congregation,
Newport, Rhode Island, August 1790

Every place you go, act according to the custom of that place.

—Ladino proverb

PROLOGUE

Max Wechsler: Being Jewish was like belonging to another world. It was not explained. I did not understand. Still I knew I was connected to some-place and something else. It had a different time zone. In this world it was the 1900s; in that one it was the 5700s. Time began so much earlier for the Jews. How could that be? The months were different too; they kept changing so that holidays came out on different days each year. That was a calendar you couldn't depend on. Yet it made more sense. The new year ought to begin when the summer ended, when school started, when everything got going again.

We weren't at all religious, but I knew about all those holidays. There were so many of them, plugging into the ebb and flow of the year, and each had its own props: nuts, little candles, palm branches, apples, cakes, spinning tops, wooden groggers. At holiday times, I would wonder: Are Jews all over the world throwing their sins into the water, fasting, eating matzoh, lighting candles?

It was like a drill, like someone blew a whistle and all the kids started rolling nuts outside the synagogue. Things appeared and went. All of a sudden, cases of matzoh were stacked up in the stores. Where did they come from?

I only spoke English, but around me were other languages, a polyglot of strange words. There were German and Romanian, and then not one but two special Jewish languages. The Yiddish sounded familiar enough, but the Hebrew—again, from another world. And both languages had a weird alphabet with hardly any vowels, and you read them from right to left, and their books from back to front.

You were living here, but you were connected back to another country you never saw, one that every once in a while people would start talking about. There was a mishmash of memories, incomplete and unfinished. I never got the whole story. A name would come up. A detail would come out. And then it would get lost. Another world. Who were they? What did they look like? What were their names? What happened?

I would stare into candlelight—there were always candles burning: at my grandmother's house on Friday nights, in the *yahrtzeit* glasses—there were all these death anniversaries of people I had never met. But they didn't frighten me. In a strange way I found the candlelight comforting and also hypnotic, a possible path into that other world.

MRS. RACHAEL CRYSTAL.

ISH FAMILY
LLS STORY OF
AR HARDSHIPS

an Is Reunited With Wif
children After Anxious
ars of Separation.

uffering all the privations
nhabitants of Polish-Russia
subject since the beginning
in 1914, Mrs. Jacob Crys-

Part One

INTO
A GOOD
LAND

The Old Stories

We Were Yankee Jews

Down South

Crossing America

New York, New York

1
THE OLD STORIES

*"For the Lord thy God bringeth thee
into a good land . . . a land wherein thou
shalt eat bread without scarceness,
thou shalt not lack any thing in it . . ."*

—Deuteronomy VIII:7–9

Jacob Marcus: I was born March the fifth, 1896. When I was four years old, we moved to Homestead, a steel mill town on the outskirts of Pittsburgh beside the Monongahela River. There my father opened a store.

Homestead was a bifurcated town. The Jews all lived in one area, and the relationship among them was very good. Nearly everyone was Orthodox and Eastern European. *Brisses* and holidays were always a time for social gatherings. The kids loved going because there was always cake. At home we never had cake.

The millworkers were mostly foreigners, Poles and Slavs. They didn't like the Jews, who considered themselves a better class. Those millworkers put in twelve hours a day for a dollar a day. I'd see them waiting for the railroad trains to come into the mills. They'd stand alongside the tracks with long poles that they'd push into gondolas heaped high with coal. Pieces of coal would fall off, and that's how they'd gather their winter supply.

Homestead was run by Irish gangs, some of whom ended up in the penitentiary. We Jewish kids had our own gang. On Halloween nights, we used to take these big long poles and upset all the toilets in the backyards. Once we went for one, and a man was seated on it. He chased us, but fortunately he didn't catch us.

I associated with one boy whose folks were so impoverished they couldn't afford to buy soap. Around about six o'clock, when the steelworkers had washed up and were going in to eat, we'd run through the backyards and steal their soap.

In those days they had bakery wagons that came to your house and sold you bakery foods. I never had pie at home, so one day I appropriated one. The baker chased me home and made my mother pay the nickel for that huge pie.

All that was part of my picaresque life when I was a child. After the age of eight, I decided to be a respectable citizen, and my life as a criminal came to an end.

We went to public school till three or four o'clock and then to the Orthodox shul, where we learned to read Hebrew. The rabbi, who taught us our prayers and about the holidays, was also the *shochet*. Every once in a while our lesson would be interrupted by someone bringing in a chicken that had to be ritually slaughtered.

◀ *(top)* Girls from Bellefaire, formerly the Jewish Orphans' Home in Cleveland, Ohio, perform in a pageant. *(bottom left)* Turn-of-the-century father and daughter on the Lower East Side of Manhattan. *(bottom right)* View of the old Jewish Orphans' Home.

I had an older brother of blessed memory who didn't know any *chachmas*. He was silently praying the 18 Benedictines in shul. Another boy, trying to be funny, jabbed a pin into him. My brother flinched but finished his prayer. Then calmly, he walked over to the big iron stove where his ice skates rested, picked them up, and slashed the boy across the face. He almost sliced his nose off. My brother didn't like being disturbed in his prayers.

When I was about six or seven, I went with my parents on an excursion railroad train to visit relatives in Connellsville. It cost fifty cents for a ticket to travel maybe thirty or forty miles. I stuck my neck out the window of the train and a voice yelled: "Put your head back in, you goddamned Jew." That is my first recollection of anti-Semitism and my first awareness that Christians have a special radar.

We moved to Farmington, a village in the hills of West Virginia, where we were the only Jewish family. The nearest town with Jews was Fairmont, twelve miles away. Once a farmer from the boondocks up in the mountains came rolling in on his Springfield wagon—that's a wagon with a lot of good springs. He sat with his children in front of our store waiting patiently for my father to come out. Finally my father walked out the door, whereupon the farmer rose up from his seat on the wagon, pointed at my father, turned to his kids, and declared: "Thar he goes. Thar is the Jew."

The locals called our store "the Jew store." My father was courteous but treated them as inferiors. Not 1 percent of his business came from the townspeople, but they looked up to him nevertheless. Any Jew who had a small store in a village became the top person because the average person was so poverty stricken and untutored.

My father made his money from the coal miners who worked in the surrounding mines. Sometimes he'd get on his horse and go into the mines to collect the money that was due him. Sometimes when the Russian and Croatian miners got arrested for getting drunk and going after their wives with a hatchet, my father would act as interpreter for them.

My father wasn't strong, but he was used to being a boss. Once when a big husky miner made some crack about a Jew, my father leaned over and swatted him across the face. The guy shut up. He recognized authority.

Howard Baer: My father used to sell liquor up around the mining towns of West Virginia. Imagine a young German Jew selling drinks to the boys up where they killed somebody every Saturday night for sport. That was tough territory. By the time the state went dry in 1913, my father had accumulated an income of about twenty-five hundred dollars a year and never really worked any more.

My mother's father had come here from Germany around 1859. When he enlisted in the Union Army, the officer recording names said, "Hell boy, you're an American now. We don't like that name Solomon. We'll call you George, after the father of your country." And George he became, even unto his discharge papers. It was so recorded on the battle monument to the 23rd Ohio in Cleveland.

They put him into the Army of Western Virginia, which lay in the hills just above Charleston. When the war was over, they didn't send them home at fifteen cents a mile; they just said, "Boys, start walking." My grandfather looked down into the valley. There were one or two Jewish families there in Charleston who must have entertained the Jewish boys on Friday nights. That's where he decided to settle. He opened a harness shop and later on, when coal became big, transformed his shop into wholesale hardware and mining supplies.

I was born in Charleston, West Virginia, in 1902. It had a population of twenty-four thousand, of which about twelve hundred were Jews. We had an Orthodox synagogue and a Reform temple, where I got my first Jewish education. Charleston, the capital of West Virginia, was a lovely place. In my growing-up years, especially around the time of World War I, it was extremely prosperous. They called it the COG City: coal, oil, and gas.

We had a very good rabbi by the name of Israel Bettan. He came as a young unmarried man and very often was our guest for Sunday dinner. When I was thirteen years old, he suggested to my mother that since the schools in Charleston were not very good, she ought to think of a better place.

Taking the rabbi's advice, she contacted her relatives in Cincinnati, who suggested the Choate School in Wallingford, Connecticut, where one had gone years before.

We took the train up. At Choate I was introduced to the headmaster,

George St. John. He asked me to spell *necessary*, which I did. He asked me who was the second President of the United States. I was right on that too. He said, "Mrs. Baer, we'd be delighted to have Howard here. We're not looking for any geniuses. We just want normal boys to lead good lives."

My mother went home, and there I was. I was put in what they called the lower school, first and second form. I lived in a white New England house named Atwater House. Mrs. St. John—her name was Clara—would come down on Sunday nights and read to us from Walter Scott and others.

The school was so damn British. On Sunday mornings, all dressed up with stiff collars, we marched down to church. Every night after dinner we had prayers and study hall.

It wasn't exactly growing up Jewish. I was in my early teens—when you're more susceptible to religion. Still I don't think it hurt me or made me any less Jewish to be exposed to all this sort of thing. I didn't take any communion. I was conscious all the time that I was the only Jewish boy in the school. But no one ever made a point of it; I never had anybody call me a damn Jew there. I got a large dose of Episcopalianism, but I also got a hell of a lot of Latin and French.

My second year at Choate, I went back early in the fall for football practice. My father came to visit me. The day before had been Yom Kippur. He wanted to know what I had done. I knew he wouldn't like it, so I said we just didn't do very much yesterday. At home I had fasted on Yom Kippur. Not at Choate. I lived in two worlds. But oh my God, no, I never attempted to pass.

Mac Berger: My father came from Romania, but he traveled around and worked in several occupations before coming here, including running a fleet of shipping boats in Cyprus. When he arrived in the United States in 1900, the Hebrew Immigrant Aid Society sent him to Texas because they were trying to build Jewish communities throughout the United States. He peddled with a horse and wagon from there to Oklahoma and on to Colorado. Finally, he settled in St. Louis in 1902 in time for the World's Fair.

That's where I was born, in 1904. I remember my father buying and selling second-hand furniture and renting out rooms: "Rooms to let—fifty cents to a dollar." I remember the oompah-pah bands and the musicians dressed in fancy uniforms playing marches on a raised platform in the park. I remember when I saw a motion-picture screen for the first time: I ran behind it to see if there was anyone there.

When I was five, we moved to Detroit because my father had heard that there was a big boom there, with Ford paying up to five dollars a day. The next year we moved on to Schenectady, New York, because my father had heard there was a big boom there with General Electric and the Baldwin Locomotive Works.

Schenectady was an old, clean city with a strong Dutch Reform influence. My father, whom everyone called Uncle Sam, opened a little store. In the summer, he'd go around with a horse and wagon selling vegetables and fruit. The wagon was decorated with a bunch of celery hanging off one side, a clump of corn hanging off the other side.

Schenectady was largely an all-American setting, but Gypsies would frequently travel through. My father would stop them and talk to them in Romanian. When we ate breakfast at a Greek restaurant on the way to market, my father would talk Greek to the people there. The counterman would call out "Orderwheatcakes," and for the longest time I thought it was a Greek expression.

There were very few Jews around, and at times I felt at a disadvantage living among all these blond, blue-eyed kids with their Scottish and English names. After staying out of school for the High Holy Days, I'd feel sheepish coming back. It seemed everyone was looking at me.

Around the time I was eight years old, my father took me on the Albany night train to New York City on the occasion of his sister's twenty-fifth wedding anniversary. It was the first time I saw a nickelodeon and the first time I was in a Jewish environment—the first time I ate chopped herring, chopped liver, lox.

I needed my heroes and found them in some of the Original Celtics basketball team, Nat Holman and all those guys, who would come to play the local team at the armory on top of the hill. It cost fifteen cents to get in. If Jewish vaudeville performers came to town, we'd go out of our way to see them. I'd also overhear my parents talking about Zionist leaders: Max Nordau and Theodore Hertzl.

I remember my parents following the trial of Mendel Beilis in the newspapers. He was a Jewish man who was accused of the ritual murder of a child in Russia: that old anti-Semitic myth of Jews needing the blood of a Christian child to make matzoh. Later his story became the basis of *The Fixer*, the novel by Bernard Malamud. Of course the event didn't directly affect us, but my parents remembered that kind of thing from Europe and were very disturbed.

Around that time, a little girl in a big fleece coat came into our store. It was a bitterly cold morning, and in order to warm up, she went near the gasoline burner we used to heat the store. Suddenly, her fleece coat caught on fire, and in seconds she was up in flames. My father ran out from behind the counter, grabbed her and rolled her on the floor. But she died nevertheless.

We felt terrible and also frightened. My parents knew they were outsiders. All their customers were gentiles. Ordinarily they didn't worry about it. Now, however, the fact that we were Jews seemed to become very important. There was a big investigation. The mayor of the town came in to visit and look us over. Luckily, nothing happened, but business did go down.

After that, we moved to Paterson, New Jersey, where my father opened an army-navy store. It was a silk-manufacturing town. Many of the manufacturers were Polish Jews who were called the "*greena*—foreign—millionaires." Living there, in a Jewish neighborhood, with Jewish friends, I finally felt I was in my element.

Al Lewis: About five or six generations on my father's side had raised great draft horses in Germany, the Clydesdale horses that Americans are familiar with from the Budweiser commercials. When my grandfather came to New York, he bought fifteen hundred acres in Walcott, near the Canadian border. It was an area of muck farms, something between mud and earth, good for leafy vegetables. We were the only horse breeders around.

I was born on a cold enamel kitchen table in the house in Walcott, a most comfortable place. It was a big country house with an enormous amount of land. At one time we had almost a hundred foals breeding. We sold horses to circuses, logging camps, miners, and breweries. Gussie Busch III, owner of the largest brewery in the world, bought his horses from us. Jake Ruppert, who owned the New York Yankees as well as one of the big breweries, would come up to visit two or three times a year. He'd stay for a couple of days, sit around the kitchen table with my father and grandfather, smoke cigars, drink beer, and talk in German about times in the old country. He'd give us kids five-dollar gold pieces, but we would only be present for fifteen minutes when we'd get shooed out.

My father was six feet nine, 310 pounds and hard as a wooden table. My grandfather was a little smaller: six feet seven, 270 pounds. It was like having two King Kongs around. Out of earshot, my mother would say, *"Sa gavane a goy,"* meaning one of their ancestors must have made it with a gentile.

We were the only Jews in a six-hundred-mile circumference, but I never had any anti-Semitic experiences—probably because of my father. I imagine what translated to the people was: "This man is a Christ killer. Look at him." The *meshuga* giant. They were probably afraid if I had any trouble at school, he'd come and tear the walls down.

My mother would say, "Your father is not intimidated by any human, animal, or machine. He is so *meshuga* that if he stubbed his toe on the tractor, he'd punch the tractor."

Outside of the house, my father didn't talk. He hit. In the feed store, somebody would sneeze "Ah-choo."

"Jew?" he'd say. "I'll show you a Jew." Bang! Bang! He used to break heads.

He would come home and tell a story of a fight at the feed store, and my mother, who was a small woman, would go at him with a broomstick. But he never raised his voice to her and never raised a hand to the children.

Actually, he was a very nice man with a great sense of humor. He could tell terrific stories. But he decided that he personally was going to part the Red Sea. That was his objective in life. Like my mother would say, *shtark meshuga*—by which she meant strong and also crazy.

He had that Prussian in him: you gotta sweat, you gotta outwork the horse. A Jewish Paul Bunyan. If you don't work with your hands, you're nothing. But I didn't want to work with my hands. I wanted to be a performer. I'd go to the circus and I'd see our horses with bareback riders on them. I saw how the audience was appreciating the performers and thought I'd like to be appreciated like that.

My mother had a brother, Jonah Needal, an itinerant Yiddish actor who, when doing the circuit, would stop off to visit us. Uncle Jonah looked like a 1920s leading man and was very flamboyant with language. But my father found him distasteful. As far as my father was concerned, the only people who worked in the Yiddish theater were sissies or *faygelers* (little birds or homosexuals). When I told him that I wanted to go with my uncle, my father had a fit.

I left my home in Walcott when I was twelve years old and went on to become a performer. My father, may he rest in peace, never came to see me. He said it was ladies' work.

Mary Klein: Both my parents died in the flu epidemic of 1918, and as we had no other family in this country, my two older sisters and I were put in foster care. There we were abused; I can remember being hungry. Evidently neighbors reported, and the next thing I knew we were in a non-Jewish infants' home in Wauwatosa, Wisconsin.

So that the three of us not be separated by adoption, B'nai B'rith became involved in our situation and arranged for us to be sent to the Jewish Orphan Home (JOH) in Cleveland. This is one of the oldest Jewish child-care institutions in the country, founded by B'nai B'rith in 1868 to care for children orphaned by the Civil War.

On a day in May 1922, when we were five, eight, and nine years old, we were sent by train, with huge tags around our necks, from Milwaukee to Chicago and then on to Cleveland. By the time we arrived, it was after midnight. Jack Girick, the assistant director of JOH, was waiting on the platform for us.

He became our surrogate father, the orphanage our home, and the people there our family. Not everyone could adjust to living in the institutional setup of JOH, but as for me, I had a wonderful childhood.

JOH was a group of nineteenth-century brick barracks-type buildings on Woodlawn Avenue in an old section of Cleveland. A hundred kids slept in a dormitory. There was a hospital, a school building, and long play yards. It was very austere and institutional looking, with hardly any landscaping beyond an occasional tree.

But if the physical environment was not beautiful, the atmosphere more than made up for it. There were brothers and sisters; children from the same family always got a chance to be with each other. The commitment was to keeping the family. The staff was generally warm and supportive, wonderful to talk to. Peg Rhul, a young and peppy gentile woman, was one of my favorites. Every evening the night nurse would leave a little surprise on my bed: a bar of chocolate, a new toothbrush. People were always hugging and kissing me. Maybe because I was so little, I seemed to be everyone's pet.

I adored books, so the library and story hour were a great outlet for me. We had baseball teams, song contests, a movie every weekend. For a while I wanted piano in the worst way so they gave me lessons. But the teacher used to prick my fingers if I didn't curve them properly, so I quit.

Once a month, we had Birthday Night. Each child with a birthday that month was allowed to pick a dollar gift. The trustee women would bake birthday cakes and bring in ice cream. The children would perform original skits and songs. For the finale, everyone would stand up and sing "School days, school days, dear old golden rule days . . ."

There were so many kids around that we were able to talk our problems out with each other without turning to the adults. I had one skate, but another girl had the other one, so we would take turns skating around the playroom. We had special friends—we called it "being in wack"—and we had to share what we had with that friend. Mine happened to work in the kitchen, so I always got extra goodies.

The food was not kosher, but the boys had bar mitzvahs, and we observed all the Jewish holidays. The big events were Rosh Hashanah and the night before Yom Kippur, when we had chicken dinners. I had Hebrew lessons once or twice a week from the time I was very little. Friday nights there was candle lighting, the cutting of the *challah*, and *berachahs*. Saturday mornings we all attended services. Each child took a different part; mine was the Shema. Jack Girick, who had himself been raised at the JOH, gave the sermon. All had some moral lesson, an example to garner from a story about being a mensch.

We went to the local public school, which was poor, working class, and mostly gentile. We made friends with what we called the "city kids." They called us the "home kids." We home kids all wore black cotton stockings and high-laced shoes; the boys wore knickers, the girls cotton dresses with aprons over them.

In the summertime, we went to camp for one week. And since we needed something to do, most of us went to summer school—which is why most of the home kids graduated from high school when they were fifteen or sixteen years old.

We did not feel particularly deprived. We had our own governors and governesses, as the workers were called; our own swimming pool, library, playrooms, craft rooms, athletic teams, drama and choral groups. We were taken on outings to county fairs and parks. We were encouraged to continue our education. In all, the orphanage gave us the opportunities to prepare for the great adventure of life.

The same year I arrived at the orphanage, Michael Sharlitt became its superintendent. He had had an unhappy childhood in an orphanage in New York City and came to Cleveland with a mission: to get the JOH children out of their institutional setting into a more beautiful environment. He detested the idea of our growing up in a poor neighborhood in huge, barracks-type buildings; and so he wrote an operetta, staged it with children from the home, and took it all over Ohio to raise funds to buy land and build a cottage-type orphanage.

In 1929 we moved into Bellefaire, named for its location on the corner of Belvoir and Fairmont boulevards. We left behind the institutional buildings in the old section of Cleveland for a pristine campus in the Heights area with the city to its back and Shaker Heights to its front.

Now we lived like wealthy kids. Instead of a hundred-bed dorm, we were two to a bedroom in Tudor-style cottages. Instead of concrete or dirt yards, we had a landscaped campus. We had beautiful new buildings including a library, tennis courts, athletic fields, and in the center a chapel where we were confirmed and where, incidentally, I returned to be married in 1939. Michael Sharlitt gave me away.

Our new neighborhood was mostly Jewish and very affluent. The students at Cleveland Heights High, which I began the year we moved, were upscale and beautifully dressed. An orphan home in the community and orphan children in school was something brand new to them. We came by bus and carried our lunches with us. We each got a coin with a *B* on it (for Bellefaire) to buy milk. After some of the kids used their coins in the candy machines, they put a knob on the end of them. So the coins became a way of identifying us.

We wore the same clothes we had worn down in the city, but here they looked out of place. Since the seventh grade, when I had taken sewing, I was making my own clothes, replacing the "out walking" dress they gave us which I hated. But still, my clothes could not compare to those of the girls at Cleveland Heights.

For gym we had always worn long johns. But here the girls wore little silk dance sets, matching bras and panties. I refused to wear my long johns; I hid them under my mattress. The cottage mother found them there, took me out of school, and made me sit in the office until I agreed to wear them. I wouldn't give in. "That's not what the other girls are wearing," I said. "I want to feel comfortable with them." Ultimately, I won out for myself and the other girls from the home. I guess I was a ringleader.

But I was never at home at Cleveland Heights High. I was the only kid from the orphanage in my homeroom, and there was no attempt at communication. In my three years there, I was not once invited to anyone's home.

With all the luxuries I was now surrounded by, I was lonesome at Bellefaire. I missed the old place. For the first time in my life, I felt like an orphan.

Meyer Lesser: I was one of sixteen children, an orphan who lived with my sister Sarah in the Crown Heights section of Brooklyn. She was married at fifteen, a widow at twenty, and as good to me as any mother could have been. But it was the Depression, and times were rough. I tried to make some money shooting pool, making deliveries for a drugstore, carrying laundry bundles up five flights of stairs for a nickel tip.

I left school in the eighth grade, but at night I would sit in the bathroom and read until my sister yelled at me to go to bed. It was a book, *The Call of the Wild,* that gave me the yen to see the world.

In February 1932, when I was thirteen years old, I hit the road. I talked this guy Hank, who was a few years older than me, into coming along. We got to the Holland Tunnel and decided to hitchhike. A car full of priests gave us a ride to Philadelphia.

There I hocked my wristwatch for two-fifty. We found a kosher delicatessen—nearly everywhere you went, especially in the eastern part of the country, you could find one—and we had a good meal for twenty-five cents. The next morning, we hitched to Washington, D.C.

It was Friday. Hank was Orthodox and wouldn't travel on Friday night or Saturday, so we had to get a place to stay. We found a synagogue and went to morning services. After, the men came over and asked where we were from. Somehow I knew if I said New York, they'd send me home. So I said Los Angeles. That became my routine on the road. When I was in the East, I said I came from a place out West. When I was out West, I said I came from somewhere in the East.

"What are you boys doing here?" they asked.

"We're looking for work."

"Do you have a place to stay?"

"No."

They had a *noch*, a synagogue fund that takes care of poor travelers. They pay a widow in the congregation to give the travelers a bed and feed them. That's how they see to it that you do not travel on Shabbos or a Jewish holiday. We spent that Shabbos at 4½ and I Street. I never forgot the name of that street.

Sunday we got on an open truck headed south. It was a windy and cold day. When Hank read the sign, "You are now entering Virginia," he threw his coat off the truck. The truck dropped us off in Alexandria, and we had to walk and walk. Hank was freezing.

A cop stopped us and asked what we were doing.

"We're looking for work," we told him.

He took us to the police station and put us in a cell where there must have been about forty other people who had been rounded up. Call them hobos if you like, but they were people who were out of work. I was the youngest. There was no room to sleep, so we all sat around and told stories. What I learned that night enabled me to get along from then on.

The next morning they let us out. "Boys, you've got to get out of town," the police said. "Let's not pick you up again tonight." We made a beeline to the railroad yard and hopped a freight train.

You catch a freight train on the fly, trying to stay on an upgrade. If you're lucky, you get into a boxcar. If not, you get into a refeer—a refrigerator car—but an empty one without a seal. It was a federal offense to break the seal.

People were traveling across the country looking for work. We'd see young women with babies, going to meet their husbands who had left home to get jobs. The women stayed on one end of the boxcars, the men on the other. Some of the women breast-fed their babies. Nobody bothered them. We gave them food, sometimes we gave them all our food because we knew we could get more. We were all in the same boat. We would sing that song "Brother, Can You Spare a Dime?" It was our anthem.

It got to the point where I knew the schedule of every train, when they left and where they were going. I also learned not to ride "silk cars," passenger trains. If you were caught, they'd throw you off a train going fifty–sixty miles an hour. I met a Jewish fellow in Chicago. Next time I met him was in California. He had been thrown off a silk car and was minus a leg.

Once we were in the Midwest and had no choice but to ride a silk car. A police searchlight woke us up. This big bruiser questioned me:

"Where are you from?"

"New York City."

"What church do you belong to?"

"I'm Jewish." I never denied the fact.

"What do you mean? Where's your horns? You Hebes are all the same. Pieces of shit."

He slapped us around, took us into the town, and put us in cells. After a couple of hours, I was taken out, put in a car, and driven to the end of town. "Listen, you little Jew bastard," the big bruiser said, "you show your face here again, you're dead."

I was in the middle of nowhere out West one time when they stopped the train. Twenty automobiles were out in a field with their headlights shining on us.

"Everybody off," a voice said.

Dozens of us stood outside the train in the darkness with the lights of the cars shining on us.

"All the white people go back."

I grabbed the ladder and swung up. There was one young black guy. He swung up, too. They shot him dead.

That incident bothered me a lot. I knew Jews were looked down upon—I saw plenty of signs "No Jews, no dogs permitted"—but blacks were treated even worse.

The blacks lived in shanties near the railroad tracks. I stopped several times in those shantytowns. They always gave me food. I would ask them if I could do some work to pay them back. They said, "That's OK." I used to feel guilty eating their food. They were so poor, but they were very kind to us.

In warm weather, I'd climb up on the top of the train. As they were all coal burners, the cinders would blow around, make your face black and your clothes filthy. I always tried to keep myself clean because I knew if you made a good appearance, everyone took care of you better.

I got off the top of a freight in Los Angeles early one morning and walked until I found a gas station. It had the most beautiful restroom I had ever seen—with two sinks. I stripped to the waist and washed my face, ears, neck, even my hair to get the cinders out. As I was drying myself, I looked up and saw an open window, and right in front of it was an apricot tree. I couldn't believe my eyes. I'd never seen an apricot tree before. I loved apricots. I leaned out the window and picked those apricots off the tree. That's what it was like in Los Angeles. No matter where you were, you were able to put your hand up and pick a fruit: an apricot, orange, a peach, a plum.

I spent a lot of time in Hollywood when Hollywood was Hollywood. For breakfast I'd go in and get a large glass of orange juice—fresh squeezed. They didn't have bottled juice. And I'd have bacon and eggs and french fried potatoes. I was drinking coffee by then: half coffee, half milk. The whole thing was fifteen cents.

In Utah I met Estelle Taylor, Jack Dempsey's ex-wife, who was appearing in a show with Arthur Tracy, the street singer they used to call him. I went backstage. "You little Jew bastard," Tracy said, giving me a kick. "Get the hell out of here."

Estelle Taylor followed me out. "What are you doing here?" she asked.

I told her I had met her husband Jack Dempsey. I didn't know they were divorced.

"Wait for me," she said. "I'll be through in fifteen minutes, and we'll get something to eat."

She took me across the street to a nice restaurant. The waiter handed me a menu. I was too bashful to order. She ordered me a steak. When the check came, she handed me money under the table so I could pay the check. That's a lady.

In Gloversville, upstate New York, I got a job working for Western Union putting flyers in store windows. I made about two or three dollars and went down to the YMHA. A young and beautiful woman was there.

"Can I get a room to sleep?"

"Where are you from?"

"San Francisco."

"There's this meeting going on in the auditorium," she said. "Take a seat in the back. When it's over, I'll take care of you."

A man on the stage was making a speech. "We have to raise a lot of money because we have a lot of Jews in Europe to save," he said.

The people in the auditorium stood up.

"I pledge eighteen thousand dollars."

"Put me down for twenty-five thousand."

I think the smallest donation was ten thousand dollars. I had never heard of money like that.

When the meeting ended, the beautiful woman took me to her beautiful house, showed me to a bedroom, and gave me some clothes. I found out she was Mrs. Schein. Her husband owned the Schein movie theaters, part of the Loew's chain. Every town had one or two of those movie houses.

That was the best place I stayed in on the road. The worst places were the Salvation Army. They made you chop wood, shower outside even in the dead of winter, and dry yourself off with an onion sack.

I preferred the jails anyday. Some had pool tables, clean linens, food.

One of my favorites was in Rutland, Vermont. It was brand new. "When you leave in the morning, please lock the door and leave the key on the ledge," they'd tell us.

But we always looked for Jews. They took care of their own. Mostly everywhere, the business people were Jewish. They owned the stores, the junkyards, the scrapyards. We'd walk in and ask for jobs. They were very, very good to us.

"Where you boys from?"

"San Francisco."

"What are you doing here?"

"Well, we're looking for work."

"Are you hungry?"

"Oh yes." We were always hungry.

They'd take us to a restaurant and order us a plate of flapjacks with syrup. It was cheap and it was filling. At the beginning, I loved flapjacks because I had never tasted them before. But after a while, I got sick of them. Once, a guy ordered me flapjacks, and while he walked away to talk to someone, I took the whole platter with the syrup and dumped it in my coat pocket. I had to throw the coat away, but it was worth it. I couldn't look at another flapjack.

I made four trips across the country. Each time, when I earned enough money to buy new clothes and give my sister Sarah a hundred dollars, I'd come home. I'd hang around for a few weeks, and then boom! off I'd go. My last trip was in 1935, when I was sixteen.

I was in all of the forty-eight states, in every large city and many small towns. I met a lot of people who wanted to adopt me. I met a lot of people who wanted to convert me. Some of them wanted to kill me. It was hardly the typical adolescence of a Jewish boy. But I wouldn't trade those experiences for anything. To this day, I'll be driving along, and suddenly I'll hear a whistle, and I'll know a railroad train's coming through. And I tell you, it's all I can do to stop myself from running out and trying to catch it.

2

WE WERE YANKEE JEWS

*"Sojourn in this land,
and I will be with thee, and will bless thee."*

—*Genesis XXVI:3*

Arthur Cantor: In the 1920s, the whole world seen from the Dorchester and Mattapan area near Boston appeared to be Jewish. I felt sorry for the occasional gentile I met; he didn't appear to be having as much fun as I was. We belonged to a Lithuanian shul in the Lithuanian community and made fun of the way the Russian Jews spoke Hebrew and Yiddish. I was told that Jews from Galicia—we called them "Galitziana"—were horse thieves, not to be trusted.

My parents, who were born in Vilna, were part of the wave that came to America in the early part of the century. They were married forty-five years, yet they rarely spoke civilly to each other. It was like the song in *Fiddler:* "Do You Love Me?" I cook for you, clean for you, take care of the kids for you. So what is love? My father was the traditional Jewish husband not knowing how to open a can. He was a salesman on the road. Many of the men were peddlers. What else could they do? They couldn't be Methodist ministers.

We lived a traditional life in a shtetl very much like the one Isaac Bashevis Singer wrote about, only transplanted from Poland to New England.

Jeff Rubin: My grandmother Sarah Cohen was born in the West End section of Boston on Christmas Eve. In honor of the holiday, the doctor who delivered her decided to enter the name "Mary" before Sarah on her birth certificate. Many years later, when she applied for a passport, her birth certificate at Boston City Hall was found under "Mary Sarah Cohen." She had to legally change her name.

A born and bred Bostonian, my grandmother defined herself as an American. She even had an American eagle license plate on the front of her car. Hardly the typical Jewish *bubby*, she was very Puritanical in her control of emotions. You don't show fear, effusiveness, outward caring. It was a Yankee thing.

Shalom Goldman: My family in Hartford picked up the New England ethos. In their own way, in a kind of sophisticated way, they had become puritanized. Later on I realized they believed they were on a mission from God to make sure the religious practices, which they could see disappearing in America, were continued. The Jews of Europe had been murdered.

◀ (*top*) A New England colonial on Maypole Road in the Merrymount section of Quincy, Massachusetts. (*bottom left and right*) Family poses in the yard, Quincy, Massachusetts, c. 1943.

Although we children were shielded from this knowledge, they felt it was up to them to carry on what was lost through school and synagogue. It was a commitment. Mostly everything else was *narrishkeit*—fun, but not going anywhere. Like the Puritans of old, they took themselves very seriously.

My grandparents ran a dry cleaning, tailoring, and clothing business that my grandmother's father had begun in 1890. My grandfather supplied the Connecticut State Troopers with their uniforms and boots. He became quite successful and was Police Commissioner of Hartford around 1935 or 1936.

But unlike the Jewish families that tended to become less observant as they moved out of New York City, mine stayed fiercely Orthodox. Until urban renewal came to Hartford and the store finally shut down in 1962, it had a sign in the window: "We close at Friday from sundown . . ."

The main message I grew up with was the Orthodox one of behavior: what you eat, what you do, all the regulations. Somehow all of that was connected in my mind to Americanism, which may explain why I grew up thinking that Thanksgiving was somehow a Jewish holiday. My family appropriated it like they appropriated so much of American culture. We had turkey, but it was done in some Jewish kind of way—*flayshedig*, no dairy— so you couldn't have Boston cream pie or milk in your coffee.

Jim Sleeper: My uncle and aunt ran a summer camp out in the country near Charlton, Massachusetts. They had an estate and a big white clapboard house, New England style, with a wraparound porch. The whole family gathered there every Thanksgiving. We would sing these old Puritan hymns like "We Gather Together," and one of the cousins would read the governor's proclamation. We were Jews, but Yankee Jews, New Englanders.

Joshua Winer: After my mother got sick, we began spending weekends with our great aunt Bertha and her husband in their house in Brookline. We'd run around in her big backyard, play Chinese checkers, and fool around with her plastic nut dispenser that had a squirrel on its back. Also we'd get immersed in Jewishness. There'd be a big pot of matzoh ball soup on the stove, and Aunt Bertha saw we finished every drop.

Four or five times a year, Aunt Bertha and her husband would take us to the Union Oyster House in Boston for lobster. She made us finish the lobster too. My older brother threw up a couple of times from getting so stuffed.

It was "eat, eat." Matzoh ball soup for the Jewish thing, and lobster for the New England thing. She wanted us to be Jewish Yankees.

Marilyn Katz: Though I was born in New Jersey, I lived in New Haven, Connecticut, from the time I was five until I graduated from high school. My mother's sister lived in Dorchester, Massachusetts, and I would come up and stay with her for the summers. My time was divided between these two New England locales.

Aunt Anita had a big apartment in one of those double-decker houses on Bicknell Street. Although there was a church on the corner, most of the people on the block and in the neighborhood were Jewish.

About three doors down from my aunt was a mausoleum-like structure, a dark and foreboding place I thought was a mansion. I became friendly with the young daughter of the family that lived there, and one day they invited me to stay for lunch.

"Do you think I should go?" I asked my aunt. "What if they serve something I don't like?"

"Just eat a little, dear, and don't say anything," Aunt Edith said. She never liked to make waves.

Sure enough, they served deviled eggs. I never ate eggs. I just nibbled a little bit.

That was how we were raised: to be restrained, polite, and low-keyed, not to call attention to ourselves. It was the example my parents and aunt and uncle set, and I was very influenced by them. Which may explain why I was so astonished the first time I saw the Krinsky family, who lived across the street from my aunt. They were Lubavitch—one of them went on to become a very close aide to the Lubavitcher Rebbe—dressed all in black with the *payess,* the *tzitzit,* the beards and the hats. I had never seen anyone like them before. They looked like Jews from a Europe of yesteryear.

We were not like that at all. Even my grandmother was up to date. She had been widowed when she was young and earned a living by managing a hotel in the Catskills. My mother and aunt were born here, so the European world was quite remote. My father and uncle used to go camping and fishing, all of that was part of the family thing.

My father was in the trucking business and had a lot of non-Jewish friends. One was an Italian fellow who was married to a Jewish woman who was as dark and swarthy as he was. She was Sephardic and as unfamiliar to me as the Lubavitchers across the street.

Being Jewish meant the values: being a good person, caring for others, honoring the family, getting together for the holidays. Either my aunt and her family would come down to New Haven, or we'd go up to Dorchester. I was the only girl, so I was always placed on a little bit of a pedestal. It was a very civilized and proper style of life, which I thought was the norm. I remember when we visited my father's family in Newark, New Jersey, I would notice how they spoke louder than we did, how they were more outgoing.

The movie *Goodbye, Columbus* shocked us—mortified us, actually. We thought it was anti-Semitic and not like us at all. We weren't JAPs. We didn't go to weddings like that. It would be an embarrassment for us to be on display. We had a feeling of wanting to be toned down. I guess the Boston Brahmin lacquer rubbed off.

Barbara Kreiger: My parents didn't want to call attention to themselves. They never bought anything ostentatious, lived very modestly. But because of the prominence of the family store, any time they bought a new car—a Chevrolet or Oldsmobile, not a Cadillac—some customer walking down the street would invariably say to my mother, "How do you like the new car we bought you?"

We lived in Shelton, Connecticut, a small industrial town of maybe twenty thousand people, mostly blue collar and Catholic. Many of my friends' parents worked in what they called "the shop," which meant B. F. Goodrich, Avco, or Sikorsky. It wasn't a suburban life; it was a small-town life, where people mostly lived in two-family houses or small apartment buildings not far from the downtown.

My great-grandfather Abraham Kreiger, who emigrated with his wife, Sarah from Russia around the turn of the century, had come to Shelton, where he started out with a pushcart. At some point, he bought a clothing and hardware store: A. Kreiger, Inc. He must have done pretty well. By the time he died in 1955, my father was set up in the third generation of the business, which was a very prominent retail feature downtown.

There were hardly any Jews in Shelton, and my parents created a kind of little Jewish island by keeping kosher and maintaining a strong sense of Jewish identity. They felt self-conscious about it, maybe even assailed, and the details of Jewish life were a barrier against the intruding gentile world.

From the outside, it might seem that the easiest thing my parents could have done was assimilate, but there wasn't even the remotest possibility of that for a number of reasons, one being the very strongly identified Jewish community out there. When I was growing up in the 1950s, there were about a hundred Jewish families scattered about the Connecticut Valley in the four little towns sandwiched between Bridgeport and New Haven: Shelton, Ansonia, Derby, and Seymour. While there may have been no Jewish neighborhood in any one town, together we formed a community that was very tightly knit.

I remember when we used to have two synagogues: the Orthodox one in Derby and the Conservative one in Ansonia. We used to go to the Derby synagogue for the High Holy Days. It was an old brick structure with a stained-glass window at the peak. The ambiance was very casual, and I was allowed to go down from the women's section to sit next to my father. From time to time during the long services, I'd go outside with my brother and sister and play with the other kids or gather horse chestnuts. We were always wandering in and out, up and down the wooden steps of the old house next door that served as our Hebrew school.

Around 1954, the two congregations merged. We all participated in the groundbreaking ceremony for the new Conservative synagogue. This was a building with a simple sanctuary of light wood, a large all-purpose room, a gym, and a classroom wing for our Hebrew school. The synagogue became the center of our lives. It was really our building. We built it, we lived in it, we grew up in it.

Every Friday night, my family would light candles, have dinner, and then go to shul. We never skipped Friday night services. This became a problem when I was in high school and couldn't go to the basketball games with my public school friends, none of whom were Jewish. I was in with a crowd that didn't take schoolwork seriously. Maybe I was compensating: Most Jewish kids did an awful lot of schoolwork. I was separating myself from that easy identification that the Jews are the ones who do the academic work.

On the other hand, being Jewish gave me a second social world that was quite wonderful. We were twelve or fifteen Jewish kids the same age, a few from each town, who formed a very tight group of friends starting from the first grade of Sunday school. So while being Jewish was sort of burdensome at times, it was very special as well.

Jim Sleeper: When I was six months old, my parents moved from Worcester, Massachusetts, where they had grown up, to Springfield because my father thought the new location would be good for business. Our house was a little four-room bungalow on a block with mostly Poles and Italians. The Diamond Match Company was at the end of the street. It was a classic white ethnic working-class scene, with the factory at the corner and the people hanging around outside. We attended a Conservative synagogue about two miles from where we lived, a big, old converted Tudor house in one of those leafy old-fashioned New England neighborhoods.

In 1957, when I was ten, my father had earned enough money to build us a house in Longmeadow, a suburb of Springfield. Symbolic of the move to suburban affluence, our new home was a seven-room ranch on a quarter acre of land, and our new synagogue a fancy temple at the edge of Springfield. Its membership must have been a couple of thousand families.

The two synagogues were not that far apart geographically, but Temple Beth El was far from a converted Tudor. Its architect was Percival Goodman, the brother of Paul Goodman. Its rabbi was Samuel Dresner, a patriarchal and imposing figure, a fantastic speaker, and a disciple of Abraham Joshua Heschel, one of the leading scholars in the Jewish Theological Seminary.

American Jews during the postwar years were moving into this kind of suburban hedonistic world of patios and barbecues and tennis courts and new synagogues that were modernistic architectural works. New England was basically Democratic, and we were enjoying the great Rooseveltian institutions, the liberal coalition, benefits that seemed to have existed from time immemorial.

We were the golden children. There was no evident constraint. It seemed like we were living in a country of limitless affluence, endless blue skies, and golden tomorrows. You would never starve. You would never have to worry. You were already on the top of the heap, living in a privileged suburb.

Ours was a benignly non-Jewish environment. Out of a population of close to two hundred thousand, there were about fifteen thousand Jews in Springfield. I experienced no anti-Semitism. The Jews were not psychically present. Maybe you'd hear an occasional crack. There were a couple of kids in junior high who used to call the Jewish kids "bagels." But overall, the Jews didn't figure in anybody's imagination. We were irrelevant to the general populace of Springfield in the 1950s.

Avrohom Hecht: I don't recall any anti-Semitic incidents growing up in Burlington, Vermont, in the 1960s, although I knew we were different. My father was the rabbi of the only Orthodox synagogue in the state: Ahavath Gerim, which means a "love for strangers." It was built by pack peddlers nearly a hundred years ago, and into my time remained a Shabbat destination for Orthodox travelers throughout New England.

The shul is a simple saltbox structure with Gothic windows and door and a high double stairway out front. One Saturday morning, my little brother fell down the stairs, and my parents had to rush him to the hospital. That incident showed me that one can violate the Sabbath to save a life.

We lived about a half mile from the synagogue, and of course we had to walk there and back every Shabbat regardless of the weather. I remember traipsing behind my father in the snow, putting my little feet in the big snowprints he made. I remember walking miles and miles with him on Rosh Hashanah so he could blow the *shofar* at the homes of people who were elderly or infirm and could not get to the synagogue.

As there was no kosher butcher in Burlington, my father rented a huge freezer from some deer hunters. He used to go down to New York City and bring back a butchered cow cut up and packaged. He'd bring down bushels of produce that he got from local farmers—apples, tomatoes, corn, potatoes—and give them away to disadvantaged people in New York. That was one of the ways he practiced and taught us *tzedaka*.

There was always the awareness that we were Jewish in Vermont. My parents spoke Yiddish at home, not only so that we could converse with our immigrant grandparents but to reinforce our separateness. When we went to birthday parties, we brought along our own food. There were the temptations, wanting the ice cream and cake the other children were eating, wanting some of the foods I knew we could not have. But that was the challenge.

Eric Portnoy: In the sixties and seventies, Barrington, Rhode Island, was very much an Anglo-Saxon Protestant town, and it was very much put upon me that I was Jewish, not on the same level as the rest. There was the institutionalized anti-Semitism of the exclusionary Rhode Island Country Club and the Yacht Club. And the subtle anti-Semitism, like all the heads turning and looking at me whenever anything related to the Holocaust or another Jewish subject was mentioned in class.

My friends' nickname for me was "Rabbi." There'd be the typical slurs. Once I went out with a girl, and right off she told me since I was Jewish, I must be rich. I took her straight home. Though I never took religion seriously, I have to admit I liked going to our very small Reform synagogue because I felt at home there.

Christmas in Barrington gave me a real feeling of being an outcast. An elaborate crèche was always set up on the town common. Years later, it became the subject of a big legal dispute. Once a friend and I smashed some Christmas lights. We got caught, and I felt terrible about it, but it was an acting out, I guess.

The funny thing was, when I was seventeen, we moved to Brookline, an almost totally Jewish neighborhood, and there I was viewed as a gentile. I ended up feeling just as isolated in Brookline from the Jews as I had in Barrington from the gentiles.

Sylvia Skoler Portnoy: It was during the Second World War that we moved to Maypole Road in the Merrymount section of Quincy, Massachusetts. We were the second Jewish family to live there. Our street got its name from the maypole that once stood at the top of the little hill at the end of the block. I used to go sledding down that hill, never knowing that the original settlers used to dance around the "Maypole of Merrymount" every first of May.

Now I think how a first-generation American Jewish girl grew up among all that history, right on the site of a Nathaniel Hawthorne short story, and took it for granted. I never even went to see the John Quincy Adams mansion, didn't know that it was part of the Underground Railroad, where Dorothy Quincy hid runaway slaves.

Our house was one of those big New England colonials, white with black shutters. We all loved it. It had a wide front porch downstairs and another one upstairs, a two-car garage, and a lovely backyard filled with lilacs in the spring. It's interesting that my father chose to move to Merrymount—the nicest section of Quincy—instead of Quincy Point, where the rest of his extended immigrant family lived. I think it was because he felt the need to be successful, to show that he had made it in this country. But I felt very isolated. Up until the third grade, I was the only Jewish kid in my class. They were mostly Irish Catholic.

Moe Skoler: We grew up with tremendous anti-Semitism in Merrymount. The priest at the local church was a disciple of Father Feeney, who would later on be excommunicated for preaching that the Jews were Christ-killers. The kids called us "sheenie." They called my brother Saul "Sammy"—I guess they thought that was a Jewish name.

Sylvia Skoler Portnoy: I remember standing on the steps of the big brick church on Saturday afternoons waiting for my friends to come out from confession and knowing they'd be mean to me. I remember their coming home from catechism after being taught the Jews killed Jesus and calling me a Christ-killer. I remember sitting on the front porch with my brother, and the kids we normally played with sitting on a porch across the street and yelling at us, "Dirty Jew, Christ-killer."

Moe Skoler: One Easter Sunday that coincided with Passover, the Christian kids came home from church and called me to come out and play. I was thrilled. We went down to the baseball field, and there they proceeded to beat me up. There were about six of them. I was only one, and I was always little. I tried to fight back, but some of the kids were in the third and fourth grade while I was only in the second. I ended up with bruised ribs, a cut over my face, and my clothes all torn. When I came home, my father was furious, more so over my torn clothes than my scratches and bruises. He thought I was stupid for going.

But I was a tough kid, and I decided that I was going to get even. I started with Kevin, the smallest boy in the neighborhood. I waited for him to come home from school, and I beat him up. Then I beat up Shaughn, and then Dick. Finally I met up with the toughest kid. We had a battle royal, and he beat me up good. But I gained a lot of respect in the neighborhood for standing up to him. Nobody in the neighborhood had ever done that. Afterwards, most of the anti-Semitic slurs and fights stopped.

We still had an awful lot of problems in school. Very few teachers were Jewish, and we were never allowed to forget that we were. One of the high school teachers gave an exam on Rosh Hashanah every year and gave every Jewish kid who was absent a zero.

Sylvia Skoler Portnoy: There was a branch of our family that lived in New York, and it seemed to me they had the real Judaism while we in New England had to cope with a Christian world. I thought they felt part of the world in general while we felt apart.

Moe Skoler: Chanukah was never a fun holiday for us. My mother bought the candles, but we didn't do eight nights and we only got one present. Christmas, on the other hand, was wonderful. Since the neighborhood was almost entirely Christian, we used to celebrate Christmas with our neighbors and exchange gifts with some of them.

Sylvia Skoler Portnoy: When we were very little, we believed in Santa Claus and thought he filled our stockings with presents. My father had seen this when he called on his customers. He wanted us to feel we were part of American culture.

He loved America and was always talking about how lucky he was to have gotten out of Russia and come to the greatest country in the world. On American holidays, we would put a big flagpole out on the top porch and the American flag would hang down over the front porch below. Every Fourth of July, there'd be a big parade down the streets of Merrymount, and we'd sit out on the front porch and watch. And afterwards, there'd be barbecues in the backyards. We'd get together with our neighbors. Those were the times we felt we were real Americans and not so different being Jewish.

Moe Skoler: There were many times I wished I was not Jewish. It was a lot of trouble; I couldn't see anything good in it. From the third grade on, I went to Hebrew school Monday through Thursday, synagogue every Saturday morning, Sunday school every Sunday morning. I couldn't play football until the ninth grade because I had to go to Hebrew school, and I resented that. And it was obvious to us that the gentiles considered themselves the better class.

Yet I always felt that my home life was better than the non-Jewish kids'. I was better clothed. I felt that our mother cared much more about us. She made us chicken or tuna fish sandwiches for lunch while the other kids ate peanut butter. All my friends always wanted to trade lunches with me. At home, our refrigerator was filled with good things. The Christian kids always wanted to come over and eat; they didn't have such good stuff at their homes. Also, we lived much more disciplined a life. We had schedules. We didn't dare not be home when my parents expected us.

Although we were not a very intellectual family, we grew up always knowing that we would go to college. Our high school was not very big, maybe there were three hundred in each class, but we got the message that education was the way to make it in America. The kids went to Holy Cross, Boston University, Northeastern, some went to out-of-town schools.

But Harvard was the epitome of an education in Quincy. And if you were Jewish and you went to Harvard, you were really something special. I was proud of the fact that my brother Saul went to Harvard. For my father, it was the vindication of his entire immigrant experience and struggle. By the time it was my turn, it didn't matter where I went to college. I was kind of left over.

Arthur Cantor: Many Jewish boys from the Boston area went to Harvard. It was kind of like the neighborhood college. Even though my mother wasn't educated, she was a very lite ite person, always reading, and she had the ambition for me to go to Harv rd. I did, but first I went to the Boston Latin School, which fed many boy. into Harvard. In that period the girls were disposable. The boys should go to college, the girls should get married.

Sylvia Skoler Portnoy: My mother had grown up in Dorchester, which was closer to Boston. She attended the symphony, the theater; it was a more sophisticated lifestyle. After she got married and moved to Quincy, she was isolated. Her family and friends were in Boston. She didn't drive.

But every Thursday evening, we'd get into the car and make the half-hour trip to Dorchester, where her twin sister still lived. Our destination was Blue Hill Avenue, the big shopping street. It was filled with Jewish stores and people walking up and down. They all seemed to know each other.

Moe Skoler: We went to Prime's, the first kosher supermarket in the United States, to buy sturgeon and lox for Sunday breakfast and kosher meat for during the week. Before Passover, we'd get an enormous order. There were all those foods we never saw in Quincy: pickles and cabbages in barrels, smoked meats, dried fruits, *challah.*

Sometimes my father would take us into G & G, the delicatessen famous for kosher corned beef sandwiches and for the Boston politicos who hung out there. And sometimes we would visit my mother's sister, which was fun because my little cousin Eunice spoke fluent Yiddish. It was a connection to a Jewish life that we didn't have in Merrymount.

Joshua Winer: My grandparents would have known every single store on Blue Hill Avenue. But my father, an internist at Beth Israel Hospital who led Grand Rounds for Harvard, and my mother, an artist, feel no connection to it. Until I was ten, we lived in Newton, a suburb many Jews moved to from the Dorchester region, and then we moved to Wayland, which is more upper class and 90 percent non-Jewish.

It was from my uncles I learned that the M. Winer Company on Blue Hill Avenue was started by my great uncle Morris Winer, a Russian immigrant. My grandfather Samuel, who lived in Roxbury through the 1930s, was a co-owner. At one time, they had a chain of a hundred neighborhood grocery stores around New England called Elm Farm. As a child, I never knew much about it; I never even saw any pictures of the stores. There was very little discussion of our history in my family.

Jeff Rubin: Among my earliest memories are those of walking up Blue Hill Avenue on the High Holidays in 1964 or 1965. I was four or five years old, and to me the mass of people on their way to synagogue and back home was a sea of legs at knee level. Everyone would be greeting each other. My father would introduce me to people he knew. There was a certain warmth to it all, a sense of being surrounded by people with whom you shared something.

My maternal great-grandparents had come to this country around the turn of the century. They settled in the West End section of downtown Boston, and after a while, my great-grandfather bought the triple-decker frame house on Abbot Street in Dorchester where the next three generations of my family were to be raised. I spent the first five years of my life there, and the next five in a double-decker house in the Dorchester-Mattapan area.

The gentile world of Dorchester-Mattapan was made up of what was referred to as "lace curtain Irish." Our elementary school was mostly Irish, with a smattering of Jews. From my experience, there was always a very easy interaction between the Irish and Jews. My best friend was Brendan McManus. I'd walk him to confessional and wait for him outside the church.

On Halloween we'd go trick-or-treating from our neighborhood to virtually the whole feeding pool of our elementary school. Then we'd stop off at the firehouse, and the firemen would give us little cups of ice cream we called "Hoodsies." At Christmas we'd go downtown to Filene's and Jordan's and sit on Santa's lap. We'd watch the animated spectacles. We certainly didn't associate Christmas with the birth of Jesus; it was just a time to get toys.

My Cub Scout pack was affiliated with St. Gregory's, the local Catholic parish. Originally I'd belonged to the Cub Scout pack run by the Jewish War Veterans on Blue Hill Avenue. But when the Jews began moving out to the suburbs, it closed down. My friend Alan Cohen and I were the only Jewish kids in the St. Gregory pack. The roster of members announced at each meeting either began with a vowel (O'Leary, O'Connor, O'Malley) or ended with one (Depasio, Esposito)—punctuated by one Cohen and one Rubin.

In 1970 our Conservative synagogue closed down. For me, that was a traumatic event. Beth Hillel was where I had had my first real exposure to religion. I knew the sanctuary; I knew the hallways. I had spent five years running around the place. Now for Hebrew school, we were bused to another synagogue in Roxbury. The feeling I had of being in a sea of warm humanity on Blue Hill Avenue was starting to give way to a sense of abandonment.

The rabbi of Beth Hillel had been attacked. Some kids apparently threw acid in his face on a Friday afternoon. He was a young rabbi, our rabbi. His home was thirty or forty yards from where my friends and I used to play. Such things were happening all around me, but as a child I had no idea of the adult repercussions of these events. All I knew was a sense of loss.

A year or so later, with the Jewish community obviously moving out of the area, our community center closed down. That was the place for our after-school activities, our annual Purim carnival. It was always crowded with people, there were always so many things to do. My brother was in nursery school at the time, probably one of the last white kids attending programs there.

He got along with the black kids just fine. So did the rest of us when they tried to effect integration and relieve crowded conditions in other Boston schools by busing black kids to our school. There wasn't any real racial tension. Nothing more than the normal schoolyard fistfights.

Nevertheless, around 1970, there were only three or four Jewish kids left in the whole school. I was one of them. I continued to walk the streets, to go from school to Hebrew school every afternoon with freedom, no fear. But by 1971, when we were one of the last Jewish families left in Dorchester, my parents decided it was time for us to go.

We moved to Canton, a suburb with a growing Jewish presence, lived there for a year, and then moved on to Randallstown, Maryland, a suburb of Baltimore. By then the infrastructure of Jewish life in Dorchester was gone. All along Blue Hill Avenue, houses and stores were boarded up, and if you drove through the neighborhood, you rode fast with the windows closed and doors locked because you did not want to be the victim of some kind of crime.

Moving from the Boston to the mid-Atlantic region was like being uprooted from American history as well as my personal history. We were now a nuclear family in an affluent suburb; newcomers, not part of what was a very insular community.

My grandparents remained back in Boston, and I missed them. I missed my Saturdays with my grandfather, going to shul with him in the morning, going downtown with him in the afternoon and tooling around Quincy Market, Haymarket Square, Faneuil Hall, the old State House while he worked in his law office. I had experienced the city, and a real love for it had been inculcated in me.

Now I felt plunked down in a place that seemed empty of meaning. The area I lived in was half Jewish and half gentile. But you couldn't tell a Jew from a non-Jew. It was totally integrated. It seemed to me the flip side of the New England experience. Judaism seemed to me not deeply rooted here as it was back in New England, where from my home I'd walked to a cemetery whose slate graves were two hundred years old.

My bar mitzvah took place the year after we moved. It was a suburban rite of passage, a small party in the house with just the family and a few friends. But after that, and through my teenage years, I developed a strong sense of Jewishness. I'm not certain where it came from, but the lost world of Massachusetts could have been a part of it, a way of seeking meaning in what I, at the time, thought was a meaningless area.

3

DOWN SOUTH

"I am a stranger and a sojourner with you."

—*Genesis XXIII:4*

Ansie Sokoloff: My mother's parents owned two general stores in Eldorado, a little town in the southeast corner of Arkansas near the Louisiana border. They sent my mother to Boston to study speech at Emerson College, where she met my father who was going to Harvard. He was a sculler and courted her in a little canoe on the Charles River.

In 1925, when I was two and my brother was five, my mother's parents said, "Come down to Arkansas. Oil is running in the street." So the four of us packed up and moved from Boston to Eldorado.

Oil was running, but we didn't get any. The people who worked for the Lionel Oil Company had great wealth and lived in enormous Tudor homes. We, however, moved into a modest house on a modest lot in a modest neighborhood. We called our home "the airplane house" because of the row of sixteen bedroom windows on the second floor.

My father, who had been raised to live a life of books, music, and art and played the violin magnificently, opened a conservatory of music where he taught violin and my mother taught what was then called Expression—speech. Every kid in town took elocution lessons so they could get up and do entertaining monologues.

Despite her example, I developed this real ugly southern accent. Years later, when we moved out West, the kids made much fun of me. I guess I sounded like Thelma's mother who lived across the street and used to shout, "Thelmer did you put the arn on the far? (Thelma, did you put the iron on the fire?)."

We did not have elegant things, but it was a bucolic childhood, barefoot time. We made fudge and sold it on the street. We hung out in our tree houses or spent hot afternoons soaking in cold water in one of our huge, silvery galvanized washtubs. Sometimes my grandmother would wake us up in the middle of the night, saying it was too hot to sleep. She'd put us in the car, and her driver Jimmy would take us to Smackover, Arkansas. We'd get ice-cream cones, and Grandma would get two-percent beer.

I remember the terrible lightning and thunderstorms, my mother standing at the window saying how beautiful the lightning was. It wasn't until years later that she told me she was absolutely terrified. Great amounts of water would fall, and after, the backyard would be filled with snails and small snakes under the stones. My brother and I would melt the snails with a match. I was always playing with the boys.

◀ (*top*) The Post Office Arcade Building in Arcadia, Florida, built by Simon Rosin.
(*bottom left*) A good catch in Arcadia, Florida, that ultimately became gefilte fish, c. 1946.
(*bottom right*) Vacationing on Savannah Beach, Tybee Island, Georgia, 1945.

But our Jewishness was very bad news. We had this unhappy feeling of being totally different. There were only six or seven Jewish families in town. There was no anti-Semitism, but at the same time there was no kosher food, no synagogue, no rabbi, no Jewish friends, nobody Jewish ever coming over. Our Jewishness was eating the Friday night dinners at my grandparents' home in the back of one of the stores—the matzoh balls and *kreplach* and *derma*. And our going to Sunday school in a little apartment over somebody's garage. It was real punishment.

Still I knew we were Jewish, and Jesus was not our Lord. I had a very good voice and was the lead singer in school. When I told my mother I was assigned to sing the part of Mary in the Christmas pageant, she said it was all right. "But don't sing the word *Jesus*," she added. "Just hum."

We were not allowed to have a Christmas tree like everyone else, but Christmas morning I'd wake up to find gifts piled up by the bed. Before Christmas, Grandma would take my brother and me to the five-and-ten-cent store, give us each a basket, and set us loose down the aisles to pick up whatever we wanted. We'd fill the baskets with jacks, coloring books, yo-yos.

When Grandma died, there was no *shivah*. Her casket was set up in our living room, where people came to call. My mother told me to go over and look. I didn't want to, but she made me. "You have to say good-bye." So I got over there and became mesmerized examining the makeup and hair.

Miriam Mayers: The Jewish families in Berwick and Morgan, Louisiana, had come from New Orleans and before that from Alsace-Lorraine. I think I was related to almost everyone buried in the Jewish cemetery in Berwick. A lot of the stores in Morgan were owned by Jews. But my family, the Leopolds, was the only one that had a store in Berwick. It was a general store one block from the river. Our house was two blocks from the river; it was one of the first in town to have electricity. We used to watch the riverboats coming down the river, and we'd swim in a part that was fenced off.

Alex Rosin: My father's father, Simon Rosin, had emigrated from Russia to Chicago. Then he went on to South Carolina, where he helped found a town called Rosinville; around the age of twenty, he got tired of that, so he got in his horse and buggy and headed south. He stopped in Arcadia, a really beautiful place on the Peace River sixty miles south of Lakeland, Florida.

He opened up a dry-goods store there and ended up being the first person in the state of Florida to have a chain of stores, with locations in Arcadia, Ocala, and Sea Breeze. He called them the Boston Stores. His wife died of diabetes the year before insulin was discovered, leaving him alone with their only child, my father: Marcus Aurel Rosin, born in 1912.

My mother's family came from Warsaw and settled in Savannah. Her father was a Paderewski, nephew of the world-famous pianist and composer who converted to Catholicism to save his skin. Paderewski is my middle name, and I've had to spell it on everything. My aunts and uncles used to call me "Alexander P." And I'd say, "No thank you, I don't have to."

When she was sixteen, my mother lost her father. The next year she married our father and moved to Arcadia, taking three of her sisters and two of her brothers with her. By the time she had her own children, it was like raising a second family.

My oldest brother was born in Arcadia. My next brother, David, was born in Arcadia too, but eight days after his birth, a drunken nurse knocked over his bassinet, and his skull was crushed by the fall. After that, my mother decided that her children would be born in Savannah. She waited till we were ten days old before bringing us home.

Arcadia was cattle country. We lived on a ranch. I learned to ride before I was three and roped my first calf when I was five. Many times we had calves whose mothers had died. I kept goats tied up to a fence post so the calves could get to them and nurse.

We'd be up at four-thirty in the morning on the ranch, ready to start the day before the sun was up. I had a special way of shouting out the back door in the morning so the horses would hear my voice as an echo and go walking up to the barn. By the time I washed up and ate a bowl of cereal, the horses would be at the barn waiting to be let in and fed.

In our backyard, we raised chickens and a garden of greens, radishes, and corn. Since my oldest brother was all thumbs, I was the one in charge. I sold the eggs, getting three cents a dozen extra for brown eggs. I had a hen who laid double-yolk eggs. That brought me some extra money. I used to plant rough lemon trees from seeds that I'd graft to different kinds of oranges and grapefruits. People bought them from me. I also rewired lamps, fixed the washing machine, did the ironing, and the like.

When my grandmother came to visit, we had to have kosher foods. We'd order from Tampa, and it would arrive on the Greyhound bus. My mother would say: "Grandma's got two chickens coming in. Who wants to go down to the bus station?" We'd get on our bikes and ride down the five blocks to pick up the chickens, salami, and corned beef.

But on the range, when we'd go out and ride for two or three days, sometimes we'd have ham or bacon with us that we'd cook over an open fire. There weren't too many things you could take that would keep for two or three days. My mother lit candles every Sabbath, but as my father used to say, the cows and the chickens and the horses didn't know Saturday from Sunday from Monday or Tuesday. So a lot of Jewish observances did get missed because we had to take care of things. We had to be practical and compromise.

In Arcadia, I went to a Methodist Sunday school to get some type of understanding of religion. I was taught about Jesus and the different Bible stories. It went in one ear and out the other. But I got to know and understand the people and was able to get along with them better.

We would go up to Savannah every summer so we kids could get some kind of Jewish education. When I was eleven, they decided we'd be better off living in a place where there were some Jewish people. So we moved down to Sarasota. My father opened up a branch law office, although he kept his law office and the house and property in Arcadia as well.

No symbolic Christian things were in our house until we moved to Sarasota. Then one year when Chanukah and Christmas came the same time, we put up a bush decorated like a Christmas tree, and my father bought me an electric train, the Lionel Scout. To this day, I keep it in a glass cabinet.

Sara Breibart: I was under two years old when we arrived in Augusta, Georgia, in 1921. My father's family was living there already, and they found him a little second-hand shoe store.

All the Jewish merchants in Augusta were on one block of Broad Street.

Most of them had little shoe stores or what they called Jewish hardware stores, which had ready-to-wear clothing. The localism for the Jewish neighborhood was Kugel Avenue, which in reality was Ellis Street.

After a while, my father moved from the little store to a bigger one and from used shoes to new shoes, although not first-class shoes. And as we had become more affluent, we moved downtown to lower Broad Street. The Savannah River flowed past the back of our house, where my parents built a room with windows all around so we could get the breeze.

In some of the small southern towns, it was not uncommon for there to be only one Jewish family, and the parents would bring their children to Sunday school in places like Charleston or Augusta in order for them to become part of a Jewish crowd. My grandparents had a tenant whose granddaughter was the only Jewish girl in McCormick, South Carolina. Her parents, who were anxious for her to have Jewish friends, decided to bring us together.

Rebecca Drucker and I were seven years old when we first met. We became best friends. Most every Sunday, her parents drove the nearly fifty miles to bring her to Augusta. Sometimes she'd spend the weekend. As we moved into our teens, Becky became part of "the little crowd"—the eight Jewish boys and eight Jewish girls in all of Augusta. We'd meet in each other's houses, roll up the rug, turn the radio on, and dance to the Hit Parade; or we'd go to this place where they had a jukebox to dance and hang around. Sometimes it would get to be eleven or twelve o'clock Sunday night when we got back. We never hurried. Becky's parents would be sitting on the front porch of my grandmother's house waiting to take her back to McCormick.

There were times Becky's father drove in, picked me up, and took me to McCormick. She always kept me separate from her non-Jewish friends. Her parents just couldn't do enough for me. They wanted that friendship.

Terry Drucker Rosin: When I was growing up in the 1940s and 1950s, I was the only Jewish girl in all of Oconde County, South Carolina. My parents had met and married in Savannah and then moved to Westminster in Oconde, where my dad opened up a dry goods store.

Westminster was a small cotton milltown with a population of twenty-five hundred—including the chickens and the cows, as my dad used to say. Outside was country, farmland. On Sunday afternoons my parents, little brother, and I would go for drives in the countryside and look at the corn and cotton growing in the fields.

The train station was right across the way from our store. When a package was due from Atlanta, we'd run across the road to watch the train pulling in. We'd get shipments of corned beef, pastrami, and salami packed in dry ice. The Passover order coming up from Atlanta was very special. It would have everything from candles to jelly to soap.

As Saturday in Westminster was payday, it was the town's big shopping day. Our store had to be open. This was true throughout South Carolina, which explains why synagogue services all over the state were held on Sunday instead of Saturday. As a young child, I sometimes went to the Presbyterian church with my girlfriends. But when I came home singing "Jesus loves me," Dad decided it was time for Sundays to be spent in shul. The nearest one was in Greenville, fifty miles away. En route, we would stop at the little towns to pick up young people for the Sunday school class.

My parents were very charitable and often donated new clothes from the store or clothes that my brother and I had worn to needy people in the community. My mother warned me not to say anything if I saw someone wearing what had once been mine, because that would make the child feel bad. Yet I remember little girls coming up to me and saying "How do you like your blouse on me?"

One of the recipients of my parents' generosity was a preacher, a thin man with dark hair who would come around to the school carrying a felt board with little cardboard figures. The teachers would stop the class, and he would tell Bible stories, illustrating them with the little figures that he'd stick onto the felt board. Whenever he told the story of Jesus, he'd say, "The Jews crucified Jesus. The Jews led Jesus to his death."

Every so often when he showed up, the teachers would come over to me and ask if I'd like to leave the classroom. I never did. I couldn't understand why they were asking just me and not anyone else. Then they'd ask if what he said bothered me. I told them it didn't have anything to do with me. Why should I feel uncomfortable? It was like the time the banker's son asked me, "Why don't you go back to Palestine where you belong?" It didn't mean a thing to me. I had never been to Palestine.

This preacher brought along a stack of little red booklets that contained parts of the New Testament. He told us if we memorized John III:16—"For God so loved the world that He gave His only begotten son, and whosoever believeth in Him shall not perish but shall have everlasting life"—we could keep the red booklet. And if we memorized the whole booklet, we would get to go to Bible school for the whole summer for free.

Now I had won a declamation contest at the age of six, beating out several hundred first graders. A picture and a story about the only Jewish girl in Oconde County winning the gold medal appeared in the *Forward*. So it was no trouble for me to memorize the verse from John. I got the little red booklet and brought it home. When my father found out what was going on, he had a fit. Very soon after that we were making plans to move to Savannah.

Susan Levin Schlechter: Birmingham is a big church-going area. There's a church on every corner, and people are into praying. Generally, they have a respectful attitude towards religion. But there was this deep vein of proselytizing; there was always the hope that we Jews would eventually see the light.

My parents got me out of Birmingham in the summer. My first sleep-away camp was an evangelical one deep in the Alabama woods. For the two weeks I was there, I fanned a lot, didn't move a lot, and learned to sing "There's a church in the valley with the wildwoods."

After that, my parents sent me north to Wisconsin and Maine, to what I called Jewish-Indian camps—they had Jewish kids and Indian names.

Zipporah Marans: In 1944 we moved from Raleigh to Savannah, where my father became rabbi of the synagogue on Drayton Street. It was a bigger pulpit for him and a bigger Jewish community. Savannah also had an Orthodox shul and Mikve Israel, the beautiful German Reform synagogue that had been founded by Sephardic Jews in the 1780s.

There was a hospitality in Savannah, that southern hospitality. Everybody was friends with everybody else. Homes were always open. French doors let out to huge gardens with beautiful flowers blooming everywhere.

Terry Drucker Rosin: I was not yet thirteen when we moved to Savannah in 1954. It was very exciting for me to leave Westminster for someplace new, especially as it was the city where my mother was born and grew up. Our new home, however, was not in the old and established Jewish community but in a brand-new neighborhood carved from a forest on the outskirts of the city. I was still in the minority, one of only three Jews in my class, the first graduating class of a new high school.

But the JEA—the Jewish Educational Alliance—was within two miles of our home, and I was there almost daily, especially in the summertime. I joined every Jewish youth organization I could, played in the orchestra, swam in the pool. I felt I had a lot to get in for all those years I had missed.

Sara Breibart: As we moved into our teens, the Jewish kids became part of a network of southern Jewry. There were dances, conventions, and get-togethers in different southern cities. Although I lived in Augusta, I knew all the Jewish kids in Savannah, Columbia, and Charleston.

Sol Breibart: The Jewish children in Charleston were in general the better students, the ones on the honor role. We were expected to behave a certain way, not get into trouble. Still there was a class distinction between the uptown Jews who were the newer immigrants and the downtown Jews whose families had been there since before the Civil War. I didn't meet any of the downtown Jews until I got to high school.

Charleston's Reform temple went back to 1749. It's the second oldest synagogue building still in existence in the United States. We called it "the Deutschisha shul" because most of its members were of German background. They were the wealthier Jews with established businesses on King Street. Beth Sholom, which was called "the big shul," went back to 1854. It was supposedly the more prestigious of the two Orthodox synagogues. The little shul, a converted house called Beth Israel, was ours. It was started in 1911 by Russian and Polish immigrants.

My father was a Russian emigrant who settled in Charleston in 1914. He worked in his brother-in-law's grocery store until he learned the ropes and then opened up Breibart Grocery, which he ran for over sixty years. It was a corner store close to the city limits that catered to the neighborhood people, most of whom were low income. Quite a few were blacks. In this neighborhood, almost every corner had a Jewish grocer. All were friendly competitors who socialized with each other.

The climate in Charleston is moderate most of the year, but it does get very hot in the summertime. Those evenings before air-conditioning, when all we could do was keep the windows open to let the breezes blow through, the Jewish families used to go down to the Battery at the tip of the peninsula and try to cool off. Originally it was called White Point Gardens, but during the Civil War it became known as the Battery when guns were actually fired for the protection of Fort Sumter and the harbor.

By my time it was a park, but the cannons were still there. The kids would play on them or run around. The mothers would sit on benches chatting and gossiping. The men were still at their business. My father kept the store open quite late in the summertime.

In our neighborhood, most of the people were not Jewish; most of my playmates were not Jewish. Still I experienced very little anti-Semitism except for the kids in the mill section I had to walk through on my way to or from school; they would call me "Christ-killer" and other epithets.

Susan Levin Schlechter: I was raised knowing that there was a polite but very clear anti-Semitism. Evidently, I heard my parents talk about Jewish and non-Jewish, about country clubs that my family couldn't join. I imagine I was scared in a very profound way as a child, but I incorporated my fears.

In Birmingham, you start swimming in May and keep on swimming till December. I was quite little when my parents got me a plastic pool for our backyard. We invited the neighborhood children over, none of whom were Jewish. I asked, "Is this a Jewish pool?" My mother said, "No, Susan. Everybody can swim in this pool."

The Jewish people of Birmingham were very assimilated, and at the same time very clearly identified. At Christmas time there was one house—ours—

that did not have Christmas decorations. And Birmingham went in big for Christmas decorations.

Alex Rosin: In the Sarasota schools, I had books stolen, spokes kicked out of my bicycle, notes that said "Go home damn Jew." One little girl kept bugging my brother and me to let her meet our mother. She wanted to see her horns. My brother tried to tell her my mother didn't have horns. She said: "Prove it to me."

Finally we brought her home. My mother sat Betty down and explained that the rays of light that came off Moses' head after he received the Ten Commandments have been depicted as horns by some artists. "But Jews don't have horns," she said. "You can look at my head all you want to."

One Friday I came back from Sarasota to our ranch in Arcadia and found my favorite cow butchered. She was a Brangus we used to call "Yo-yo" because every time you pushed her, she came right back. Her mother had died giving birth to her, and I had raised her. She got to be fourteen hundred pounds.

When I saw her head and torso lying there that Friday, I knew right away that this was an anti-Semitic act. I also knew whoever did it would be back, and I was ready for them with a thirty-thirty rifle and a thirty-caliber police special pistol. I caught them. I made them swim the Peace River. I marched them. I tracked them the eight miles to jail.

Another time, someone burned the shape of a cross and the word "JEW" onto our lawn with fertilizer. I never did catch the one who did that.

Artie Allen: The Klan was still around in the mid-sixties and early seventies. I heard stories, like the time they burned a cross in front of the ZBT Jewish fraternity house in Tuscaloosa.

Brenda Robinson Wolchok: My mother told me stories of how the Ku Klux Klan would march down the street of McCormick during the Depression when she was a young girl. They lived above the store, and they would run and hide in the back.

Sara Breibart: The Ku Klux Klan was always marching down the main street of Augusta. Heck, we knew they were anti-Jewish too, but we'd go watch them marching anyway. My parents were afraid. I guess it was pretty scary, but we kids just looked at them and laughed.

Artie Allen: In the 1970s there were no Jewish day schools in Montgomery, and the public high schools were not very good. So my parents sent us to St. James, the Catholic school.

In the ninth grade, a guy told me my desk was better than his and I should get up and give it to him. He called me a no-good Jew boy. Then he kicked me, and my desk flipped over. I got up, grabbed him by his red hair, and hit him as hard as I could. He was wearing braces, and his gums just started bleeding all over the place.

I was the noseguard on the football team and remember the religious ceremonies after football games, invoking Jesus' name, praying, listening to the coach tell you that Jesus was a Jew. When you said you couldn't play on the High Holy Days, the coaches would say, "I don't care what you have to do, you're going to play football."

My brother and I each got the blue-gold award for being the best senior athlete in the high school. I was amazed. I was sure we would never get it because we were Jewish.

Always, I felt a sense of alienation, of not being free to speak my mind. I realized if it weren't for the blacks in Montgomery, the Jews would have been treated like the blacks were. They took the brunt of all the discrimination, all the time. But we Jews never felt entirely at home either.

Brenda Robinson Wolchok: I had only one real anti-Semitic experience growing up in Savannah. That was in high school, when a Christian friend put my name up for a sorority. "I don't think that's a problem," she said when I told her I was Jewish. After speaking to her president, however, she called me back. "I'm so sorry," she said. "It's not that we don't like you. It's just that our customs are so different from yours."

Susan Levin Schlechter: In their sophomore year, the gentile girls in Birmingham joined sororities. It was kind of a rehearsal for what eventually would happen at the University of Alabama or other colleges throughout the South. You could rank these sororities; there were layers. You knew which ones had the most young women who were going to be debutantes.

There was no pretending. Nobody rushed anybody Jewish. Ever. Ever! It was all done so politely. Still, I never forgot it. The only reason I was being excluded was because I was Jewish. I was probably so consumed with that rejection that I didn't think of what was much more scary to me—the issue of race. For after all, I had the privilege of my skin color.

Ansie Sokoloff: It's hard to believe that in my lifetime, blacks had their own box office at the movies. In Eldorado, Arkansas, they could not buy tickets where we did and could only sit in the balcony. They could not enter any restaurant or store. They could not pass you on the street.

Even though we were living right in the middle of the Depression, we had two black women in to help: Della who did the laundry and Brooksy who did all the cooking and cleaning. There was a little house in our backyard that Brooksy and her family lived in. She raised her children there. When they got sick, we got the doctors. We loved them and cared for them, but it was the way we cared for a little puppy. Still we never questioned it, never thought about it.

Sara Breibart: We grew up with a black nurse named Ella. She was grossly underpaid, of course. When she got married we all went to the wedding; she was like a member of the family. But at the same time she was not a member of the family.

Susan Levin Schlechter: We lived in Mountain Brook, a tiny suburb over the hill from the city of Birmingham. My ancestors had come there as peddlers in the 1880s. By the time I was born in 1945, my father, uncles, and grandfather were the owners of the New Ideal Department Store, a major downtown store. Almost all the major department stores were owned by Jewish families, and we knew all of them.

Birmingham was founded during Reconstruction. It remained like a third-world country for a very long time. I recall hearing: "We don't have to really obey the Thirteenth, Fourteenth, and Fifteenth amendments because we didn't get to vote on them."

We lived in separate and unequal worlds: "white" and "colored." Two water fountains, four restrooms, separate upstairs sections in the movie theaters, separate entrances. If I was ever on the bus with a nursemaid, I sat in the back too. Colored people worked in our home. They raised me. They held me. They loved me, I guess. Some worked in our store, but they did not wait on customers.

We never, ever socialized with them. You lived in your affluent neighborhood in a beautiful house with carefully tended grounds and constant inequities. The mature man who tended the yard you called "boy."

Our all-white high school backed on a forest. On the other side was the black high school. We could hear their music. "Oh, yes, that's the black high school band practicing," we'd say. They could have been on Mars. No one thought about it. That's the way it always was, and the way it ought to be.

I knew about Bull Connor, but the explanation was that the people who were causing all the trouble were "outside agitators," and if "they" just left "them" alone, we and the blacks we would work this out. Years and years of apathy.

Whatever Martin Luther King and his followers did—and I couldn't swear that I heard the name Martin Luther King when I was growing up— it was always "they" or "the other" and had very little to do with us. It wasn't even a matter of keeping up appearances. It was just go about your business, and mind your business, and don't cause any trouble, and everything will be okay.

I remember that Sunday when the church exploded, and the four little girls were killed. We heard a tremendous blast from all the way over the hill. We didn't know what it was at first. Then we were stunned. We felt so terrible. But we did not do anything. I don't want to make the leap, to make any connection to Nazi Germany, although I have thought about the "good Germans."

In our home, race was never discussed. We simply did not talk about it. We all felt silenced, especially those of my parents' generation. There was a whole system, a conspiracy of silence. If I didn't have a voice, it was because every signal I was given implicitly and explicitly was to not have a voice—not as a girl, not as a Jew.

I had had a whole life of being told to be well mannered, decorous, polite. You would never just say "Yes" to anyone. That would have been rude. It was always "Yes, ma'am" or "Yes, sir." I was trained to keep and replicate my place and to be quite grateful. In a million years, it would never have occurred to me to do anything other than what I was told.

Although my parents did not talk about what was happening, I saw they were being affected by the boycotts, the sit-ins at the Woolworth's lunch counter. These actions began to take an economic toll on downtown Birmingham. Still there was very little discussion except that we'd have to tighten our belts. We'll work this out, they said. Don't worry, you'll be taken care of.

I guess we Jews must have felt so marginal that we couldn't possibly make a stand for blacks. We were part of the group that existed in the South where you were Jewish in your home, but out in public you try to look like everybody else. You never deny that you are Jewish, but you also don't make waves. You simply do not do that.

Ansie Sokoloff: Just after my father passed the Bar in Arkansas and was set to accept an invitation to join a very prestigious law firm, he got a telegram stating that his Uncle Sam in Cheyenne, Wyoming, was very ill and he should come at once. My father took the train that day.

He ended up staying for seven or eight months. Every time he said he had to get back home, Uncle Sam said, "You can't leave me. You're my favorite nephew. Stay and help in the business." Finally, my father decided that since he couldn't go back to Eldorado, he would move the family to Cheyenne.

When he called with the news, my mother was overjoyed. All of us had just had malaria. It was beastly hot. She sold the house—lock, stock, and barrel—put us in the car, and took us touring. She didn't want us to leave our part of the South without seeing it. First we went to Baton Rouge because she wanted us to see the capitol that Huey Long had built. It was so hot there, we had to spend most of the day in the swimming pool. We went to Natchez, Mississippi, and then to New Orleans so we could sample the food. Then she sold the car, and we took the train to Denver.

My father met us at the station in Uncle Sam's giant cream-colored Pierce Arrow that had two jump seats in the back and headlights that stuck out in the front. We climbed in and set out on the long drive to Wyoming. "Wait and see what a beautiful house I bought for you in Cheyenne," he said. "You'll all be so happy there."

4

ALL OVER THIS LAND

*"Lift up now thine eyes, and look from the place
where thou art, northward and southward
and eastward and westward."*

—*Genesis XIII:14*

Ansie Sokoloff: My roots in Wyoming go back to my great-grandfather Max Idelman, a Polish immigrant. In 1864 he boarded the Union Pacific Railroad in St. Louis and took it to Cheyenne, where with two brothers he opened the Yellowstone Tobacco and Liquor Distributorship. They had a three-state territory and sold liquor to the Indians.

Max made a fortune. He took his second wife on a year-long honeymoon trip around the world, and then he built her a mansion outside of Cheyenne. It had the only ballroom in the state; Teddy Roosevelt spent a night there on his way across the country.

Max had one son, Sam, who was from his first wife. Uncle Sam never married but took care of all his nieces and nephews, sent them to college, built them homes.

When we arrived in 1935, Uncle Sam had been settled into two rooms at the Plains Hotel, one for him and one for a nurse. He spent the rest of his life living in that wonderful western hotel and going out every single afternoon for a drive on the prairie. Cheyenne is all prairie. I had never seen land so flat.

Every Sunday night, we'd have dinner with Uncle Sam in the Plains Hotel. It was elegant. They'd give you little finger bowls with flowers floating in them and serve sherbet between courses to cleanse the palate.

In 1935 there were one hundred fifty Jewish families in Cheyenne out of a population of thirty thousand. Maybe all but three were immigrants, Orthodox. They were very hard workers who lived in the backs of their stores, ate this strange food they had to go down to Denver to get, and had these strange accents. I thought they were foreigners. They were always talking about money and kept their children from socializing with any non-Jews. On the holidays, I was brought to the little shul they attended. I hated it.

Many of them became very well off. They had the big retail stores in town, the Western Ranchers' Outfitters. Their huge families intermarried with one another: the Starks, the Zuckermans, the Vetas. They moved on to the boards of banks and developed a lot of political clout.

As for me, once again I had no Jewish friends, not one. I can't tell you how uncomfortable I was being Jewish where all the Jews were a clan. I had nothing in common with them.

◀ *(top)* Western pageant at inauguration of Governor Fuller Warren, Tallahassee, Florida, 1948. *(bottom left)* Max Idelman and associates before his Yellowstone Tobacco and Liquor Company in Cheyenne, Wyoming. *(bottom right)* Childhood pleasures in Eldorado, Arkansas.

I was twelve years old. Adolescents don't like to be different. They all want to be invited to the same parties and be part of the same gang. I couldn't move into the Jewish group. They were too foreign to me. The Christian kids, on the other hand, were the kind I had always been with in Eldorado, Arkansas.

They became my gang. My best friend was Catholic, my second best was Episcopalian. I sang in churches on Sunday mornings. I was part of the Court of Frontier Days, the biggest rodeo in the world. I rode in the Pioneer Day Parade on a big old wagon. I did not live a Jewish life.

In truth, I never had any problems except once. It was on Halloween, and we were a gang of eight boys and eight girls trick-or-treating. A guy opened the door and made some comment about "your people." The kids sheltered me. They said "he's a crazy old man." I didn't hear the word "Jew," but I understood what he meant. It was the only time, but very painful, like a knife, an accusation.

At first, my parents had no Jewish friends. My father became the only Jewish member of the Cheyenne country club. The other Jews disapproved. There was some conflict. I got snubbed a bit. I guess they thought that we were snobs.

But my father liked community work. He became president of the Salvation Army, the Chamber of Commerce, the Lions Clubs' Rocky Mountain District. And then he went on to single-handedly run the United Jewish Appeal drive. He did all the collecting, made all the calls, filled out the slips, had the speakers come.

My mother, who thought Jewish and felt Jewish, became president of the Sisterhood. At home, she taught elocution and practiced speech therapy to kids with harelips or cleft palates.

In the late 1930s, the Hebrew Immigrant Aid Society was sending Jews to Cheyenne. Whoever had no place to go came to us. We had frequent musicales. We had seders, always with non-Jews present. My father took great joy in explaining the services to them.

I lived in Cheyenne until I was seventeen. Then I went off to Northwestern. The other Jewish kids who went away to college went to the University of Wyoming at Laramie, or the University of Nebraska, or the

University of Colorado. Most, however, stayed in Cheyenne and married a child of one of the other Jewish families.

Barbara Krause: When they got married, my father brought my mother to his parents' farm outside of Carthage, South Dakota. My grandfather had started out in this country as a peddler, going from place to place. But he had a dream of owning land, something a Jew couldn't do back in Russia. Finally he saved enough money to buy a farm and some livestock. He grew crop corn and wheat.

The farm is still there. It's out in country so desolate you could drive for miles and miles and not see anything. The single tree on the property is the one they planted. When my parents lived on the farm, it was the 1950s, but it could just as well have been the 1850s. There was no electricity. They had to go to the well to pump water. At one time, my mother said, the chickens were living in the house with them.

My older brother was born premature and had to be left in the hospital, which was fifty miles away, for a number of weeks. My mother vowed that she was not going to go through one more pregnancy on that farm. When she was pregnant with me, they moved near her family in Sioux City, Iowa. After, we moved to Mitchell, South Dakota, together with my father's parents.

My father and grandfather started a produce market. Then they went into fabrics and feathers. Their store was in a huge, drafty building made of pink cinder blocks and filled with tables laden with bolts of cloth as big and round as a tree trunk and up to ten feet long.

Farmers would bring in great quantities of feathers that my father would sell to pillow and quilt manufacturers. He always kept big sacks of goose down and pheasant feathers in his car. Even though he drove a nice new Mercury, my mother refused to ride in his car. She just couldn't stand the smell.

There were only four Jewish families in Mitchell. I had no Jewish friends. My parents were very reluctant to have us seem too Jewish. We were told to play down any differences and take part in the Christian programs in school. Still everyone knew we were Jewish. I did not experience much anti-Semitism, but there was a boy who would drive his bicycle by me and scream, "Get off the sidewalk, dirty Jew!"

Once a high school teacher asked me to deliver a little talk about Judaism. Students asked me questions, but I didn't know the answers. I guess I was a little ashamed of being Jewish.

At home, we hardly practiced any religion. I was not bat mitzvahed; my brother was not bar mitzvahed. We never had a seder. On the High Holy Days, we stayed home from school, visited my mother's family in Sioux City, and put in a few hours in shul. I found it boring. It was as if we went so we could say we did our duty.

Yet my parents were very concerned about my marrying a gentile. As a result, I did not have one single date during my whole high school time. I missed out on the proms, on the normal social life of a teenager, and I was very resentful.

When I was sixteen, my parents sent me to New York City as the family representative at my father's youngest brother's wedding. I was taken to see *Fiddler on the Roof,* of all things. I attended a seder. I had never been to one before, and I was so afraid of doing something wrong and making a fool out of myself. When it came time to spill the drops of wine, I spilled the whole thing. I was drowning in *Yiddishkeit,* overwhelmed. I was just happy to leave.

From such beginnings, I ended up marrying a Lubavitcher. We have five children, *kineahora.* My parents think I'm crazy.

Robert Yaffe: In the 1950s and 1960s, Omaha was an oasis in the wilderness. Beyond the city line were endless cornfields. Kansas City, the nearest city of any import, is one hundred eighty miles away. Chicago was ten hours away.

The sense of isolation was intensified if you were Jewish. That was probably one of the factors that solidified the Jewish community and made it unique. Jews lived in a Jewish neighborhood and had Jewish friends. There was heavy synagogue affiliation in three well-attended synagogues. We went every Saturday even in the winter, and winters in Omaha can be pretty bad. At the Sunday morning Junior B'nai B'rith bowling leagues, we filled up all twenty-five lanes. We also had a Sunday basketball league for Jewish kids, which my dad wanted me to join. But I hated it—the smell of the gym, the fact that the other kids were good and I was not.

The previous generation had created an infrastructure of Jewish accomplishment in Omaha. One of the largest jewelry stores in America is a Jewish concern originally owned by a Jewish family, the Borsheims. A major supermarket chain was begun by Abe Baker, a Russian-Jewish immigrant.

Rose Blumpkin, another Russian immigrant, came to Omaha in 1917 and turned 100 in 1993. A harsh-looking tiny woman who wore her black hair in a kind of bun, she'd drive around her small carpet store in a little scooter cart, pull up beside a customer, and offer a deal. That store became the Nebraska Furniture Mart, America's largest furniture store and a multimillion-dollar enterprise.

My grandfather, Nathan Yaffe, came to Omaha from Russia and started the N. S. Yaffe Printing Company in 1906. It exists to this day. I can still smell the ink, see the printers slab it onto the presses, hear the noise while my father takes me around and explains the process to me.

My parents and most of their friends were successful in business. They were people of accomplishment, and we were expected to accomplish as well. The push was for us to become professionals.

I felt different, but different in the sense of better. We had three high schools in town: Tech, West Side, and Central, known as "Little Israel," which was largely Jewish and a good enough school to be nationally ranked.

In our community, financial problems were few, divorce was relatively unheard of, conspicuous consumption was kept to a minimum. We were living an all-American, upper-middle-class suburban Jewish life in the middle of nowhere. It was strange if you thought about it.

Leon Toubin: There's something about Texas that makes it like its own country. In school we would sing "Texas, Our Texas," every single day just like it was the national anthem.

There were a lot of Jews in the area around Brenham when I was growing up, and being Texans was a big part of their identity. Mainly they were descendants of German Jews who came there before the Civil War. Many of the original settlers intermarried because there were no Jewish girls around then. Today there are all these Jacobs, Goldbergs, Foxes. I know a sheriff who says, "We were probably all Jewish once, but we're Lutheran now."

My mother's parents came about 1875 bringing their parents with them. They were small people, particularly the grandparents. Monday mornings, my grandfather would put a pack on his back and go out calling on little farms in different places as far as he could walk, selling needles and thread. He'd be back Friday before sundown. When he got enough money together, he bought a horse and a wagon. Then he could carry a little fabric, some pots and pans. Soon he was able to buy another horse. Finally he had enough to open a store.

Brenham was a good trading area. People used to come from twenty, thirty miles away. Salesmen used to come in and set up shop for the small merchants to look at the wares. At one time there were seventeen Jewish merchants in little stores. All made a living selling shirts and pants and sundries. One of my uncles made a living fixing umbrellas. How he did that is still a mystery to me. But he had eleven children, and they seemed well taken care of.

B'nai Abraham, the oldest Orthodox synagogue in the state of Texas, was right near the Brenham fire station. The fireman on permanent duty was the *Shabbos goy*: he'd turn the lights on and off. In the late 1930s, when they began having trouble getting ten men together for the daily *minyan*, I began to be counted—even though I was only eleven years old. They'd send me to the corner service station to make the calls: "We need one more, we need two." The men would always say, "Get started. I'll be there."

But for the High Holidays, there was more than enough. All the Jewish people for miles around would come to Brenham. There was no hotel in town. Everyone stayed at my grandparents' house, sleeping on the floor, the porch, whatever. The shul was right behind Grandpa's property. People would cut through a hole in the back of his garage so they didn't have to walk all around the block.

Karol Musher: Laredo is a small Texas town located on a steppe on the Mexican border. When I was growing up, it was a benign kind of place, no pressure. There were three drugstores, a couple of drive-in carhop places, two movie theaters. On Sundays my father would take me to see double features in the air-conditioned theater so we could escape the Texas heat. It was a dry heat though, and in the evening it wasn't bad. People would sit on their front lawns, visit with one another.

My father had been a farmer in Lithuania, and after he worked for a while as a peddler around Laredo, he turned to farming again. It was starting to become lucrative when he had a very severe heart attack and had to give it up.

My mother then opened a fabric store called La Victoria and taught herself the business from scratch. It was a large place, the first shop on the right-hand side after you crossed the bridge from Mexico. We sold all kinds of material, from fine lace to coarse cotton. I can still smell the fabrics, feel the irritation in my nose and eyes from the wools and woven goods.

The customers were mostly Mexicans who bought large quantities and smuggled their purchases back across the border by wearing the fabrics under their clothes. I'd see them go into the back room and come out looking twenty pounds heavier. I did not understand what they were doing. My father would say, "It's better not to ask."

My mother was the entrepreneur. My father never, never liked business but tolerated it because it was the livelihood. He sat on his stool wearing a yarmulke and studying Torah. He had the whole thing memorized. Looking back, I just can't imagine how such an intellectual person survived in a world like Laredo.

We were part of a Jewish community of about fifty families, Eastern European immigrants who came into the United States via Mexico. They learned to speak Spanish before English. In many ways, Laredo was more Mexican than American.

Marv Stein: I was one of two gringos in my grade school in Pueblo, Colorado, and maybe one of four Jewish kids in my high school of two thousand. Fifty percent of Pueblo's population was Mexican. As for Jews, there were never as much as a hundred families. People asked a lot of questions.

I grew up eating borscht, chopped liver in its myriad forms, and our own version of smoked salmon—recipes my grandparents brought along with them. But I also ate a lot of green chili.

Pueblo is in a natural bowl. We can document 295 days of sunshine. It's flatlands, very different from most of Colorado. Roads throughout the state might be closed because of the snow, but in Pueblo people will be playing golf in the sunshine—in their shirtsleeves. It was an idyllic place to grow up in, with the hunting, fishing, running around free, seeing the mountains in the distance.

My grandfather, who had come over sometime in the late 1860s, ended up in Pueblo, where the steel-mill economy had attracted quite a number of Jews. After a little lollygagging around, Grandpa became Pueblo's first police chief. He stayed on the job for twenty years. The fact that he had no criminal justice experience was immaterial. His major responsibilities were keeping the kids in school and the cattle in their own pastures. He also had to take care of the occasional drunk. For this, he was paid forty dollars a month. He carried a Colt revolver, which he did not bring into the synagogue.

Although Grandpa had gotten out of the sheriff job more than twenty years before I was born, the old-timers around town would still stop me:

"Your grandfather was always breaking up the fight in the pool hall."

"Your grandfather was always writing me tickets for my letting my cows come onto the streets."

Grandpa's trademark was a white horse that was taller than he was. He was a little guy, but people thought he was tough. I always figured his bluff was a lot bigger than his bite.

He lived with my grandmother above Stein's Food Market, a little retail grocery they started with two cousins for seven borrowed dollars. Once, when a woman came into the store and ordered ten cents' worth of meat for dinner, Grandpa gave her ten times that amount.

My father asked him, "What the hell are you doing?"

Grandpa said, "She's got eight kids. She can't get by on ten cents' worth of meat."

My father turned to him and said, "*We* don't have anything to eat."

Grandpa just didn't understand business. Fortunately, he never had much to do with the store.

My father was not your typical Jewish father. He loved to shoot guns and was one of the top skeet shooters in this part of the world. I was my father's shadow. Since he left school in the third grade, he thought nothing of taking me out of school for weeks for hunting or skeet-shooting trips. He always felt you could learn as much traveling and keeping your eyes and ears open as you could in the classroom.

For a couple of years, I used to sit on my front porch and watch Clark Gable, who was stationed at the Pueblo Army Base, drive by in his big convertible. But it was no big deal. The kinds of people you see in all those westerns, we saw the real thing in town all the time.

David Elcott: I was a Valley boy, growing up in the 1950s in a suburb between North Hollywood and San Fernando. The Valley was rural country then, pretty and green. Down the block was a farm; fruit trees were all around. I learned to ride a horse about the same time I learned to walk. We shopped in a general store.

At that time, you could buy a house in the Valley for seven or eight thousand dollars. A lot of people from the Ozarks, from the Midwest were moving in. It was a brand-new area, and everyone was struggling to make it. There were no established institutions. We helped build two Catholic churches nearby. Our synagogue was California Conservative. You put on a *kipah* but that was it. I never saw a pair of *tefillin*—didn't even know what they were—until I was fourteen years old.

Disneyland opened when I was five. It became my model of what was beautiful. Even though we heard they didn't hire minorities, we went once a year and loved it. It was clean and wholesome, not a speck on the street. America the way it wants to see itself.

Leonard Goldstein: My parents were American born and well-off. We enjoyed an all-American style of life of Sunday afternoon drives and summer vacations. The Depression didn't seem to affect my father's insurance business at all.

The sign on the railroad trestle in my hometown of Trenton, New Jersey, read, "Trenton makes, and the world takes." The west end of Trenton, where I grew up, was where the Jews who had already made it lived. It was a prosperous-looking neighborhood of big houses and manicured lawns. Our home was right on the Delaware River.

The west end's synagogue was Conservative. All the Orthodox synagogues were downtown, in the old Jewish section. There people lived in small houses and above stores. On *yuntif*, downtown Trenton was as closed up as a ghost town.

My grandfather, Joseph Finn, lived downtown. He had come to Trenton in the late 1800s and had established himself in the wholesale produce business. He was Orthodox, but modern and liberal. In the early 1900s, he bought shares in Bank Leumi when it was just beginning. It was not a business investment but a commitment to Zionism. That was very unusual among the Orthodox in those days, because they believed the Messiah would have to come before the Jews could return to the Holy Land.

Grandpa was president of an Orthodox synagogue that remained very much in the Old World. They'd auction off *aliyahs*—the honor of being called up to recite a blessing—and the higher the honor, the higher the price: "*Drei taller* (three dollars) to come up to the Torah. Do I hear four?"

The west end was Americanized while downtown evoked Europe. I got my *Yiddishkeit* from my grandfather and his downtown world. He knew English perfectly, but he'd speak Yiddish to me all the time. He wanted to be sure I could speak what he feared might become a dying language.

Sam Popkin: The guys I hung around with spoke Yiddish a lot so that other people wouldn't know what they were talking about. They were a bunch of older guys who handled the smuggling of whiskey from Windsor, Ontario, to Detroit and then on to my hometown of Toledo, Ohio. They kind of adopted me, gave me a little money to go along for the ride.

Toledo was a wide-open town then, with gambling places and a big numbers business. Most of the gambling halls were owned by Jewish people with names like Jew-Murphy, Frisco Lew, Cowboy, Billy Sunday, Shadow, and Alcatraz. Lots of them also ran legitimate businesses and had nice families. They'd come into the synagogues from time to time, and always they made big donations.

As I was a boy from the boys, it meant nothing to me when guys from the Purple Gang, primarily a Jewish gang based in Detroit, used to come down to Toledo to do business with the gangsters there. Even the biggest gangsters, the Licovili and Al Capone gangs, came to Toledo for business.

Sometimes the guys who ran whiskey were caught by the law and put in jail. I remember mothers taking children to visit fathers and uncles in the jail downtown Toledo. But usually they were released after a couple of days and went back to the business of making and selling whiskey.

On the whiskey-smuggling rides, we'd go in these big trucks from Detroit to Toledo along old Route 25. One driver would try to bump the other into the ditches alongside the highway because the first truckload of whiskey to reach Toledo got the highest price. It was good-natured fun, something like drag racing, only with trucks. Nobody got hurt, and the same night, both drivers would get together in Toledo and have a couple of drinks. The guy who ended up in the ditch would tell the bumper, "I'll get you next time."

These guys were all good jokers. One was named "Okay Harry" because every other word he used was "Okay." Another was "Firetop" Sulken because of his red hair. Unfortunately, he wound up in the penitentiary.

Sometimes when we got to Detroit, we'd stop off to eat at Boesky's Delicatessen on Twelfth Street in the Jewish area. We'd take turns: a few of the guys would go in to eat while a few would remain inside the truck, guarding it with their guns. Then we'd switch.

Boesky's was an old-time deli, not too fancy on the outside but very clean with big banquet rooms downstairs for bar mitzvahs. There was a huge variety of all kinds of food: marinated herring, different smoked meats, chopped liver, gefilte fish, delicious soups. Celebrities were always dropping in. I met both Jimmy Hoffa and Walter Reuther there—at different times, of course.

Mr. Boesky was a Russian Jew, a very fast talker and a humorist. He dressed beautiful, always in a different suit. "Sam," he used to say to me, "stay out of those gambling joints in Toledo." I often wondered what advice he gave to his son, Ivan.

Brooks Susman: Weinstein's Delicatessen, in the Squirrel Hill section of Pittsburgh, served Reuben as well as corned beef sandwiches. The top of their menu read: "When in Shaker Heights, go to Corky's and Lenny's."

On the second floor, above Weinstein's, was a betting parlor. As a kid, I used to wonder why beefy Jewish men with large cigars would stand outside Weinstein's on Sunday mornings; finally my cousin Henry Katz, who spent a little time at the state's expense in the workhouse, told me what went on upstairs.

Pittsburgh had the elements of a frontier town even into the postwar years. There was a wildness among the kids, even the Jewish kids. A young man's entrance into manhood, for three dollars a pop, was just a short drive away in Wheeling, West Virginia. You could get anything you wanted in Wheeling for a price.

The Sesquicentennial of Pittsburgh in 1958 was essentially a watershed time between the old steel-mill and the present paper-pushing Pittsburgh. When I was growing up during the postwar years, Pittsburgh was still a nineteenth-century mill town, not the twenty-first-century city it is today. It was a time when Jews owned one white shirt that they wore for Shabbat, because why else wear a white shirt? It would turn gray in twenty minutes. Streetlights would be on during the day. From the third floor of my house, I could see the Bessemer converters open at midnight to let out the heat from the cauldrons of steel. The sky would turn bright as day.

Steel was Jewish—Levinson, Jones, and Loughlin (even though the name didn't sound it)—and Pittsburgh was a hub of German Jewry, a very important center of Reform Judaism.

In the postwar years, my family moved to Squirrel Hill, Pittsburgh's up-and-coming Jewish suburb. Within a six-block radius of our home were my two sets of grandparents, my mother's sisters and their families—the whole *mishpocheh*.

Squirrel Hill was divided by Forbes Avenue into two very different sections. North of Forbes, where we lived, was the German-Jewish section with beautiful single-family homes. South led into Stanton Heights, the Eastern European–Jewish area of attached homes and small apartment buildings.

In my age group, there was no relationship between the Reform German Jews and the traditional Eastern European Jews. That was just the way it was. It was a snobbish thing. The Reform Jews were wealthier. You aspired to be a north-of-Forbes Squirrel Hill Jew.

Most of the German-Jewish kids went to Squirrel Hill's high school, Taylor Allderdice. It was a unidimensional environment. You bought your shirts and pants at Brooks Brothers or you weren't accepted. You had to look the same, speak the same, belong to the proper high school fraternities and sororities.

I had a sense that the world was Jewish, totally. I hardly knew from Christianity. And to me there was one Judaism: Reform. Conservative and Orthodox Judaism did not exist. I never saw a *tallit* or a yarmulke. The only import traditional Judaism had on my life was those second-day-*yuntifs* that I had to go to school. "If there's a service you go. If there isn't, you're in school," my mother would say. So I went—to a school so Jewish that the only kids there were the Reform Jews whose parents made them go. The few Christian kids took off knowing nothing would take place.

Jacob Marcus: I remember hearing about Jay Leonard Levy, the rabbi of the Reform synagogue in Pittsburgh in the early years of this century. People talked with wonder and amazement about him. They said he didn't keep kosher and wore a dog collar like an Episcopalian.

Brooks Susman: Solomon B. Freehof, probably the most noted Reform scholar—renowned even among the Orthodox for his scholarship—was rabbi of Rodef Shalom, the prominent Reform congregation in Pittsburgh. He drew his biggest crowds, into the hundreds, not on Shabbat but on Sunday mornings when he delivered his lectures. He sermonized in the old sense of the word, for forty-five to fifty minutes.

On the High Holy Days, the crowds would be too large to fit into Rodef Shalom, so services were held at the Shriners Hall down the block from Forbes Field. One day in 1960, when the Pirates were in the World Series, Rabbi Freehof—who adored the Pirates—went to the game after services. He had invited Assistant Rabbi Fred Schwartz to join him. Rabbi Schwartz, embarrassed to be seen at the ballpark in the striped pants and morning coat they wore for the High Holy Days, put his trench coat over his outfit. I think it was 112 degrees outside.

For the *shofar* blowing, my French horn teacher would stand in the wings and produce these perfect dulcet tones with her horn. Meanwhile, out on the *bimah*, someone would be holding the shofar aloft. Lenny Bruce would have loved it.

Growing up in Pittsburgh, I always thought I was living in the East.

Then I moved to New York, and I realized the Allegheny Mountains separate the East from the rest of the country. New York Jews are used to seeing a piece of lox sliced in front of them. Midwestern Jews get pre-sliced, prepackaged lox. That's the essence of midwestern Jewry: It's prepackaged.

Morris Kerness: Duluth, Minnesota, and Superior, Wisconsin, face each other across Lake Superior. In my day, Duluth was the conservative, proper town. Superior was the wide-open town with all the whorehouses. We went there many times.

Dan Kossoff: Duluth was a beautiful city with hills, like San Francisco. Superior was the tough port town of wall-to-wall bars and honky-tonks. But Jews in both cities were one community, very insular and closely knit.

Is Crystal: In the early years of this century, iron ore was discovered north of Duluth. The little range towns like Hibbing, Virginia, and Chisolm, five to ten miles apart from each other, beckoned for workers. Jewish people arrived and opened general stores. Some of the towns came to have fairly nice-sized Jewish populations.

In 1913 my father left Galveston, Texas, where he had been sent by HIAS and joined his brother in Duluth. He worked seven days a week, ten or more hours a day, and at the same time went to night school to learn English. In 1917 he bought a little deli downtown. By 1920, when he had become fairly well settled financially, my father returned to Russia and brought my mother, sister, and me to America.

During the crossing, my father told us all about Duluth: what the store was like, how all the children in Duluth went to school. I couldn't wait. At last, I thought, we were going to America: the *goldeneh medina*, the land of gold that my mother, uncle, and grandparents had talked about all the time. Though my mother and sister were pretty seasick most of the way, I was so excited that my folks had a tough time holding me down. I kept climbing up on the railing, and they were afraid I'd fall into the ocean.

We stopped off at Ellis Island after disembarking, but since my dad was already an American citizen, we didn't have to go through Immigration. My very first day in America, I had a Hershey's chocolate bar. That's how I started off. We spent a week with family in New York City and really saw the town before moving on. We arrived in Duluth on May 12, 1920. The snow still covered the ground. The next day, the *Duluth News Tribune* ran a story about our arrival, and I began school.

Morris Kerness: Issy and I are about the same age. We met the day he came to Duluth and have been friends ever since. The first thing I did with him was get some United Cigar coupons and shoot craps. Naturally, I took the money from him. He was a greenhorn.

Is Crystal: They used to sing a Yiddish song about a *greena kuzina*, a beautiful girl, full of life and joy, who comes from the old country to America and loses her bloom and vitality from working in the sweatshops. But that didn't describe our experience in Duluth. The cold was never a problem for us. We dressed for the season. The cars would go up the icy hills and slide down. We got used to it. We skated, skied, went sledding—all the winter things.

Morris Kerness: We'd start up on Tenth Street with our toboggans and slide all the way down the steep hill to First Street. The only thing that wasn't fun was walking up the hill with the sled again.

Winters in Duluth were very cold. It hit forty below many days. But it is a beautiful city, sitting on a hill at the head of Lake Superior. You can see the whole panorama of the lake, and deep forests, and Wisconsin on the other side.

Is Crystal: From the time we came and through the early forties, Duluth had a population of about thirty-five hundred to four thousand Jews. The rest were Scandinavian, Irish, Polish, and German. We did not feel the anti-Semitism in Duluth the way they felt it in Minneapolis, which was one of the strongest hotbeds of anti-Jewish feeling in the whole country. We read about that in the newspapers all the time.

Morris Kerness: Even though I had many non-Jewish friends, I felt different from the gentile population. I'm only five feet four, but I was a tough kid. Issy was gentler than me. He'd turn the other cheek; I didn't.

Issy's house was about eight blocks away from mine, in the nicer part of town where most of the merchants lived. We lived in the Jewish neighborhood up on Ninth Street, the regular ghetto. Two blocks north up the hill were the Polish people. We were always fighting. They'd call us "sheenie" and "kike." But I'll tell you what: we busted a few heads.

The Jewish ghetto was a radius of four to five blocks of modest one-family homes. The fathers were mostly peddlers. They'd park their wagons in front of the houses, and the horses would walk around by themselves to the barns in the back alleys. They knew the way. You didn't see many cars around Duluth until the mid-twenties. My father had a neat, meticulous harness shop on First Street. He was a very honest and hard-working man. Like the other men in the ghetto, he was Orthodox—poor but proper.

Franklin School was right near our ghetto, and 80 percent of the kids were Jewish, so on the High Holy Days they practically closed the school down. We had a teacher by the name of Mrs. Thor who was very mean. Every now and then, we'd come into the class, and she'd go: "I smell gefilte fish."

Once a kid named Frank Rachman was absent for a couple of days. Instead of sending truant officers, the teachers used to walk over to the houses during recess to find out why someone wasn't at school. So it happened that Friday morning, Mrs. Thor went to Mrs. Rachman's house.

Our mothers knew all about Mrs. Thor. That day Mrs. Rachman offered Mrs. Thor some gefilte fish. Mrs. Thor sat down at the table, and Mrs. Rachman gave her a plate with a couple of fish patties. Only they weren't boiled. Mrs. Rachman sat there and watched while Mrs. Thor bit into a raw patty. Mrs. Thor never smelled gefilte fish again.

Is Crystal: Almost every store on Superior Street was owned by a Jewish merchant: the bookstore, the clothing store, the linen store, the appliance store. They were open on Saturdays, but on Friday nights and the High Holy Days they were closed, and it was pretty dead downtown.

There were three Orthodox shuls in Duluth. Though they had Hebrew names, we called them by the street each was on. There was also Temple Emanuel, the Reform temple, for the German Jews and those who had already made a few bucks.

When someone died, the body of the deceased would be placed on the floor and surrounded by lit candles. Then they laid it down on a plank and took it across the river to the Jewish cemetery in Superior, Wisconsin—just like they did in Europe. Later a law was passed that required the body be enclosed in a box before it was carried to a grave.

Summers in Duluth were beautiful, nice and cool with the lake. Back in the twenties and thirties, peddlers from New York and Chicago who sold umbrellas, fancy handkerchiefs and such would come up for the summers. Their headquarters became our store. They'd sit around and discuss world and Jewish affairs, read aloud from the *Forward* and other Jewish papers.

After a while, my dad's store became the meeting place for the steady stream of Jewish people who came from the East. It was a kind of checkpoint on the way west, a place to get kosher food, to speak the *mama-loshen*. A lot of them would keep money in my dad's safe. They all wore beards—which may be why I thought they were very old.

Our store catered mainly to foot traffic, but we also had the so-called carriage trade. In the early days, they drove up in horses and wagons. In later years, they drove up in chauffeur-driven limos. These were the money barons who made it on lumber, grain, or shipping. They lived in mansions. It amazed me to see them come into our little store to buy caviar or marinated artichoke hearts, fruit pickled in brandy and cognac. We developed a friendship with them. It's hard to say what their inner feelings were about dealing with Jews, but outwardly they were very friendly.

My father knew how to make wine out of raisins or grapes—beautiful stuff. At Christmas he'd make a special batch, bottle it, and give it out to the non-Jewish customers. We had a wonderful relationship with them.

In Europe, my sister and I knew nothing about Christmas. Here we learned about it in school. Once a Jewish friend from a wealthier family sold us a bill of goods, telling us if we hung up stockings, they'd get filled with toys and other presents. We tried it, but all we got was coal and orange peels and potatoes. That was our parents' way of telling us Christmas wasn't our holiday.

Going out with a *shiksa* was frowned upon. You had to do it behind your parents' backs. When you took one out, you did it to have a good time. When you wanted to develop a relationship, you took out a Jewish girl. My mother used to come down to the skating rink—skating was a big thing in Duluth—to see that I was not skating with a *shiksa*.

There was a lot of camaraderie among the Jewish boys and girls in Duluth. We rarely ate *trayf*; we kept as kosher as we could. That's how my dad's store became such a hub: kids could get a kosher meat sandwich there.

A bunch of ten or twelve boys and girls would often drive up in a truck to the range towns fifty miles or more outside Duluth. In a town like Hibbing, there might be thirty or forty Jewish kids. Their parents were anxious for them to meet Jewish kids and were glad when we came up. They were very, very prosperous. Companies made billions of dollars up there. The schools were beautiful, and the kids got their school supplies for free.

In Duluth, a lot of the Jewish boys sold newspapers on the street, but my father didn't want me to do that. He also didn't want me hanging around the pool hall with the Damon Runyon kind of group.

Dan Kossoff: Is Crystal and my dad were boyhood friends. They took dancing classes together. By my time, much of our social activity revolved around Duluth's Jewish Community Center, where we played basketball.

Is Crystal: There was a strong Zionist group that took in Duluth and Superior and all the range towns. Every summer they held a picnic in the park, and that was a good place for the boys and girls to meet. They always had a speaker from some place, traveling cantors, actors from the Yiddish theater, people from the Workmen's Circle, socialists, union organizers. They were kind of an intellectual group, people of renown from New York. Some Sunday nights, my dad would close up the store to go hear them.

Dan Kossoff: Generally, anti-Semitism wasn't open, but under the surface, everyone understood it was there. The Northland Country Club was the greatest symbol: it was off-limits to Jews through the 1960s. During the winter, we used to sneak up on the slopes there and ride down on toboggans.

Always in the back of my mind was the idea: here we are, Jews playing in a place that is off-limits to us.

Dinah Crystal Kossoff: In grade school one of my best friends was Kathleen Dinhamm, the daughter of an orthodontist. Her parents would take me along to Northland Country Club and Pike Lake, a private swimming club. Even though I was very young, I knew Jews couldn't be members at those places, and going there gave me an uncomfortable feeling.

The Jewish families would make the hour-and-a-half drive to Patterson State Park. My father often left the store late in the afternoon to have dinner with us in the park. We were always wishing the temperature would reach seventy degrees, which was my mother's minimum requirement before we could go swimming in the lake. Most of the time, the water was so cold, you'd go in and get numb.

Morris Kerness: At one time, Duluth had about 120,000 people. About thirty years ago when they got the St. Lawrence Waterway, they thought the town would grow to about half a million. But instead, we're down to about eighty-five thousand. At one time, Duluth had a Jewish community of four thousand families. Today there are about three hundred.

Is Crystal: Hibbing used to have at least three hundred Jewish people. Only seventeen live there today.

Dan Kossoff: The exodus began in the late fifties, when the iron range began to run out of ore. The economy went down, and most of the young Jewish people moved away.

Morris Kerness: The kids grew up, made money, and moved out of town. There was nothing for you here unless your father had a store. You had nothing to come back to. You became a doctor or a lawyer and moved on.

Dinah Crystal Kossoff: Duluth was my growing-up town, and it was a wonderful, wholesome place. I couldn't walk down the street without seeing someone I knew. All my cousins, aunts and uncles, my grandparents were there. Everybody I loved was in that town. But unlike our parents, our generation went on to college, most of us to the University of Minnesota. Afterwards, many stayed in Minneapolis or they went on. Very few came back. We loved growing up in Duluth but didn't want to stay. I guess it was just too small a town.

Blu Greenberg: My grandfather Moshe Genauer came to America in 1905, at age twenty-six. The impetus was one more pogrom in the Ukraine. He was taken out of a yeshiva and sent to America to pave the way for the rest of the family. It was during the time of the Alaskan Gold Rush. Figuring he could do better following the Gold Rush path than competing with all the other peddlers on the Lower East Side, he boarded the Northern Pacific Railroad and headed west. In Seattle, he met some Jews who needed a tenth man for a *minyan,* and he wound up staying there.

He was a peddler, buying and selling used clothing. One day he walked four miles out of town to buy some suits from a man. He came back to his little room, laid the suits out on his bed, and found a diamond brooch in one of the pockets. So he turned around and walked all the way back to the house of the man who had sold him the suits.

A woman answered the door. "I'd like to speak to your husband," my grandfather said.

She saw a man with a beard and a hat, obviously Jewish, speaking with an accent. "You can't bother my husband," the woman said. "You were here already. What do you want?"

"I didn't buy a diamond from your husband," my grandfather replied. "I bought a suit."

Her husband turned out to be the president of Rainier National Bank, and he rewarded my grandfather's honesty with an unlimited line of credit. This enabled my grandfather to open up a men's wholesale clothing business and bring over his wife, my uncle, and my father, then aged two. And that is how I came to grow up in Seattle, the beautiful city of hills. The business became successful and supported six families the next generation. Today the name Genauer is one of the names synonymous with the Seattle Jewish community.

Marc Angel: Turkish and Greek immigrants began settling in Seattle around the turn of the century. The greenery, the mountains, and water reminded them of the old country, and they were able to earn a living in the fishing industry. A handful of Sephardic Jews followed them. They made a little money, sent for their relatives, and started a small community. By 1910 there were about six hundred Sephardic Jews in Seattle, almost all of whom lived in the section known as the Central District. It wasn't a fancy neighborhood—the Jews were very poor in those days—just modest one-family frame houses, a working-class area. Japanese, Filipinos, and blacks lived there as well as Jews.

In 1908 my grandfather Angel left the Isle of Rhodes, where his family had probably been living since shortly after the expulsion of the Jews from Spain, and came to Seattle. He worked as a shoeshiner and cobbler, and by 1911 earned enough to send for my grandmother and seven children. My father was the youngest and the only one born in the United States. My mother's parents came here from Turkey as teenagers, met and married here.

My mother's father used to tell the story of how when he first came to Seattle, there was no Sephardic synagogue. He and a group of Sephardim went over to the Ashkenazic synagogue. Here they were, Sephardim who spoke Judeo-Spanish (Ladino), had names like Romey and Angel, and looked like Arabs or Greeks or Turks. The Ashkenazim didn't think they were Jewish.

Finally, some of the Sephardim wrote to Dr. Mendes, the rabbi of the Spanish-Portuguese Synagogue in New York. He wrote to the Ashkenazim: "Yes, these are Jews. There is such a thing as Sephardic Jews."

Blu Greenberg: When I was a child in the thirties and forties, the Ashkenazic and Sephardic communities of Seattle were separate. A marriage between an Ashkenazi and a Sephardi was looked upon almost as if it were an intermarriage. My grandparents' home was a block away from the Ashkenazic shul we attended. Halfway down the block in the opposite direction was the Sephardic shul. To us, the Sephardim were very strange—a group apart. Jews, but like a different sect.

Marc Angel: The Ashkenazic kids used to call the Sephardim "Mazola" because they cooked with vegetable oil. The Sephardic kids called the Ashkenazim "schmaltz" because they cooked with chicken fat.

We attended the Ashkenazic Hebrew Day School where the Hebrew words were pronounced differently, the melodies for the prayers and Torah were different. Half the time, we didn't understand what the teachers were talking about. They'd say something like "On Chanukah, Jews eat *latkes*," and we'd wonder, "What are *latkes*?" We had never heard of them. On Chanukah, we ate a kind of fried dough dipped in honey. We felt cornered, a certain degree of alienation.

Blu Greenberg: Despite the differences, my father had friends and business associates in the Sephardic community. By the time we were growing up, the communities were beginning to come together, and the children of both groups became friends.

Marc Angel: There was a lot of bad blood early on. Not that it was anyone's fault. The two groups just didn't understand each other's culture. That does not seem so strange when you consider there were enough differences even between the Greek and Turkish Sephardim for them to have their own separate synagogues. Ezra Bessaroth, where we belonged, was for the Jews from the Isle of Rhodes. Bikur Holim, where my mother's family belonged, was for the Jews from Turkey. My grandfather Romney was one of its founders, and in 1919 he became its president. Both shuls exist to this day.

Blu Greenberg: We attended a magnificent Ashkenazic shul with a great dome and a beautiful chandelier. I was fascinated by its thousands of little tiny crystals. The shul was a very familiar place to me, like home. I had great freedom there: I could go in and out, run about with my friends in the yard or play games of rolling walnuts in the vast basement of the shul.

Despite the different groups, the Jewish population of Seattle was very small, and the Orthodox a small portion of that population. It was inevitable, I guess, that we would come up against anti-Semitism. My experiences puzzled me more than anything else. Like I couldn't understand why Mary Jane who lived down a different hill wouldn't let me ride my bike on her block because I was Jewish. What did being Jewish have to do with it, I wondered.

Or that morning I was walking to school with my two sisters, and the kids on the next block called to us from their porch: "Hey girls, are you Jewish? Oooh, you killed Jesus Christ."

I remember looking down at my freshly polished white shoes and wondering why I didn't see any blood. If I killed somebody, I thought, there ought to have been some blood. That day when we came home for lunch, we asked our mother who Jesus Christ was. She asked why we wanted to know. And we said, "Because we killed him."

Perhaps these events did not deeply affect me because I loved being Jewish. Being observant was not a burden. It was ingrained in me that living the life of an Orthodox Jew was something special and wonderful, a great gift.

Also, I was so enveloped in the life of my large extended family. I had four uncles and aunts and all of their children nearby. The sense of a family and community as being so essential was implanted in me at a very young age.

Marc Angel: There were about thirteen thousand Jews in Seattle out of a population of half a million when I was born in July 1945. And if you scratched just a little bit, you would find that every Sephardic Jew in Seattle was related by blood or by marriage. So there was a very strong feeling of home during my childhood. I felt I was in a place where I belonged.

Many years later, when I had moved to New York and had a family of my own, I began going back to Seattle in the summers with my wife and children. It is still such a beautiful city, and I took pleasure in visiting the old neighborhood, in pointing out the Hebrew school and synagogues and the houses that had once belonged to my parents, aunts, and grandparents. Until one summer we drove past my grandparents' house and found all the windows boarded up and on the door a sign that said "Condemned."

It was hard to accept. That house was the symbol of my Seattle childhood. I can still picture the peach tree out front, the cherry tree in the back, the little garden with its string beans, tomatoes, and eggplant.

And inside, all the people, the joyous get-togethers—there was always an excuse for a celebration or party—the people dancing around the living room to Turkish music. My mother, a redhead, very bright and full of life, would play her castanets. My uncle Jack would add his tambourine. We'd sing along. Sometimes my uncle Dave would show movies that he took on his vacations. To tell the truth, a lot of his film never came out, but we had a good time looking anyway.

Although we knew about the tragedies of the Jews throughout history and had observances that reminded us of them, these were remote events. We thought we were lucky. We thought everything we had was the best. We thought Jews were the happiest, luckiest people in the world. I didn't know there was such a thing as an unhappy Jew until I came to New York.

5

NEW YORK, NEW YORK

"Blessed shalt thou be in the city."

—*Deuteronomy XXVIII:3*

Neil Postman: If you're writing a story of growing up Jewish in America, in a way you're writing a story of growing up in New York. New York is the most Jewish city in the world. A white Anglo-Saxon Protestant from Kansas who's in New York for three months starts to get Jewish.

When I grew up in the thirties and forties, there were three and a half million Jews living in a city of eight million. There were roughly two million Jews in Brooklyn alone. When they called Brooklyn the borough of churches, we didn't know what the hell they were talking about.

Irv Saposnik: My East New York neighborhood in Brooklyn was an ex-clusively Jewish world. The worst part of it was the narrowness and insularity, the smugness. The best part was the feeling of sanctuary and closeness.

Murray Polner: We were poor children of poor immigrant parents who spoke with Yiddish accents, living in an overwhelmingly Jewish part of the world. Hardly any of us seemed to notice what we lacked. We were at home.

The Brownsville section of Brooklyn, where I grew up, was a cohesive, easily definable community of God knows how many people, most of whom were Jewish except for a strip where a lot of black people lived. We would go there to hear "sepia music"—jazz and blues.

Al Lewis: At the age of twelve, I moved from Walcott in upstate New York, where we were the only Jews in town, to Brownsville in Brooklyn, the largest Jewish ghetto in the world. I got up in the morning and walked ten blocks this way, ten blocks that way, and I was surrounded by *Yidden*. There was not one store in Brownsville that was not Jewish. The "geshmacht" (smell) of the food from the kosher delicatessens, the knishes, the charlotte russes—it was all there. I was caught in a landslide. I was buried in Jews.

I never saw a live poultry market before I moved to Brownsville. My aunts would pick their chicken out and give it to the *shochet*. He'd kill it a certain way. Then they'd give three cents to the fat lady with the bloody apron and she'd pluck it as fast as a machine.

I never saw a fish market until I went with my aunts to buy fish. Every week, all the kids would gather round the bathtub as Aunt Molly filled it

◀ New York City scenes in the 1920s.

up with water and threw the live fish in. The fish would swim, everybody would go crazy. But the sad part came on Friday when Aunt Molly got ready to make her gefilte fish. She'd take the fish out and put it on a board. All the little kids would plead, "Don't kill it, please don't kill it. I like that fish." She'd bang it with a rolling pin. The kids would scream and cry. It was a trauma. Till next week when she bought another fish home.

What I didn't know about live chicken and fish markets, I knew about horses. I'd grown up on a horse farm. My little cousins found this amazing. The only horses they ever saw were those the peddlers used.

"You . . . you touched a horse?" they'd ask.

"I saw them crap. I saw them pee."

"You did?"

I was the only one in all of Brownsville who saw that.

In all of Brownsville, there weren't any Jewish horse breeders like my "meshuga tata" (crazy father). But there were plenty of Jewish gangsters: Abe Rellis, Pittsburgh Phil Straus, Banjo, the boys in Murder, Inc. They hung out on the streets. We didn't know—or we didn't want to know—the infamous acts they were involved in, that they were murderers for hire, would ice-pick a guy to death for two hundred dollars. All we knew was they were not so *oy-oy-oy*.

What clothes they had! They shopped at Leighton's in Manhattan, the clothing store of clothing stores. We'd spend twenty-eight dollars for a suit at Crawford's or Howard's. They'd pay three hundred bucks a pop. We didn't make that much in a month, in three months.

Murray Polner: We used to take a wide swath around them, but one Saturday night, Bummy Davis's brother was shot in a bar, and we followed the trail of blood with fascination.

Neil Postman: After my father got married, he became rather protective of my mother's five unmarried younger sisters. One of them, the legend says, was dating Louis Lepke Buchalter, the head of Murder, Inc. The legend goes on to say that my father, who didn't approve, went to Lepke and told him to stay away—which would have taken a lot of courage, if it were true.

Roz Starr: One day my mother and I were walking down the street in Brownsville, and we passed this well-dressed, dark and smiling man who always sat outside the coffee shop. "She's a beautiful girl," he said to my mother.

My mother said, "You should hear her sing."

He said to me, "Come over here, honey." He sat me on his lap and I sang. When I finished, he gave me a quarter. Afterwards whenever I passed by, he always made me sing, and he always gave me a quarter. In those days with a quarter you could go to the candy store all day. Later on we found out he was Bugsy Buchalter of Murder, Inc.

Morris Friedman: I remember how glad I was to learn Burton Turkus, the D.A. who prosecuted the members of Murder, Inc., was Jewish. My entire perspective on public life was whether or not it was good for the Jews. If I heard someone was incarcerated, the first thing I wanted to know was whether he was Jewish. I sought out Jewish heroes to identify with, people like Hank Greenberg, Barney Ross, Sid Luckman.

Al Lewis: The stars of the Yiddish theater were my heroes. They were geniuses: David Keseel, Ludwig Zatz, Menashe Skolnik, Boris Tomashefsky, Molly Picon, Jacob Kalish, and Muni Weisenfreund, who went on to become Paul Muni. Yiddish theaters were all over New York City. Around 1935, on a given Friday night, people would have a choice of twenty-six theaters to go to. Live shows, a drama, a musical. Ordinary people finished a week's work and said, "Let's go to the theater."

People got all dressed up. Women who worked as seamstresses for nine, ten dollars a week, would put on the one good dress they owned that maybe they bought for six dollars in Klein's on Union Square and go to the theater to have a good cry. It was a tremendous event. Back home in Walcott, I had never seen anything like it. Who would be in the audience? A horse?

Manny Azenberg: My father's brother was the bohemian of the family, involved in Jewish and later English theatrical productions. His real name was Vuluff Azenberg, but he changed it to Wolf Barzell; *barzell* means "iron" in Hebrew. The show he did I remember best is *The Skipper Next to God* because John Garfield, the Marlon Brando of my time, was in it. After the show, we went backstage. The name on the dressing room door was "Julius Garfinkel." There was a Jewish boy's hero: Jewish *and* a tough kid from the streets. I went back to the neighborhood having met John Garfield. That was good for two or three months.

Irv Saposnik: On the street, our heroes were Danny Kaye and Steve Lawrence, guys who had made it out of our neighborhood. But they were the impossible dreams. They had leaped so far that they were fantasies.

For a couple of months, our hero was Cal Abrams of the Brooklyn Dodgers. He was the toast of the National League, hitting well over .400. Everybody was trumpeting him; it looked like we had another Ted Williams. Then he went away on a road trip, and boom-boom. He just fell, fell, fell.

Murray Polner: For many immigrant children, baseball became an Americanizing process. My father worked six and a half days a week. But one hot summer day, I made him go with me to Ebbets Field. I cheered for the Dodgers as any nine-year-old would. When we got home, I said "Dad, we're going to do this again and again."

That evening my father was sitting outside on the street, and somebody asked, "Alex, how was your day?"

"*Oysgemattert farloirener tog,*" I heard him say—an exhausting, wasted day.

Irv Saposnik: You had to be a Jewish kid to understand the appeal of the Dodgers. We related to them in ways I suspect no other ethnic group in Brooklyn could. They gave us something to identify with. We were able to use them as a magic carpet of possibility, a way out of our confinement.

The blacks had Jackie Robinson, who became a batting champion and Most Valuable Player. He prevailed. That was one kind of experience. Ours was identifying with how the Dodgers always came up short, second place to the victorious goyim: the Yankees. Having pain and defeat as part of our inheritance, this was easy to understand. And they played into our messianic hope, our looking into the future. The Jews were waiting for next year in Jerusalem. The Dodgers were waiting for next year to win the World Series. We saw baseball in a Judaic context and followed it with religious fervor.

Shalom Goldman: Although we were part of a pretty vibrant Orthodox community in Hartford, the feeling was the real religious fervor of Judaism was in New York. You had to go there to experience it.

Once my father took me to see the Satmar Chasidim in Williamsburg, Brooklyn. I got swept up in the ecstatic quality of it all, but at the same time I was traumatized. Here I was, a typical-looking American Jewish kid surrounded by all these Chasidic kids, nasty little boys who were tweaking my cheeks and screaming at me in Yiddish, *"Und vee iz doner payess?"*— Where are your earlocks?

Roz Starr: My mother, who was deeply religious, saw to it that we spent every Shabbos in the shul across the street. I liked going. It gave me a sense of the sacred and a feeling of security. Maybe the men being on one side and the women on the other had something to do with it.

The pledges of cash for *aliyahs* still ring in my head:

"Rom's Bakery for the best-tasting strudel and rye bread in Brownsville pledges eighteen dollars."

"Cohen's Butcher Shop is pleased to pledge *chai* times two and a half for the best flanken around."

"Gordon's Glatt Dairy, with all the special foods you need for your holiday table, happily pledges twenty-five dollars."

The pledges were thirty-second free commercial spots. The whole congregation was a target audience. But I always wondered how, in those days before tape recorders, they remembered the pledges—and how many of the pledgers made good on them.

Mitchell Serels: The rabbi at our Sephardic synagogue in the Bronx came from Tangiers, as did my father. We went there until they built the Cross-Bronx Expressway, which cut through the neighborhood and made it too difficult to walk to. The congregation was mostly Spanish-speaking Jews from Greece and Turkey, plus a few Cubans. Next door to the synagogue was a brotherhood building, a place to play cards and hang out. Every year the women had a bazaar that raised a lot of money for the congregation. They picked up clothing that were seconds or used, worked very hard sewing and repairing them, and sold them at a rummage sale. They also did a lot of cooking—the stuffed pastries, baklava.

Murray Polner: There was a neighborliness in the Jewish communities of New York. Even when people were not cordial, they looked in on and cared for one another. During the Depression—when people were dispossessed from their apartments, their furniture placed out on the sidewalks—my mother would lead a battalion of women. They'd find places for the dispossessed to stay, call on the boys hanging around to carry their furniture to a safe place.

Neil Postman: Our Flatbush neighborhood was like a little shtetl, although a fairly affluent one. All along Avenue J, the main shopping street, were appetizing stores catering to the Jewish clientele: Elfenbein's and Ebinger's bakeries, two kosher delis, at least three candy stores, and of course a very popular Chinese restaurant. A Chinese friend once told me that the thing Jews and Chinese have most in common is their love of Chinese food.

Every Friday night, my brother Jack, sister Ruth, and I had this routine of going to the Chinese restaurant. This was before Jack went into the Army, when I was eight or nine and Ruth was maybe twelve. Jack had one dollar. The dinners were thirty cents each, and the tip was a dime. We'd get egg drop soup, an egg roll, and chow mein. And then a little bowl of ice cream with a fortune cookie. To show you how dumb I was—and we did this maybe thirty times—every time I was just about finished with my chow mein, my brother Jack would say: "I think I lost the dollar. We don't have any money to pay, and this means we have to wash dishes." And I would believe him. You would think after ten times . . .

Although my neighborhood was primarily Jewish, the local elementary school, P.S. 99, had Christian as well as Jewish kids. And that was wonderful. The public schools gave us the sense that though we were different, we were all Americans.

We had no problem singing the Christian songs at Christmas time, although we thought "Deck the halls with boughs of challah" was a hilarious twist. None of the Christmas songs had Jesus in them. "Mary" was in a few, but my grandmother's name was Miriam and she was called Mary. So that was okay. We didn't feel less Jewish in any way for singing these songs or for drawing turkeys on Thanksgiving or Santa Clauses on Christmas. We weren't Christians. We were Americans.

The Midwood Movie Theater on Avenue J was an important vehicle for our Americanization. One can make the case that there were never any Americans like the characters we saw in the movies, but every group needs its ideals. They were wonderful people: Mickey Rooney and Judy Garland. And Andy Hardy's father, Louis Stone—there couldn't be an ounce of anti-Semitism in a man like that. There was a sweetness to those movies that we related to.

Marilyn Cohen: Hollywood created images of what I thought America was, people who looked like June Allyson and Van Johnson. We looked nothing like them. It was only later in life that I realized why I adored the Arthur Scyzk illustrations in my book of Andersen's Fairy Tales. His figures looked like Eastern European Jews.

My father worked for Macy's and marched in Manhattan in the Thanksgiving Day Parade. What could be more American than that? Yet the legacy I had from my family was that we were outsiders. You can never tell when the political climate might change and you would no longer be welcome.

Until I was ten, we lived in the Bronx, where almost everyone we knew was Jewish. In 1949 we moved to Flushing, Queens, which was mostly empty lots at the time. I thought it was like living in the country. There were no other Jews in the neighborhood, but because most of the people were Italian, it was okay. They had a warm feeling for Jews. But I did feel strange as the only Jewish child in my elementary school class, especially at assembly when they read a passage from the New Testament.

Herb Kalisman: I felt we first-generation kids in my East Harlem elementary school were looked at by the mainly Irish teachers as if we somehow weren't clean. They would inspect our fingernails, look behind our ears—things they didn't do with the second- and third-generation kids.

Gail Eiseman Bernstein: Many of our teachers were single Irish ladies, very strict and stern but not without humor and occasional flashes of affection. After third grade, I began getting some Jewish women teachers and, every so often, a man.

Neil Postman: One day Mr. Moses, our fifth-grade teacher, was going over our math homework. He said "Neil, problem three," and I did it. "Mildred," there were Mildreds in those days, "problem four," and she did it. Then he got to Elliot Cohen, and Elliot said, "I didn't do my homework."

"Why not?" asked Mr. Moses.

"Because I didn't want to," Elliot answered.

Every kid who was in that class will remember that moment. You could say your mother was sick or your grandmother was dying. But to say "I didn't want to" to a teacher was out of the question. We all agreed this can mean only one thing. Elliot is destined to spend his life in Sing Sing.

Murray Polner: The teachers in the public schools, the librarians on Stone Avenue, where I first discovered books—they encouraged us to read and to search and to investigate. There were many Christians who treated us children of the immigrant working class with honor and respect and brought us into the life of the mind. Never once did I hear an anti-Semitic remark.

My father infected me with the love of Jewish history and Jewish literature. But it was a young, heavy-set teacher at Tilden High School, a Protestant from New England—the first man of that kind I had ever met—who infected me with the love of American and European literature.

Karl Bernstein: It wasn't until I was in the eighth grade that I met a Protestant kid. Up to then, all I knew were Jewish, Italians, and Irish who used to call out "Dirty Jew, spit in your shoe" and start up fights. But there were so many of us around, I never had the sense of being a minority.

Manny Azenberg: In the Mott Haven section of the Bronx, near Yankee Stadium, the Irish were part of the neighborhood. The Italians were across the train tracks. Harlem was across the river. And being Jewish was conflictive, endlessly conflictive.

You knew it internationally because everybody was getting killed in Europe. You knew it in the Bronx because if there were eight of them and four of you, they'd beat you up. Although if there were eight of you and four of them, you'd beat *them* up.

Being Jewish meant other people could take a whack at you. You'd walk past the church at 163rd Street and Morris Avenue and make the sign of the cross across your chest so they'd think you were Catholic and wouldn't beat the hell out of you.

Neil Postman: In my neighborhood, there was an easy connection between the gentile and Jewish kids. One of my Christian friends, Sonny Allen, could do things with a Spalding in our stickball games that were unbelievable. It would curve about four different ways before it got to you. I often went to Sonny's house. At Christmas, though, their tree had a smell that was very alien to me. For some reason, I preferred not to smell it.

Sammy Rutigliano, who went on to become head coach of the Cleveland Browns, was one of the four guys who played two-on-two basketball in the gym at the Young Israel of Flatbush on Coney Island Avenue. Our agreement with the *shammes,* or caretaker, was he would let us play, and we would participate in the evening prayers whenever he was short of a *minyan.* He was always short of a *minyan.* He'd ask, "Are you all Jewish?" We'd say "Of course." Sammy would come along; they'd stick a yarmulke on his head, and he'd become part of the *minyan.*

We formed a basketball team and sold raffle tickets to raise money to pay for our jackets. We wanted them to be flaming scarlet with the team name—"Hawks"—written in yellow on the back. When the *shammes* of Young Israel found out about it, he told us he could get the jackets for cheaper than the guy we were dealing with. So naturally we gave him the order. But what he didn't tell us was that he intended to get "Young Israel" onto the jackets somehow. When we got our flaming scarlet jackets, the word *Hawks* was written in yellow on the back, but added on were the letters *YI*—without any periods. We became known in the neighborhood as the "HAWKS-YI!"

Once this *shammes* made some bigoted remark about a Christian. We were horrified. I never heard anything like that in my house. It was a very Jewish but also a very American home. World War II was a great binder. When you got killed it didn't make a difference what you were.

My two older brothers were in the army, overseas. During the war if you had a son in the armed forces, you hung a star on the window. If he had been killed, you put up a gold star. We'd see these gold stars hanging in the windows all over the neighborhood. Because of the war, you had to be good. You knew your parents were frightened out of their minds. Every time the doorbell rang, it could be a telegram from the War Department saying, "We regret to inform you. . . ."

Kids were not so silly. Part of their general behavedness was that the general atmosphere was more civil. But part of it was also that a war was going on, and not a war like Vietnam. A war that everyone believed in and everyone who could fought in. So you didn't want to be trouble.

Jeff Solomon: When my parents got out of Germany in 1938, they came to the Washington Heights section of Manhattan, where there was a big community of German refugees. There was a social scene, something called the Prospect Club, where my parents met. Although they felt very much American, many German Jews in Washington Heights continued to feel part of Germany even after the Nazis came to power. They couldn't get over this longing for the Germany they remembered with all its culture and art.

Addi Friedman: We were part of the large German Jewish community on the Upper West Side of Manhattan. We knew very few gentiles. My parents did not want us to have non-Jewish friends. They never said as much, but it was understood. They felt Christians disliked Jews and that it was better for our safety and our world that we didn't mingle with them. Jews had to live among Jews.

We were members of the West Side Institutional Synagogue, where many people prominent in Jewish life belonged. The Horowitz Maragareten family davened in the pew in front of us. But there were five or six other synagogues that we could attend if we wanted to hear another rabbi speak.

We could go to the Jewish Center on Eighty-sixth Street, or we could walk across the park and hear Rabbi Joseph Lookstein at Kehilat Jeshrun. There was a little Young Israel around the corner on Eighty-fourth Street between West End Avenue and Riverside Drive. As we got older, my sister and I would congregate with boys and girls after services, walk down to Riverside Drive, and talk of things.

Daniel Musher: The boundaries of my existence were 66th Street to 101st Street and Park Avenue to Central Park West. Just about everything I did and everyone I knew were within those parameters with the exception of 111th Street, where I went for my violin lessons.

My grandfather, Mordecai Kaplan, had begun teaching at the Jewish Theological Seminary at the beginning of the century, when Solomon Schecter brought him in as a professor. He went on to become the head of the teacher's college and then the dean. By 1955 anyone who was a Conservative rabbi in the USA had studied with him. I remember how he used to walk all the way up to the Seminary on West 121st Street and Broadway. That's how he got from one place to another—by walking, very fast and straight.

Morris Friedman: The Jewish communities of New York afforded the possibilities of an intensive Jewish education. When I was five years old, my father decided that we should move from Far Rockaway, Queens, to Borough Park, Brooklyn, so that I could be educated in a yeshiva. At the Hebrew Institute, I attended Hebrew sessions in the morning and English in the afternoon.

Sundays, school ended at one o'clock. I'd go home, have something to eat, and get driven by my father to my mother's sister in Rockaway, who taught me violin. Yeshiva was not enough for European Jewish parents—their son had to be a violinist, too. I hated it. And once my lesson was finished, my father asked my uncle to interrogate me on what I had studied all week, the chapters in the Bible, the prophets.

That same kind of questioning took place with Samuel Mirsky, an extraordinary scholar and rabbi at the Young Israel of Borough Park. Friday nights in the winter, we would finish dinner about six and make a pilgrimage in the dark to his home. He'd ask me probing questions about what I had been learning all week. I felt a lot of pressure to excel.

Mitchell Serels: I attended the Akiba Hebrew Academy in the Bronx. It was a progressive school, influenced by the theories of John Dewey. We called the teachers in the secular department by their first names. Most of them had been blacklisted from the public schools because of their left-wing associations. They taught us a lot of freedom songs. They took us to the English principal's living room to watch the inauguration of President Eisenhower on television and made negative comments.

Lucille Brody Noonan: My brother and I attended the Ethical Culture School on Prospect Park West in Brooklyn. We lived nearby on Eastern Parkway, which was a broad boulevard reminiscent of the Champs-Élysées in Paris with islands where people could stroll or sit on benches and watch others passing by. Our world was the Botanic Gardens, the Brooklyn Museum. Both were right down the street.

My parents had rebelled against their Orthodox upbringing in Europe and became Ethical Culturists. As a result, we didn't attend synagogue. There were quite a few in the area, though, like the Brooklyn Jewish Center and Union Temple.

Since I attended a private school, the kids in the neighborhood, who were Jewish for the most part, thought I was exclusionary and would not play with me. I had to hang around with the doorman whenever my mother sent me outdoors to get fresh air. But because my mother was a grande dame who raised us to believe we were superior to everyone else, it never bothered me.

Gail Eiseman Bernstein: Being a member of Union Temple at 17 Eastern Parkway was tantamount to having arrived. It was a world of accomplished people, professionals or business people, all American-born. They came to Temple dressed in their finest and conducted themselves with aplomb. In 1954–1955, my parents were copresidents of the Young Married group; and at the end of their tenure, my mother was awarded a pair of sterling silver candlesticks.

From what I understand, in Catholicism you are assigned to a parish according to where you live; in Judaism you can join whatever temple you want. There were people who joined temples in fancier neighborhoods because they thought it would be a step up. Union Temple was five stories up. It had a sanctuary and balcony, a suite of offices and classrooms, a tremendous ballroom, and a health club with swimming pool and gym.

Union Temple was modern, rational, and Reform. Young Judea on Bedford Avenue and Linden Boulevard was Old World, emotional, and Orthodox. My grandfather was part of the *minyan* of this little shul. Dressed in his neat suit and spiffy white shirt with detachable collar, he attended services every morning and night. And on the High Holidays, I visited him in shul, dressed in my new hat, coat, and shoes. Because I was a little girl, I was allowed to sit downstairs with him and the other old men.

Two very different kinds of Jewishness occurred simultaneously during my Brooklyn childhood: the Orthodox *Yiddishkeit* of my grandfather's world and the Reform Americanized world of Union Temple, where the men and women sat together, services were in English (the occasional Hebrew prayer was transliterated), and the choir sang to resounding organ accompaniment.

At Union, I came across kids who lived in the beautiful apartment buildings on Eastern Parkway near the Brooklyn Museum. Many went to private schools: Packer Collegiate Institute, Berkley, Brooklyn Friends. Once my father scheduled an interview for me at Packer. I had a temper tantrum. I was *not* going to school with those snobs.

My parents' social life was built around Union Temple. Saturday nights there was a synagogue function, or members went to one another's homes. I remember the elaborate dinners my mother staged; how she planned the menus, worked for days cooking and coordinating, the beautiful tables she set with sterling and her best china. My father was a school principal, and we didn't have a lot of money, but we were on the periphery of an upper-class environment.

There were real social strata among Brooklyn Jews during the forties and fifties, before the suburban push: those who lived in East New York or

Brownsville as opposed to those who lived on Ocean Parkway or Ocean Avenue or Eastern Parkway.

In seventh grade, I invited a girl to my house. The next day she said, "My mother said you have to come to my house first." She had a "hoo-hoo" Lenox Road address. Her mother grilled me: what did my father do, where did we go to temple, a whole litany of questions. That was my introduction to social snobbery. Despite their being part of the Union Temple world, my parents weren't like that at all.

On Sundays I'd go to the Lower East Side with my mother and aunt, and it was another world. I loved all the noise and crowds, the interesting little stores. Although the counters were too high for me to see over, I was always imagining what was behind them.

Max Wechsler: My mother usually went to the Lower East Side on Sunday afternoons to visit her mother in her little apartment, a walk-up in a tenement on Eldridge Street. And every so often, especially when I was little, I went along. Usually we took the train, but on nice days, we would walk across the Williamsburg Bridge, which was about eight blocks from where we lived. We'd walk down the streets, and I'd notice how quiet Sundays in Brooklyn were. All the stores and schools were closed; nothing much seemed to be going on. It was a day when business stopped.

As we crossed the bridge, my mother and I would stop a couple of times to look down at the East River, which was always a dull shade of gray. Behind was home, my familiar Brooklyn world. Ahead were the tenement buildings and old factories on the Manhattan side. At least once during our crossing, our conversation would be interrupted by the subway train roaring by, making so much noise we couldn't hear each other speak.

It seemed to me that the Williamsburg Bridge separated my two worlds. Brooklyn was the new world, an orderly and organized place where people spoke in English. It was America. Manhattan, which I only knew as the Lower East Side, was the old world, a noisy and chaotic place, that place of confusion where my relatives had come from.

We walked off the bridge straight onto Delancey Street, a wide avenue, filled with traffic and people running around, buying, selling, shouting at each other in a combination of languages and accents, and I felt I was plunged back into that world. I had crossed a bridge from a place that was sleeping to a place that never slept. "Don't these people ever get tired?" I wondered.

We'd turn onto Orchard Street, which was narrower and lined with push-carts and people spilling into the gutter. There were old men in long black coats and hats, women with kerchiefs around their heads. The signs in the store windows were in Yiddish. The atmosphere was one of congestion and clamor. It seemed every kind of item was available for sale: pots and pans, all kinds of clothing, hardware, leather, books, furniture.

We always stopped off at this one appetizing store to pick up some things for my grandmother's supper. It was a long and narrow place with glass counters along one wall and barrels of tomatoes, pickles, and sour kraut along the other. And once she stepped inside, it seemed to me that my mother became just like the people of the old world. The guy behind the counter knew her. They spoke to each other in some combination of Yiddish and Romanian. He'd give me a sour tomato and a slice of pumpernickel bread. I'd stand around enjoying my little treat while my mother had him cut a few slices of sable and fill a little container with herring in cream sauce with sliced onions. She'd also get a slice of "shoeleather" for me, a sheet of dried apricot stuck to a sheet of paper. That was my treat for the subway ride on the way home. All the rest of the day, I looked forward to eating it. How I loved that sour taste.

Karl Bernstein: Like so many others, our family had started out on the Lower East Side. When they moved to an apartment on Grand Street with central heat, it was the first big step up. The next move was across the East River to Williamsburg. Some of the family still lived there when I was a kid. We'd visit my father's Aunt Lena and her husband Jake, who had a laundry on Berry Street and lived in the back. I felt sorry for them. Williamsburg seemed so old and ugly. The houses were mostly tenements, and there were hardly any trees. But that's where my father came from; it was a place of origin. From there the family spread out to the neighborhoods of Brooklyn and then to Queens and Long Island.

Shalom Goldman: I returned to the Lower East Side in the 1950s, many decades after my grandparents had gotten out. When I was around eight years old, my parents were divorced. My mother took the three children and moved from Hartford to Jackson Heights, Queens.

We went from a house in a Connecticut town with a thriving Jewish community to a very small apartment near the elevator train in a largely German neighborhood. At first my brothers and I were sent to an upscale Hebrew day school in Queens. But after a while, we didn't have the money to go there anymore. So I was sent to Rabbi Jacob Joseph, a European yeshiva on Henry Street and East Broadway on the Lower East Side.

It was an entirely new world, the flip side to the Connecticut experience. In Hartford, everything had been totally safe and open. Here I had to take the subway every day. Puerto Rican kids waited for us at the East Broadway stop. They would scream "Jews" at us—something I hadn't heard before—and attack us with chains. Most of us weren't scared. We fought for our turf in the park, fought on the corner for who could play stickball.

The kids at the yeshiva came from families who hadn't made it, or they were refugees or children of refugees, kids born in DP—Displaced Persons—camps. My grandparents probably didn't like my being thrust into this environment. It was back to the past. But they must have been ambivalent about it because it was very Jewish.

Everyone joked that the yeshiva was airlifted out of Warsaw before the Germans bombed the ghetto. The ceilings were twenty feet high. It was dingy. It was dirty. The bathrooms were disgusting. The paint was peeling. All the books were old Board of Education rejects. You would walk into the school, and there would be beggars in the hallway, old *Yidden* who would ask for a few pennies. Later you'd see them out in the street, huddled over containers of coffee.

Some of the teachers were survivors. What was important to them was not the German murderers. It was that there was something sacred and significant that they had destroyed, and this school was an attempt to recreate the Talmudic Academy that had existed.

The yeshiva was totally integrated into the Lower East Side, an open space with people wandering around, talking to each other in Yiddish, hanging out in the cafeteria downstairs. I got some understanding about a whole way of Jewish life that had been wiped out. It didn't strike me with sadness then. It was more like, "how interesting."

We'd arrive at eight-thirty or nine. The morning was all Talmud or Bible taught in Hebrew and Yiddish. At two o'clock there were secular studies taught by public school teachers who had finished their regular school day and were totally burned-out or by people who couldn't get a teaching license or had their license revoked.

My English literature class at four in the afternoon was taught by these bohemian poets who lived on the Lower East Side and were picking up a couple of bucks. They introduced me to the whole world of literary New York. But the English part was like Talmud Torah is to other kids—supplementary. We didn't take it seriously. It wasn't important to us. American Civil War history? Who cared? It wasn't our Civil War.

The atmosphere was totally chaotic. The school cafeteria was run by these two women who were survivors. They were insane. When you got them angry, they would scream at you in Yiddish and throw food. Spaghetti would be flying through the air.

We usually ate out at either the kosher deli or the dairy restaurant. Once in a while, we'd sneak into the Garden Cafeteria around the corner from the school. It wasn't a kosher place so it was forbidden fruit. We'd have to watch out or the rabbis would catch us. But it was where all the Yiddish writers hung out. We'd see them sitting together in intense conversation, smoking cigarette after cigarette.

At lunchtime the pushcarts would come around selling knishes, chestnuts, baked potatoes. The pushcart peddlers were bent-over old people. I don't know if they were refugees—for all I know they were refugees from two blocks away. But they were surely refugees from life.

Across the street from the school was some kind of old age home for mendicant Jewish scholars called the *Anshei Ma'amid*—"men of distinction." The rabbis would send us over there with cups of tea. It was a *mitzvah*. To me they seemed a million years old. They were all from Europe, and I'm sure they got a lot of pleasure out of seeing and talking to these little Jewish students.

I'm romanticizing about it now, but to be honest, it was repressive. They would hit you on the knuckles like they did in Catholic schools. They would scream at you, curse you. In Hartford, it had been Dr. Spock: we were spoken to like we were adults. On the Lower East Side, we were spoken to like we were street kids.

I was the *vilder kind*, "the wild child," always being thrown out of classes. But in a kind of osmotic way, I learned a lot. We didn't get the rote thing like what you get in supplementary schools. We got the real thing: the life of the mind in a very limited sphere. We didn't talk about Henry David Thoreau and the goyim. It was the life of the mind as the Jews understood it—like the thirty-nine categories of work you can't do on the Sabbath, which may seem like triviality but not if you're part of that world. It's not just memorizing them but finding out how these categories were arrived at.

On the Lower East Side, I discovered humor and irony, and that was what saved me. It struck me as comic. Not that I was laughing; I was pretty unhappy at the time. But the richness of it all: the Jewish bookstores, the walking out at lunchtime and listening to all the Warsaw characters, the importance of conversation, the constant talking all the time, they never shut up.

How did I get from this *faschlechta* (badly behaved) school where they were throwing things out the windows to being a college professor at Dartmouth? There must be some explanation.

"My roots in Cheyenne, Wyoming, go back to 1864."

(below) "We moved to Farmington, a village in the hills of West Virginia, where we were the only Jewish family."

"Grandpa became Pueblo, Colorado's first police chief."

Eldorado, Arkansas, scene, c. 1927: "We did not have elegant things, but it was a bucolic childhood."

"My great-grandmother, who emigrated with her husband around the turn of the century, had come to Shelton, Connecticut."

"At last we were in the 'goldeneh medina,'
the land of gold that my mother, uncle,
and grandparents had talked about all the time."

"My family picked up the New England ethos."

"In the Brownsville section of Brooklyn, we were in an overwhelmingly Jewish part of the world. We were at home."

"We lived a traditional shtetl life, only transplanted from Poland to America."

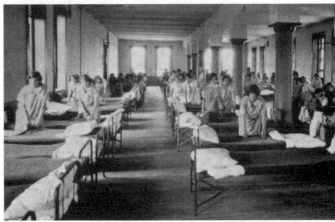

(top left and right, middle) Scenes from the Jewish Orphans' Home (JOH), Cleveland, Ohio, c. 1922.

(bottom) Bellefaire in the Cleveland Heights section—the cottage-type orphanage that replaced the institutional-looking JOH in 1929.

The cast of an original JOH production.

Crystal's Kosher Delicatessen in Duluth, Minnesota, c. 1924, when a two-ounce jar of caviar went for thirty-five cents. "Jewish people like good food."

(top) A prominent retail feature of downtown Shelton, Connecticut: the Kreiger family's clothing and hardware store in 1950.

(middle) A New England custom peddler. "Many of the men were peddlers. What else could they do? They couldn't be Methodist ministers."

(bottom left) "My father was always talking about how lucky he was to have gotten out of Russia and come to the greatest country in the world."

(bottom right) "There were times we felt real Americans and not so different being Jewish."

(*top left*) The only Jewish girl in Oconde County, South Carolina, with her parents and little brother in the postwar years.

(*top and middle right*) First and second generation "All-American kids."

(*bottom left*) "When I was growing up, there were roughly two million Jews living in Brooklyn, New York"—including this family of immigrant parents and their American-born daughters.

(*bottom right*) The eighth-grade class of the Seattle Hebrew Day School in the spring of 1959.

Part Two

IN OUR TIMES

Tikkun Olam—
The Repair of the World

Shoah

The Precious
Promised Land

6

TIKKUN OLAM— THE REPAIR OF THE WORLD

"And thou shalt not glean thy vineyard,
neither shalt thou gather the fallen fruit . . . thou
shalt leave them for the poor and for the stranger."

—Leviticus XIX:10

Caroline Katz Mount: My father quoted from "The Sayings of the Fathers" all the time: Don't tell a hungry man about the good meal you just had; don't tell a crippled man about how much you enjoyed walking through the park. We grew up with the sense of possessing a very rich heritage by virtue of our being Jewish, a high moral ground.

Herb Kalisman: To most people, the expression *Es iz shver zu zein ah Yid*—"It's hard to be a Jew"—refers to the anti-Semitism, the hardships Jews have endured. But to my father, it meant the extra concern, the moral responsibility a Jew must undertake.

It was the custom among bakers to fill poultry bags with rolls and bread after work and bring them home to the family. During the Depression, my father would start out for home with three bags. He'd pass through the Union Square station, where hundreds of people were sleeping in the corridors, and invariably he'd hand out the bread and rolls. By the time he came home, he never had more than one bag left.

Menachem Katz: Bubba Rivka, who lived with us, got more mail than anyone else in the house. That was because she was always collecting money and sending it to various charities. Most of the money she collected was from friends and relatives who came to visit us.

My father was terribly embarrassed because everyone she asked felt obligated to give as they didn't want to offend her. His cousin, in particular, would complain to my father about being hit up for money whenever he walked in the door. He was quite tight with the dollar and made a big issue out of it. Of course my father would never reprimand my grandmother, but he complained bitterly to my mother, who would complain to my grandmother, who totally ignored my father's recriminations and continued to collect money.

Is Crystal: The shuls in Duluth had long tables lined with saucers called *pishkes.* Every saucer had a little sign in Hebrew: "This is for the Talmud Torah." "This is for the hospital." "This is for the people who don't have food." "This is for the Jewish National Fund." The men would go around and drop a penny or two in this dish, a nickel or so in that one. If something

◀ (*top*) Children holding banner at the Sholem Aleichem Folk Institute School, Bronx, New York, c. 1925. (*bottom*) A contemplative moment during the consecration ceremony, Temple Israel, Lawrence, New York, c. 1955.

was real close to the heart, maybe they'd drop in a dime. Once in a while, a big shot would come by and throw in a paper dollar.

Irv Saposnik: My grandmother kept a whole collection of *pishkes* under the sink. It seemed to me that there were constant visits by these bearded old men, representatives of the various charities. They would sit down at the table. She'd serve them tea in a glass with sugar lumps and share long conversations with them. Then she'd take out the *pishke* for their particular charity. They'd open up the box, spill out the change, and count it up.

Murray Polner: All of the synagogues, all of the Talmud Torahs had illustrations of poor Jews, posters of Eretz Israel, and collection cans. Everybody gave, no matter how little they had. Every Passover we worked with the local Talmud Torahs collecting food and delivering it to people who were out of work or in need. My parents taught me that you've got to reach out, be a humane mensch. They were Jewish to their bones, deep in their bones.

When, to the horror of our parents and grandparents, many of us fled from their ritualistic orthodoxy looking for a larger world, we carried along their humanism, their quest for peace, the sense of commitment, caring, and charity that is bedrocked into Jewish life—what has come to be called *tikkun olam,* "the repair of the world." For many Jews I knew, this notion of doing for others emerged in left-wing activities.

Herb Kalisman: My father had a ready-made audience sitting around the old kitchen table in our apartment up on the fourth floor of a building in East Harlem. The two young men who were courting my sisters had not been schooled in Marxist politics. They hadn't read the *New York Call,* the socialist paper that my father read, or the *Forward,* in its infancy then. Being Jewish was not only being ethical, he told them. It also was being political and intellectual.

But when he began to talk about Bertrand Russell propounding free love or marriage for companionship, my mother would chime in, "You have four daughters. Is that what you want for them?"

My mother went along with my father and voted Socialist. However, she had her doubts. "Socialism is a wonderful thing," she'd say, "but where are you going to get the people who are honest enough to live it out?"

Flora Berger: My father came from an observant and well-to-do business family near Odessa. He didn't like the way the factory workers were exploited, and he would get up on a soapbox to rail against his parents who owned the factory. He made so much trouble for them, they sent him to America.

Even though he owned a dress shop here, he remained a committed socialist, beginning as a clerk and moving up to treasurer of the Cloak Makers Union, Local Number One. He was a rabble-rouser, very politicized, and totally nonreligious.

Murray Polner: Even though many people in the neighborhoods of New York came from shtetls in Europe and had little formal education, there was a large degree of cosmopolitanism among them. Workers were intellectuals and vice versa. This connection was a real contrast to the artificial demarcations of today. People like Abraham Cahan, the founder of the *Forward,* Clara Zametkin, Morris Hillquit, and others worked alongside working people and developed roots among them as well as a method of translating their rage into a kind of political action.

My father was intensely anti-Communist. He and his father had experienced the Bolsheviks in Russia after World War I. "Stay away from them," he'd warn me.

Marnie Bernstein: My father came from the Ukraine and had lived through the Revolution. The furriers' union he had to belong to was Communist-dominated. These experiences made him fear and hate anything tinged with the Communist influence. He said the only good time in Russia was during the short period when Kerensky was in power.

My mother's family, on the other hand, remained pro-Russia even after the Hitler-Stalin pact became known. When my uncle had to select a birthdate for himself in order to become a citizen, he picked the day of the Russian Revolution. These conflicting attitudes towards Russia and Communism were the source of much friction in the family.

Alan Lelchuk: I knew, or felt, my father's entire perspective—his baggage, so to speak—was Russian and leftist.

The decision for him to come to America was made when his father was murdered by a Cossack in his little shtetl outside of Minsk. The family decided to send the youngest one to America to make some money and return. That was my father, Harry.

He arrived in 1918 and spent the rest of his life trying to get back. Of course he never made it. He came close when I was one year old, having saved enough money for us to go to Russia, ostensibly for a vacation. We were on the passenger liner when my sister got one of her perennial bad earaches, and the doctor aboard the ship advised us to not make the crossing. My father said, "No, we're on ship. We're going." But my mother overruled him—it was one of the few times she did. We got off the ship. My sister went into medical care. And two or three days later it was September 1, 1939, and Germany invaded Poland.

His family never made it out. They all perished. He missed them greatly. All his life, he wanted to be reunited with them. It was as if his true life was there. He was closest to me when he was describing that life. He would take me on his lap and draw pictures of the house and stables his family had owned. He expressed warmth when he talked to me in Russian, especially when he explained how the Russians were defeating the Nazis at Stalingrad and Leningrad. The homeland for him always remained Russia. Here in America, my father was in perpetual exile.

He ate like a Slavic person, adoring salty fish, borscht, and *schav*. I remember visiting him in some of these dank cellars where he worked as a milliner making ladies' handbags, hats, and embroidery. He'd sit by his machine and eat a hunk of farmer's cheese along with thick dark bread and salt—a very Russian meal. During Passover and other holidays, he took great pleasure in making his own *chrane*—horseradish. The test for it was: if you were able to walk into the kitchen and breathe easily, it wasn't strong enough.

In our small apartment, he had his own private library. There was this Empire secretary with a pullout desk and three windowed shelves on top filled with books. And there were books in other places, many in Russian. He had political books and literary books: Marx, Trotsky, and Lenin; Dostoyevsky and Tolstoy. It was only in later life that I found out the interesting parts of the man. He had records of the Russian Army Chorus with black and gold RCA labels. And he would take me to the Stanley Theater, the Russian émigré hangout on Fourteenth Street in Manhattan.

I spoke Russian as a little boy until my mother insisted that I drop it. The household was Russian only on his side. She was born in this country and didn't want anything to do with it, especially because of my father's political leftism.

He was not an actual member of the Communist Party, but he felt himself a communist and a Jew. This was imparted to me as much from my mother's attribution as from what he told me; my father did not talk to me particularly about politics. But because he grew harsh and bullying towards my mother, I resented him and that became a resentment of his left-wing politics.

When I went with him to his club on Sunday mornings, I noticed the other men would always kid him about his leftism. It made me feel protective of him but at the same time not want to associate with him. He was the chief Red of them all.

The ironic thing about my father's leftism was that his family had been prosperous in Russia; they were timber merchants. Nevertheless, he believed in the Revolutionary Movement, in the need to change economic and social conditions.

There was this discrepancy in his life—how well-off he had been in Russia and how poor he was in America. The golden land was not so golden for him. He was a terrible businessman, an arrogant semi-intellectual, a man of misjudgment who always picked the wrong partners. One way or another, he always went belly up. He wound up most of his life working for other people at a machine.

Once or twice a year, he dressed me and himself up and took me to see the great soccer teams from Europe. He was a European gentleman. He loved soccer. Of course I hated it: soccer wasn't American. And I hated him for dragging me to those slow, irrelevant games. I wanted very much to be an American. For me, the ultimate patriotism was the Brooklyn Dodgers and the American game. My father never went to a baseball game.

As I grew more Americanized, he grew resentful. He felt it was a departure from him, from his Russianness. I think that hurt him very much. I was his hope of being a Russian boy. When I was about fourteen, he left.

Sidney Helfant: The teachers in the Sholem Aleichem school I attended were all atheists, communists, and socialists. We were regaled with stories of the Russian Revolution. One teacher in particular loved to recount his parading in Moscow in 1917, waving the red flag. But oddly enough, there were no attempts to indoctrinate us.

My parents weren't worried about my being poisoned by Communism. We were immune to that crap. My mother had experienced so many people whose idealism was phony. At one point our landlord was a Communist. Our neighbors' maid—the Glassers were fortunate enough to be able to hire a woman to take care of the kids—was a Communist. She took all the books out of their bookcase and replaced them with books by Marx and Lenin. It was a joke. No one took it seriously.

My mother, who never had more than two or three years of formal education, but was nevertheless very wise, called the Communists *Communistlekh*, a Yiddish diminutive that means "little Communists." But the implication was contemptuous: it suggested people who thought themselves very important but were in reality playing at a game.

Without explicit instruction, my mother taught me to be a reactionary with a small *r*. She was always wary of new things, careful to be less than overjoyed at first glance. She took to heart the old adage: be careful of what you pray for.

Murray Polner: I inherited my father's anticommunist feeling, but I couldn't help but notice the Jewish connection to the left, which meant everything from Franklin Delano Roosevelt hero worship to the socialists, communists, and anarchists.

Herb Kalisman: When I was a kid, it was still possible for a Socialist candidate in East Harlem to win an election—which is why come election time, my father was a poll watcher, proudly walking around sporting a red tie, making sure that no one was electioneering. The Tammany guys were always trying to pull an election fraud.

Neil Postman: The family interest in politics started with my grandfather, Abe Postman, who owned a saloon on the Lower East Side on the border between the Jewish and the Irish neighborhoods. Both Jews and Irishmen came to this saloon, and in those days the food was free. There'd always be a lot of fights, and my grandfather, so the legend goes, was a terror, who had an extraordinary ability to stop fights. He was involved in local politics, Tammany Hall.

In the 1920s and 1930s political life was much more personal than it is today. When a child got in trouble, Catholics could go to a priest or Jews could go to a rabbi, but they also went to local political leaders. That was the strength of the Democratic Party in New York. They delivered for their constituency. But come election time, they expected you to work and to vote.

Murray Polner: A local Democratic Party candidate, Mr. Miller, would pursue people from the Saratoga Avenue El train station and shriek at them if he thought they hadn't voted or hadn't voted right.

Neil Postman: I remember a Thanksgiving when I was six, and my father was out of work. The doorbell rang. I opened the door. There was a guy with a big package: turkey, sweet potatoes, cranberry sauce, the whole thing. It was a gift from the Democratic Club.

Murray Polner: Every Saturday before Election Day, an extraordinary event took place on Pitkin and Saratoga avenues in Brownsville: Politics Night. On each of the four corners, speakers up on soapboxes, an American flag beside them, would exhort the crowd to vote for the Democratic Party, the Liberal Party, the American Labor Party, the Communist Party, the Socialist Party. Sometimes there was even a Republican.

Neil Postman: There was a rumor that there was a woman in the neighborhood who was a "Republican." She was almost a mythical figure. Word would go through the neighborhood: "The Republican is in Hoffman's Grocery Store." And everyone would go to see.

I did have an uncle who was a Republican—a Jewish Republican! Uncle

Carl was also a Giant fan. That fit: a Republican *would* be a Giant fan. But nobody took him seriously. There had to be a fool in every family.

Yitz Greenberg: There were no Republicans, not in Borough Park. It was a version of the Biblical injunction: "If I forget thee o Jerusalem . . ."—"If I vote Republican, let my right hand wither. . . ."

Murray Polner: By and large the Jews I grew up with had an enormous sympathy for Zionism, left-wing politics, the New Deal, and FDR.

Balfour Brickner: I was seven years old when FDR won the first election. I remember the New Deal, the CCC (Civilian Conservation Corps), the NRA (National Recovery Act) stickers on the backs on cars. I remember the first hundred days, the economic turnaround and the steam that Roosevelt generated.

Neil Postman: President Roosevelt had been president from the time I was one year old, and I grew up believing that the president had to be Roosevelt. To have a president who spoke in this patrician, elegant way had a terrific effect on me. We heard two voices in our house all the time: Franklin Delano Roosevelt and Red Barber, who a lot of us thought was Jewish. They made us aware of the power and grace of language.

Murray Polner: I was twelve when Wendell Willkie was running against Roosevelt for his third term. I revered Roosevelt, but I said to my friends: "Well, Wendell Willkie seems like a pretty good guy." They tried to beat me up.

Yitz Greenberg: FDR was the great man. He saved Jews, we thought. America had not become anti-Semitic thanks to him. The rabbis talked about him. When politicians campaigned on Thirteenth Avenue, huge crowds turned out to hear his name invoked.

Arthur Cantor: Jewish people are not supposed to worship graven images, but my mother used to kiss this little bust of Franklin Roosevelt that was on top of the big old radio. That was very characteristic of Eastern European Jews. The women especially were nuts about him. He was always defending the Jews in one way or another, or at least we thought he was.

Balfour Brickner: We did not know what was going on behind the scenes at the Evian Conference, the Bermuda Conference. We didn't know that FDR was telling Cordell Hull that under no conditions do you let Jews into America.

7

SHOAH

"O Lord God, to whom vengeance belongs,
Thou God, to whom vengeance belongs,
Show Thyself."

—Psalms 94

Henry Birnbrey: In 1938, when I was fourteen years old, I arrived in Atlanta and met my "American family": Fanny Asman, a widow with a son who lived in Atlanta and a daughter who lived away. I formed an immediate and beautiful relationship with her although I did not, at the time, speak a word of English. I had left my parents behind in Dortmund, a big beer town around the area of Essen and Cologne. My ancestors had lived in Germany for four or five hundred years.

It was a strange time. Along with the pain of parting from my parents I had a sense of the adventure. I don't think any of us had any understanding of what was about to happen in Germany. We expected to be reunited.

Over the last years, the environment in Dortmund had become more and more restrictive. Jews not permitted here; Jews get out of here. The nice Jewish school in our community was closed down, and we had to move into a slum school. There was the constant assault of the marching, the flags, the singing of anti-Semitic songs. Without a uniform or some form of swastika insignia on my clothes, I stood out. But after dark, my friends in the Hitler Youth would take off their uniforms and come over to my house to play.

It was a very lonely existence. Food became scarce, as did fuel for heating. My father lost his business. He was accused on a trumped-up charge, and the judge, who was a friend of his, told him to abandon his business so the accuser would think he had been sent to a concentration camp. We had heard about the concentration camps. We did not know what they meant, but the prospect was frightening enough.

My parents tried desperately to get out. I can't tell you how many things they signed up for: Palestine, New Zealand, America. They took the first opportunity that came along: my emigrating to the United States through the Birmingham, Alabama, section of the National Council of Jewish Women, which sponsored a number of German Jewish children to be placed with American families.

All alone, with the one suitcase of clothes I was permitted to carry, I went to the American consulate in Stuttgart. There I met up with other kids from different parts of Germany. We proceeded, on our own, to Hamburg, where the ship was docked. It was a German ship with swastikas all over it.

◀ (*top*) Abraham Peck with his parents in the Landsberg am Lech DP Camp in Bavaria, 1949. (*bottom*) The S.S. *Navemar* in 1941—the last boat of refugees to reach sanctuary in the United States.

Nevertheless we were treated respectfully, probably because we were international passengers.

My parents hoped that when I got to the States, I could get an affidavit to get them out. But as it turned out, that was not possible. People in America did not understand the urgency.

Before the year was over, I learned of my father's death. He was taken from his home on Kristallnacht and beaten so badly that he died the following month. It was a great shock to me. Halfway through my year of saying *Kaddish* in the Conservative synagogue in Atlanta, my uncle wrote with the news of my mother's death. She had been a sickly woman, always on special diets. I assume with the food shortages and the general situation, she just couldn't go on.

I ended up saying *Kaddish* for a year and a half. There was a daily *minyan* of about a hundred people in that synagogue—some saying *Kaddish,* others just attending prayers. The camaraderie among the people there was so comforting to me. Some became lifelong friends of mine.

The Jewish population in Atlanta was about thirty-five hundred then. The synagogues, kosher butchers, and community center were all in the same area. Atlanta was not free of anti-Semitism. I recall a high school teacher who made hurtful remarks; the Ku Klux Klan was an active presence. At patriotic events like the Fourth of July, there was always some anti-Semitic and racist rhetoric. But there was an enormous difference between all of that and Nazi Germany. The overwhelming part of the community did not believe it; in Germany everybody believed it.

American freedom was something new to me. School was much less serious and businesslike, the standard of living much higher. During my first year of high school, I became a Junior Red Cross delegate to the national Red Cross convention in Washington. I attended parties in the White House and met Mrs. Roosevelt. Ironically, that was the first week of September 1939—the week Germany invaded Poland.

Addi Friedman: The morning of September 1, 1939, I came down the stairs and almost tripped over our little fox terrier. I was so startled to see my mother sitting in the living room, crying. I thought something terrible had happened to my father or my sister. Then my mother gestured to the newspaper on her lap, and I saw the headline that Hitler's army had invaded Poland.

After that, I began to live with a vague terror. A sense of peril began to invade my life. There was this villain Hitler who was going to come and destroy my parents, my sister, and my home. I became afraid to go to sleep at night. I thought Hitler's planes would fly over our house and bomb us.

Neil Postman: Around the time I was eight years old, I began to hear about Jews in Europe being punished, if not killed. My childhood had been quite idyllic except for this major thing: the war and the Holocaust, and I'm lumping the two together. It was frightening to know you could be killed not for anything bad that you did but just because you were Jewish.

Blu Greenberg: Asa Gisca was a girl who lived down the hill from us in Seattle. Everyone knew her family were Nazis, and I understood that meant something terrible. But what it meant I, as a child, could not really comprehend.

Dorothy Gottsegen: Nearly all my neighbors in the Ridgewood section of Queens were German. They spoke German, they read German newspapers; it was like Germany transplanted. And they were pro-Nazi. We had a picture of FDR in our living room. They had a picture of Hitler.

Oddly enough, many of the stores in the neighborhood were owned by Jews. My father had a grocery until he was driven out. When I was about five years old, my brother and I went down to the store one day and saw that a gigantic Jewish star had been drawn across the window. My father was scared off. I was scared, too.

Once, after I had scarlet fever, my mother lit sulfur candles to disinfect the house. That's what they did at the time. Somehow the fumes seeped into our next-door neighbor's apartment. She came out screaming at my mother, "You're trying to kill me, you dirty Jew!"

I grew up hearing "you dirty Jew." I heard it from the German storekeepers when I went around collecting for the Jewish National Fund, a little kid with a little *pishke* who wandered into the wrong store by mistake. They'd take me by the back of the neck and throw me out. I even heard it from my friends every once in a while. I was the only Jewish child in my class. Though I usually had no problems with the kids, whenever we got into arguments my Jewishness would surface.

One day two boys in my class invited me to come along with them to the delicatessen owned by the father of one of them. We lay down on our tummies and looked through a window into the basement of the store. A Bundt meeting was going on. Here were all these men from the neighborhood dressed in Nazi uniforms and carrying on. There were Nazi flags and swastikas everywhere.

My parents were European born, very liberal. They hated Nazism. How they remained in that neighborhood until I was thirteen, I'll never understand.

Addi Friedman: In 1940 we moved back to Riverside Drive on the Upper West Side of Manhattan. I was fourteen and my sister twelve, and in this very insular Jewish society we were now part of, the war seemed fairly distant. But we got to know a great deal because our parents were part of a contingent that tried to reach the ears of President Roosevelt.

Our parents did succeed in bringing over a woman from Germany. Hannah Koppel had been a caretaker in the Jewish girls' home in Germany where my mother was placed as a child, and she had been very devoted to her. As she had no place to stay, she moved in with us.

More than anyone else, Hannah Koppel brought home what was going on in Europe. She was close to sixty at the time, a kind and loving person with blue eyes, blonde hair that was graying and pulled back in a bun, and a face that was very sad. She would tell us wonderful stories about her childhood but would never go beyond that. She couldn't adjust to America. She lived in her past, a haunted and helpless human being.

Hannah would receive letters long after the events they described had taken place. Usually they had been smuggled out. In some cases, the writers had been killed by the time the letters arrived. They told about the desperate situation—how her brother, his children, other relatives had perished one by one. We wept for her.

I was very fond of Hannah and had great compassion for her, but to tell the truth, there were times my sister and I felt her living with us was an intrusion. She was so very Germanic, and as we grew more and more aware of what was going on, we developed a dislike for everything German, including the language. It had become like a curse. We hated it, but we had to speak it with Hannah.

We had grown up speaking German and English interchangeably. Our nanny only spoke German. My mother had spoken to us in German; she had taught me German grammar and script, which is a kind of calligraphy. She was very familiar with German literature. Germany was the representative of high culture to us. Then all of a sudden it became the enemy. I began to become annoyed with the German Jews in our community who continued to be proud of their German origins. I didn't want to have any part of it.

We would see our mother weeping. We saw the tears in our father's eyes. We lived with it. It became part of our lives. We couldn't understand why this wonderful United States of America, which was supposed to be a haven for all, was not doing something about the terrible things that were happening to the Jews in Europe.

Balfour Brickner: Secretary of the Treasury Morgenthau visited my dad in our home in Shaker Heights, Ohio, during the winter of 1942–1943. Morgenthau showed him photographs that had been smuggled out of concentration camps. Torture and death. I saw a picture of a man hung up by his testicles.

Dad looked at them and said to me, "Get Silver on the phone."

My father took the phone and said: "Abba, this is the story. Morgenthau is here, and I have seen photographs." And then my father described what he had seen and said, "We are going to hold a Madison Square Garden rally."

Murray Polner: My father took me to the rallies at the old Madison Square Garden on Eighth Avenue where people like Rabbis Stephen Wise, Abba Hillel Silver, and Barnett Brickner spoke out, along with the Socialists and the Jewish Bundt. I think we also heard from Mayor Fiorello La Guardia and Senator Herbert Lehman—the first a half-Jew and the second a member of the German-Jewish "elite," but two politicians we Jews in Brownsville trusted and revered, indeed loved.

Brownsville's adults knew, or at least strongly suspected, the worst about events in Nazi Europe. My father and many of his friends, immigrants from the Ukraine, read about it in the Yiddish newspapers and magazines. I saw that my father, mother, and grandmother were troubled, and that troubled me. I knew they had relatives living in zones conquered by the Nazis, but we received no mail from them all during the war. After, we learned that many members of my father's large family were killed. I remember when a single postcard came. All it had was one sentence, in Yiddish: "Father is dead."

Ruth Perlstein Marcus: As a result of the efforts of Raoul Wallenberg, my father's one brother came over when I was eleven years old. I was lying in bed—I'm sure they thought I was sleeping—and I overheard my uncle talking to my father in Yiddish. They took the people, he said, and they didn't even shoot them all, they just threw them into pits and buried them alive. He said he saw the people pushing up the dirt trying to get out. He told my father how they took his sister who was pregnant, cut her open, took the baby, and left her to die.

I made believe I was sleeping. I understood they did not believe that we children should hear such terrible things. They were so horrible, nobody would believe them. How was it possible? I had never experienced anti-Semitism. Our Chicago neighborhood was so Jewish that our one Italian friend told everyone she was Jewish just so she could fit in.

Manny Azenberg: I was still a kid when the war ended and the State Department contacted my mother with the news that her father and three sisters had been killed, and other relatives too—seventy in all. She was kind of *non compos mentis* for six months. I was sad, but I didn't know any of those people. The full impact of what happened hit me years later. You went past tears.

Yitz Greenberg: When Warsaw fell, a cousin who was in the Polish Army fled and was able to come here. He lived with us for a year or two until he got settled. I would overhear him crying at night. I would overhear my parents' whispered conversations and understand they had a tremendous intensity of feeling in reaction to him and to what was going on.

About a year after the war, a second or third cousin who survived a shooting in a pit with her daughter came to visit us. By now I was maybe fourteen and allowed to sit with them a while. They were saying they were the only survivors. And then I was told to leave. The idea was you don't talk about these things in front of children.

But a year or two later I was complaining one day, I guess very bombastically, about how the Jewish people were not observant or religious enough when my father turned to me in anger. "You have the nerve to denounce the Jewish people in the name of God?" he said. "After what happened, who should be more ashamed—the Jewish people or God?"

I was stunned. My father never spoke about the Holocaust. And yet he had this anger. He never stopped observing, never stopped teaching, but he had this anger at God. It was something I never forgot. It haunted me for years.

Karol Musher: My parents didn't talk about it much. Even so, the anti-German message was loud and clear. Both had lost dear relatives. My father received a letter describing how some very close gentile friends betrayed his sister. There was clearly a bitterness. The incredible love of learning remained, but there was some loss of absolute blind belief, a falling away.

Stephen Solender: It was a subject we could not discuss. I am the oldest son of the oldest son of Samuel Solomon Solender, a man who had this very strong conviction that no Jewish child should have to grow up in an orphanage. During the first part of this century, he went from community to community becoming the director of its Jewish orphan asylum. Then, one by one, he placed the children in homes until he was able to close the orphanage down. My father for many years was the national director for the Jewish Welfare Board. Traveling around the country with him, I saw him motivate thousands of young people to come into Jewish communal service. In the process, he motivated me.

But the Holocaust has always been too sensitive an issue for us to discuss. I have been impatient that their generations did not do more. And I think they feel I don't appreciate how much they did at that time and how difficult it was for Jewish leadership to assert itself in the 1930s and 1940s. I don't know how much they knew. I'll never know.

Jim Sleeper: From 1945 to 1948, there was all that frenzied activity to resettle the DPs and the refugees. And then Israel became a state. All that psychic energy went to positive things. There was a great deal of denial.

Brooks Susman: My generation of baby boomers grew up not learning about the Holocaust. Our parents hid it from us. They didn't want us to be injured or brutalized by it. "We went to war. We beat Hitler. It can never happen again. You don't need to know about it."

Jeff Solomon: During the mid-fifties, I would see relatives and friends of my parents with numbers on their arms. I never asked what they were. Sometimes I'd hear my parents, my uncle talking about things that happened before they left Germany: how my uncle was beaten up or how my mother was thrown out of school. But about the larger issues, they were silent. Whether they were shielding us or themselves, I don't know.

Barbara Kreiger: My first clue of what had gone on came when I was around eight years old. I mentioned something about Hitler to a friend of mine. Maybe I had heard the name in school. And my friend said, "Shhh, don't you know who he is? He killed the Jews."

He knew. His parents had told him. My parents had never spoken about it. In public school and the early grades of Hebrew school, I learned nothing. I had no idea what he was talking about. I was ashamed that he knew and I didn't. And I was very ashamed at having mentioned the name without even knowing whom he was. It was traumatic. Then I started to learn.

Yitz Greenberg: The subject of the Holocaust did not come up at Brooklyn Talmudical Academy. Nevertheless, when I took the Regents exam, I selected the topic "Unwanted" from a choice of subjects and wrote about the Jews of Europe trying to escape. Wherever they went, I wrote, they were greeted by a big sign saying "Unwanted." Finally, they were rounded up and lined up in front of the gas chamber, and there, at last, they were greeted by a big sign saying "Wanted."

Manny Azenberg: There were survivors at Camp Kindleveilt, the Zionist labor camp that my father managed in Highland Mills, fifty miles outside of New York. Many of them were in their twenties. Anyone who came with a number on his arm got a job as a waiter or a counselor. They didn't play basketball. They were special. You always dealt with them carefully. What could you ask them: "Who did you fuck to live?" "Who did you kill to live?"

Natalie Cohen Monteleone: After my grandfather died, my grandmother rented the upstairs of her house to a refugee named David. My grandmother used to call him "my boy" although he was close to my parents' age.

Whenever I saw David, he was sitting on a rocking chair on the front porch, rocking back and forth, hardly saying anything except "Hi" to us all. He knew our names.

There was something wrong about him. I couldn't say what, although I felt it had something to do with one of those hush-hush topics.

Marcia Lee Goldberg: The subject of the Holocaust was sort of passed over in my religious school in St. Louis shortly after the war. I thought of it as something like the Queen Esther story. Many years later, when I became involved with the Holocaust Commission, I learned that Rudy Oppenheim, one of my favorite teachers in the school, a man only ten or fifteen years older than I, was a survivor himself.

Artie Allen: No matter how hot it got, and it gets pretty hot in Alabama, Reverend Leib Merenstein always wore long-sleeved shirts. That was because he didn't want anyone to see the numbers tattooed on his arm. He was the sole survivor of his family. But he rarely discussed it. In the South, people don't talk about their tsuris very much.

Reverend Merenstein prepared the kids from the Montgomery Conservative synagogues for their bar mitzvahs. He was also the *shochet,* so his car was full of feathers and had a funny smell. But he had access to great corned beef sandwiches that he'd bring us for a reward.

He was a very short man who spoke with a heavy accent. I was very short too, and Reverend Merenstein used to say it was wonderful to have someone shorter than him in the class. He was our only connection to what happened to the Jews under the Nazis. At home, in school—no one ever spoke about it.

Frank Rich: I guess it's a cliché that there were a lot of Jews during the 1950s and into the 1960s who wanted to ignore the Holocaust and didn't tell their kids anything. That was not the case with either of my parents. They talked.

It was pretty hard not to stumble upon the Holocaust. I read *The Diary of Anne Frank* when I was five or six years old. It was one of the first "adult" books I read. I remember how it struck me, how it grabbed me because the book speaks in a child's voice. *The Diary of Anne Frank* was a best-selling book, a huge hit Broadway play, then a very successful Oscar-winning movie. At the same time there was *The Wall,* which I saw as a play; the books *Exodus* and *Mila 18*; and the movie *Judgment at Nuremberg.* The movie *Exodus* came a little later. I think we'd all be fairly embarrassed to look at that movie now. But at the time . . . I remember the song and the bombing of the King David Hotel. When I was about ten, I saw *The Pawnbroker.* It had a big effect on me. I find it absolutely amazing that the Holocaust escaped people. If you wanted to find out, the information was there.

Robert Leiter: I saw *The Pawnbroker* when I was about fourteen, and it shook me down to my toes. The quickness of the changing images: a comfortable middle-class life torn apart, the horrible background of Harlem, the father and son in a boxcar. I had never felt so frightened.

That same time, my grandmother was reading a book about Auschwitz. I used to stare at the red and black cover with its picture of Eichmann's head and a swastika and overhear my grandparents' whisperings about the horrible tortures and medical experiments described in the book.

Phyllis Taylor: I became quite obsessed; I'd read everything I could about it. It was horrific, that sense of absolute vulnerability. It happened once; it could happen again. Just by the fluke of where I was born, I had been safe while others perished. I used to stand in front of the mirror, look myself in the eye, and say, "You're a Jew, and if you had been there, you would be dead." At summer camp, whenever we gathered around the campfire, I'd see people in the flames.

Frank Rich: It was such a formative thing for me in terms of what Jews have been through to survive, this one and all the holocausts that came before it. The fact that one of the times the Jews had been treated so criminally was so close to my own lifetime had a tremendous impact on me. Here was something that was writ large, and it hadn't happened hundreds of years ago. It had happened five years ago.

Marc Angel: I was one of two Jewish kids in my ninth-grade class when we were shown a film that showed the stacks and stacks of shoveled bodies. I guess the idea was to make us feel the horror. Instead I felt a scorching shame. How could such things have been done to the Jews? For the first time in my life, I had the feeling of Jewish powerlessness. For months, even years, I couldn't bring myself to talk about it.

Mike Lecar: When I found out what happened, I was ashamed. I wondered how the Jews could have let the Nazis do that to them. I thought the Germans couldn't have killed that many if the Jews didn't cooperate. It would take more effort to kill that many cows. Even a slowdown would have saved a lot of lives. I was embarrassed that these people who marched to their deaths without fighting were my people. I was a tough kid, and if somebody tried to do something to me I fought back.

Max Wechsler: I was minding my own business on a Sunday afternoon, listening to the Yankee game on the radio, when my sister's current boyfriend came into my room. He had been going out with her for a few weeks and was a refugee—thin, bent, broken. He spoke with a thick accent. I'd always thought of the DPs, those former concentration camp inmates, with a little bit of contempt. How could they have let what happened happen? The few times anti-Semitic slurs had been hurled at me, I always fought back. But from what I had learned about these people, they went like sheep to be slaughtered. That was something I could not understand.

Now this guy was in my room—hovering over me, intruding, switching the station on my radio to some classical music. There were a few brief moments of objection on my part. Then my mother intervened: "He's a guest. Let him listen to whatever he wants."

He might have been a guest, but he was an unwelcome one. And someone whom I had absolutely nothing in common with. Baseball was what you listened to on the radio. You didn't listen to classical music.

Yet somehow, in the weeks and months that followed, this man and I developed a relationship. He told me about the Nazi sadists and a German nation that went mad. He spoke about people losing all their dignity, having their heads shaved, forced to work in subzero temperatures with the thinnest of clothing.

The whole subject began to take on a personal dimension. The names of the camps and their commandants, the maps of Poland, Germany, and Czechoslovakia formed and reformed in my mind just like the makeups of the baseball teams and their rosters. Only baseball was such an upside to my teenage life whereas his chilling testimony cited horror after horror. I learned what a ghetto was, what it was like to have to wear the yellow star, what it was like to have German shepherds nip at your fingers and your knees, what it was like to be separated, cut up, carved up from those you loved, what it was like to see your family die.

Hundreds of hours of conversation with him changed my macho American-Jewish boy stance, made me see and feel the enormity of what had happened. The shame I felt about the European Jews not fighting back was gone. In its place was compassion and sympathy for all of their losses and a rage and fury at the Nazi murderers. Ironically, we had traded information. He schooled me in the Holocaust, and I got him hooked on baseball.

Abraham Peck: I was born in May 1946 in the displaced persons' camp in Landsberg am Lecht, Bavaria, the town where Hitler had written *Mein Kampf* in his prison cell. In December 1949, I emigrated with my parents to the United States. Both my parents had survived the labor camps and after liberation found each other through the network of survivors who gathered in Prague. With the exception of a couple of my mother's nephews, they were the sole survivors of large families.

Through their wisdom or lack of wisdom, Jewish-American officials settled us in the middle of a black ghetto in Waterbury, Connecticut. For the better part of my childhood, America was black America to me.

Our black neighbors could not believe that Jews were poor, as we were, nor that we would live among them. As for my parents, they had had very little contact with black people except for those among the liberating troops. But they soon became comfortable with them. A uniformed white policeman brought back the memory of the horror, but our neighbors represented no threat. A number of the men had been liberators, had seen the concentration camps. They were able to relate to the things my father talked about in a way few others could.

Although my mother was unable to talk with me about what had happened, my father was obsessed with the need to bear witness. From a very early age, I learned about specific tormentors. There was Kuhnemann, the lame dwarf who walked around the labor camp with a huge German Shepherd. Depending on his mood, Kuhnemann would either shoot a prisoner at random or allow the dog to tear the victim to shreds. There was Hans Biebow, the handsome administrator of the Lodz Ghetto, who made enormous amounts of money off the labors of ghetto inmates while hastening to deport them to the death camps. Whenever friends of mine came to the house, my father would start telling them about these people, about what he had lived through. They would look at me as if to ask, "Why is he telling us this?" It was so embarrassing that after a while, I stopped bringing friends home.

My father was very aggressive, very angry at the world. That too was an embarrassment for me. "Where were you when I was in the concentration camps?" he would ask. "Where was American Jewry? Where was God?" Such themes were part and parcel of my growing-up years in the 1950s in our intimate nuclear family. Until I made friends and met other families, I thought no one had grandparents or uncles or aunts.

To say that I was everything to my parents is an understatement, and I felt the burdens. But I also felt American. I played stickball like everybody else. I loved sports. I was into rock and roll.

On the other hand, I shared my parents' sense of being apart from the American Jewish community. I was uncomfortable with the Jewish kids I went to shul or to Sunday school with. Growing up in Waterbury, I did not experience that sense of survivor solidarity that those who grew up in places like New York, Los Angeles, or Montreal might have had. It was like I lived in two worlds. Most American Jews had come to this country because they wanted to. My parents had no choice. They had no civilization to go back to in Poland.

Shocked and stunned by their experiences, my parents remained re-moved from American Jewish life. They retained the feeling that European culture was superior, that there was a closeness among people in the shtetls that didn't exist in this country.

My mother maintained her faith in God, but my father had great diffi-culty accepting the existence of a religious deity. What they were both com-mitted to was belief in the Jewish people and their continuity. They affirmed a Jewish future by having me.

Israel was everything to them, the ultimate vindication of their experi-ence. In later years, regardless of how little they had, they continued to send clothing, food, money. It was never enough. But though they were prepared to make *aliyah*, they finally decided that the experiences of their lives had made it too difficult for them to live in Israel.

Although there was no way my father would buy a Volkswagen or any other German product, he ended up earning a living because of his knowledge of German. His job at Timex, which was headquartered outside of Waterbury, was as liaison with German component makers of Timex's machine tools. It was a very difficult situation for him.

In 1958, when I was twelve years old, we bought our own home. By virtue of his working hard and being white, my father had been able to move us up to the middle class. Our house was next to a monastery and St. Margaret's Catholic School, and our garden went right up against the schoolyard fence. My mother was a wonderful gardener, and she soon discovered the monsignor at the monastery also had a love of gardening. They became very good friends. The monsignor would come up to our house for coffee, and the two of them would talk about flowers and plants for hours.

Still, Christmas and Easter time in Connecticut brought back memories of Polish priests talking about the death of Christ and the blood of Christ on the hands of the Jews. Fear became the operative feeling in our household and along with that, the just plain lousy feeling at the mass marketing of Christmas. There was a while I thought maybe Santa would come on Christmas morning despite who we were. He never showed up.

David Elcott: My mother had come from an upper-middle-class family in Dusseldorf, near the Dutch border. After their home was destroyed on Kristallnacht, they knew they had to get out of Germany. She and her brother were able to get work permits in England, and they brought her parents and sister out.

From the time I was born in 1949, I was raised as if all the people in the family who didn't get out were still alive. We knew they were dead, but through the stories we heard, they lived. In school, I'd join the rest singing "Land where my fathers died . . ." knowing that none of my fathers died in America. They all died in Europe. But I was so happily Jewish, so grounded in being Jewish. After all, American history started in 1620, but my history started four thousand years ago.

It was the memories of my mother's Europe that impacted on me—not the Holocaust but a Europe that was a living, vibrant community. The melodies we sang, the stories we told, the rituals we followed were all from the synagogue my mother's family had attended in Germany. This was what they held onto in Los Angeles, a place without a Jewish past, a Jewish life. I lived in a strange presence.

My mother would read to us from the diary she kept as a teenager in Germany. It was a story of her victory and survival. She wrote of Nazi kids forming a chain to block her as she rode her bicycle and how she plowed right through them, knocking them down. She wrote of screaming "You cowards!" at the Nazis when they came to arrest my grandfather, of crying "Go ahead and shoot me" to the SS man. Because she asserted herself, because she got out before the total degradation and destruction, that period was for her a time of defiance and victory.

Not so with her father. He had been a very proper German burgher whose self-definition lay in his ability to take care of his family. But they put him in prison, and he was unable to get himself out. It was his children who arranged his emigration; he could not save his parents, sister, or cousin. His world was destroyed, and he became a broken man.

After my grandfather died, my grandmother came to live with us in Los Angeles. She became a surrogate parent, a pivotal figure in the life of the family. Every one of her children and grandchildren was sure she loved him or her best.

What my grandmother brought with her was a strong attachment to the German culture. She could quote Heine, Schiller, and Goethe. That was the real Germany, she said, the culture of Bach and Beethoven, of German Christians who shared their views. The Nazis were not Germans. "How could they share my culture?" she demanded. To her death, she maintained that Hitler was Austrian, that the people who destroyed her home did not come from her area but were imported from elsewhere.

The message I received from her, and from my parents as well, was one of victory. My mother's immediate family had gotten out of Germany and survived. My American father was a successful soldier of a war that we won. We were powerfully, culturally Jewish, historically grounded, victorious in war. Yes, six million Jews had been killed, but Germany had been devastated. Israel was an established Jewish state. I did not deal with the Holocaust until much later.

Jim Sleeper: The period of amnesia ended with the Eichmann trial in 1963. The trial brought to the surface a lot of things that people had suppressed, ripped that all wide open. A nation was suddenly riveted. The scenes of the Jews in Israel, listening to the loudspeakers broadcasting the trial, standing in the streets in silence . . .

Susan Levin Schlechter: Before there was silence. Now there was all that talk about the six million. As a child I would sometimes ask, "Does the rabbi always have to talk about that?" No matter where his sermons went, they always came back to the six million.

David Landau: Growing up in the eighties, it seemed to me I had always heard about the Holocaust. I was five or six when the movie *The Holocaust* was shown on television. We talked about it in regular school and Hebrew school, but it didn't have much of an impact on me.

Then one day our Hebrew school teacher was absent, and the principal took over the class. Rabbi Aidelson was a little man, not much older than my parents, yet he seemed like someone from my grandparents' generation. He spoke with a heavy accent, was easily excited, and hardly looked imposing. But when he said, "*Yeladim* (children), I am talking to you; and when I am talking, I expect you to listen," even the rowdiest Talmud Torah kids would shut up and pay attention.

This day he didn't have to tell us to be quiet because, for over an hour, we sat spellbound as he recounted the story of his life during the years of the Holocaust. He was a small boy, part of a very religious family living in Poland, that hot September in 1939 when the Nazis came. He told us how they were forced to leave their home, were herded into a ghetto, and later on after the ghetto was liquidated were deported to a concentration camp called Budzin. The only German in that camp was Faix, the commander. The other SS were Ukrainians, dressed in black uniforms. They had volunteered to help with the Final Solution.

Rabbi Aidelson was one of eighteen children put to work in the kitchen, cleaning and peeling potatoes. One midday, he told us, the Ukrainians came and chased all the children out into the middle of the camp where Faix was sitting on his horse. Rabbi Aidelson was the last one out. He ran to the end of the line of children, clicked the heels of his wooden shoes together, and saluted. He had never done that before or after, and he still doesn't know what made him do it. You were not allowed to greet a German, he said.

Faix pointed at him with his horsewhip, indicating he go back to the kitchen. As he started running back, he heard the sound of gunfire. The other seventeen children were machine-gunned to death.

Rabbi Aidelson went on to tell us that when he first came to America, he never talked about these experiences because no one wanted to hear about them. "No one wanted to touch the wounds," was the way he put it. But even though I was only a kid of ten or eleven when I heard his story, it touched me in a way the made-for-television movies never had.

Abraham Peck: As I shared my parents' wounds as survivors, I also shared their anger. The survivor was often not quite the Jew that American Jews wanted to have here. He was regarded as suspect, not quite kosher. Because we did not fit into the American Jewish community, I was able to relate to black rage against white America and become involved in black liberation group activities.

Jeff Solomon: The mystery surrounding the Holocaust, the impotence associated with it, made the Kennedy-Nixon race a defining time for me. I began to appreciate how democracy in the United States operates and what actions I could take.

Phyllis Taylor: Not only did the knowledge of the Holocaust mold my view of the world being an unsafe place, it also molded my character in terms of my not wanting to be a "good German," someone who could continue to live in a normal way when horrendous things were happening.

Brooks Susman: We had been brought up on the notion of hope, without the realization of Holocaust. Maybe that's why Vietnam became such a watershed for my generation.

Stephen Solender: My generation was so traumatized by the Holocaust that it enabled and ennobled us to be much more assertive in our adult lives than the previous generations had been.

Abraham Peck: The subject is all part and parcel of an experience that I still do not understand. We talk about the Holocaust; we memorialize it. But on some level, I don't think we comprehend the way our Jewish identity has been shaken and obliterated.

8

THE PRECIOUS PROMISED LAND

"Hear the word of the Lord, O ye nations . . .
'He that scattered Israel doth gather him
and keep him, as a shepherd doth his flock.' "

—*Jeremiah XXXI:10*

Stephen Solender: I'm from the generation that was born in the Depression, grew up during the Holocaust, and experienced as children and teenagers the birth of the State of Israel and its first years of struggle. That's part of our memory.

Yitz Greenberg: The Holocaust was something that people wanted to put behind them. The focus now was Israel. For religious Jews there was almost a kind of messianic quality about it. We prayed for it, dreamed of it.

Addi Friedman: I used to imagine Palestine as a little medieval city of nooks, crannies, and towers—a dusty place of Arabs with daggers and Jews living in walled towns. I dreamt how wonderful it would be when there was, at last, a Jewish state.

Moe Skoler: We used to listen to the news every single night at the kitchen table. We tried to find out what was going on. In 1946–1947, we began to hear stories about Jewish refugees trying to get into Palestine, and we began paper drives all around Boston, gathering and selling newsprint and sending the money to Palestine. I was no more than eleven when I was unloading trucks of newspapers.

Balfour Brickner: Our favorite pastime as kids was picketing the British consulate in Cleveland. Our struggle was to create the State of Israel.

Yitz Greenberg: From the age of about twelve on, I went out with Jewish National Fund boxes into the Brooklyn subways to collect money for Israel. It seemed the riders on the West End line, which ran through Borough Park, didn't give much. The best subway was the Brighton Beach line. Somehow Jews gave more money there.

   The technique was to get on a train with a box in each hand and stand in front of the doors. As soon as they closed, I would shout, "Open the doors!" Everyone would look up—at which point I'd continue, "Open the doors of Israel to new immigrants!" It was a great attention-getter.

◀ (*top*) Young participant in the Salute to Israel Parade, c. 1975.
(*bottom left and right*) Photos of family in Israel.

Manny Azenberg: My father was a Zionist, always a Zionist. A self-educated man who spoke five or six languages, he was born in Poland and lived in London before coming to America. In 1919 he worked directly with Chaim Weizmann at the Second Zionist Congress.

Zionism was always around the house. We sent money to plant trees in Palestine; we dropped the coins in the Jewish National Fund box. My father worked for the Zionist Organization in New York. In the summer, he managed the Zionist Camp Kindleveilt. It was joy. I was under pressure in school, at home, in Hebrew school, on the streets of the Bronx. At camp there was none of that. You played basketball, you swam, you necked, you had color wars with blue and white teams. You had social dancing and Israeli dancing, you sang Hebrew songs—dozens of them, early 1940s Israeli songs about the Palmah. They sank into you.

Adults visited the camp, people like Golda Meir and Abba Eban and also people who painted houses, worked as butchers or in the garment center. Nobody rich, a very active group of working-class, lower-middle-class first-generation or immigrant Jews. They were not educated, but they knew the value of education. These were people who discussed and listened. These were people who read four newspapers: *The New York Times,* the *New York Post, PM,* the *Forward.* You saw the papers laying around the camp.

Famous Yiddish and Hebrew writers came up to talk. We kids weren't invited to the lectures. We wouldn't have gone anyway; we just wanted to play basketball. But we were surrounded by an atmosphere. It didn't hurt. We bumped into people who were committed. Coming back to the Bronx was culture shock. I started thinking about the next June.

We grew up in a traditional Jewish home. Friday nights, we waited for my father to come home, had challah from the G & R Bakery on 161st Street, said *Kiddush,* ate gefilte fish and chicken. We went to shul on the High Holy Days, and we had a seder. But as time went by, religion diminished in our lives. We moved from being pulled by religion to being pulled by Zionism.

When I was fourteen and my sister was ten, my father took us out of school and up to the Waldorf Astoria to meet Chaim Weizmann. This was the day before he went to Washington to persuade President Truman to recognize the State of Israel. Secret Servicemen escorted us into Weizmann's room. I had seen pictures of him in our house, and I expected him to be about seventeen feet tall. So I was surprised to meet this little man who had spots on his bald head and was going blind.

He asked me when I was going to Israel. "Next year if there's peace," I said because that's what I'd been told to say.

But he chastised me: "There will be peace."

And I, of course, agreed right away: "Don't worry, there will be peace."

As we were leaving, Weizmann said to my father, *"Tsvay feiner kinder"*—two fine children. It was like George Washington telling your father "nice kids."

Whatever my father was or wasn't, he was a Zionist. He had a passion about it. You were respectful about that passion no matter what. He sat at the kitchen table listening to the radio while the United Nations voted on partition. They ticked off the names of the countries. When they got to Uruguay, which put it over the top, he just sat there and cried. But in many ways, his job was over.

Balfour Brickner: When that vote was taken in Lake Success, we all went crazy. Who would've believed the state was going to be established? It was a justification of my dad's life.

Mike Lecar: My father died in 1943. He had been a great Zionist but did not live to see the fulfillment of his dream. After Israel became a nation, I began having this dream in which my father had not died after all. He was alive, living in Israel where he was working as a spy. One day I would go there, and I would see him again.

Alan Lelchuk: Burt, a dear older brother type who lived upstairs from me, had enlisted in the Air Force as a seventeen-year-old and got shot down over Germany in a B-17. He had about forty operations to get out the pieces of the experimental German glass bullets that broke into parts when they exploded in his body, but he never fully recovered. He was arrogant, caustic, and cynical. Nevertheless, when Israel was being formed, he decided to go to Palestine and fly with the early Jewish Air Force. He became part of a small group of American flyers, not all of whom were Jewish by the way.

My father thought it was crazy for Burt to make this heroic gesture, and they had arguments over his going there. I was about ten years old then, and Israel was beginning to take on some concrete reality for me.

Marnie Bernstein: In September 1948 I entered fifth grade and Israel celebrated its first New Year, 5709. For me these two events—one personal and one historic—are forever entwined.

I can still remember that September morning, sitting in a classroom in a Brooklyn elementary school, my neatly folded hands resting on a desk that was bolted to the floor, listening to the teacher talk of the usual first-day-of-school things. Much as I and the other children tried to pay attention, we kept glancing out of the fourth-floor classroom window where the spire of the Coney Island parachute could be glimpsed in the distant sky. Our teacher must have sensed our longing for freedom because she smiled at us and said, "Summer is over, and now we must turn to the business of learning." But leaning against her desk, her hands crossed on her lap, she suggested that this would not be such a terrible thing.

We looked at her with some curiosity. She neither looked nor sounded like the martial matrons we were accustomed to at P.S. 177. She was graceful and pretty, dressed in a long flowing skirt and silky blouse tied at the neck with a bow—a "New Look" outfit, that romantic reaction to the military-inspired dress of the war years. "This year," she told us, "we will study American history, and you will learn how lucky you are to be living in this wonderful country."

She did teach us American history as well as all the other subjects, but without the strict regimentation we were accustomed to. Gone were the marching drills. Instead we put on musicals and produced class newspapers. Our teacher seemed to us the epitome of peace and loveliness, and none of us knew her immediate, intimate connection to war.

It was not until much later that I learned she was the widow of Mickey Marcus, the United States Army colonel who had been one of the chief architects of the military strategy that won Israel its War of Independence. A World War II hero and the only American soldier buried at West Point who died in the service of a foreign country, Colonel Marcus was a victim of "friendly fire" in June 1948, just at the war's end.

That September Mrs. Marcus returned to her teaching job, and I became one of her students. Sitting there that first day of school, yearning for the pleasures of a summer just past, how could I have known that just three months before, David Ben-Gurion had embraced our teacher tearfully and told her, "Emma, he was the best we had."

Irv Saposnik: You felt tremendous pride associated with the creation of Israel. It compensated somewhat for the embarrassment you felt growing up around people who had one foot in the Old World: the seltzer man who carried loads of bottles on his back up four flights of stairs, the rabbis and Hebrew teachers who walked the streets with a timeless tread, the *pishke* man who came once a month to collect the pennies my grandmother put into the box for charities in a Jerusalem that only I would ever see.

Marnie Bernstein: We had a Yiddish record, *"Vee ahin zol ich gehen?"*— "Where shall I go?". The singer recounts how he tries to go here, go there, but nobody wants him. Then the mood of the song abruptly changes from pathos to pride, as he sings: "Now I know where to go/Where my folks proudly stand/Let me go, let me go/To the precious Promised Land."

Something new had been added to my personal universe, a land far away and very different, and at the same time totally familiar. I saw Israel as a complicated combination of the pictures in my Golden Library *Bible for Children,* a place of modern apartment houses with terraces that overlooked the sea, and a Jewish world of family and stores like home. My mother had one sister who'd remained in Romania with her husband and children after everyone else emigrated to America. Miraculously, all had survived the war and reunited in Palestine in 1947. My cousins were married now and starting families, and these people I had never met began to take on the dimensions of reality.

I'd seen their photos in family albums: dark, serious figures in heavy suits and coats. Now they were wearing sundresses or shorts, squinting into the camera lens from the bright sun. Where Europe had seemed to me a place of perpetual winter, Israel was eternal summer.

All kinds of items began coming into our home: a sheaf of postcards of Israeli sites that folded up like an accordion, a letter opener with a little map of Israel in the handle, a turquoise ashtray with the Hebrew letters for Israel forged in brass along the edge, copper trivets engraved with belly dancers, bottles of colored sand arranged in a pattern, camels carved out of wood. Exotic names of places like Ramat Gan, Tel Aviv, Haifa, and Bat Yam—names that made me think of gardens and orange groves—entered our vocabulary.

The guttural Yiddish I had heard all my life was giving way to a new kind of pronunciation that was so appealing. In Israel, we learned, they said "Sha-*bat*" instead of "*Sha*-bos"; "Yom Kee-*poor*" instead of "Yum *Kip*-per"; "Sha-*voo*-ith" instead of "Shveese." And the songs—"Hatikvah," which gave me the chills; "Tzena-Tzena" and "Hava Nagila," which we danced the hora to; and Arabic melodies in a minor key—flooded my consciousness.

A mythology was taking shape, with a cast of heroes dressed in short-sleeved white shirts or military uniforms. There were founding fathers like Chaim Weizmann and David Ben-Gurion, and Golda Meir, a founding mother, as well. My favorite was Moshe Dayan, whom I thought as romantic and dashing as Errol Flynn. We heard about the land of milk and honey, of gardens growing in the desert, of girls fighting in the army alongside the men. We heard about *Sabras,* the native Israelis, who like the fruit they were named for were tough on the outside and sweet on the inside. Everything was bright and modern and so totally opposite from the Jewish image I'd had until then.

David Bisno: I didn't know about Israel until I got to Harvard in 1957. The German-Jewish milieu in St. Louis was very anti-Zionist. It wasn't until Israel became a success, as I saw it, that the Jewish community there turned around and accepted its existence.

Balfour Brickner: The Reform movement was classically anti-Zionist, and the job of people like Abba Silver and my father, Barnett Brickner, was to move the American Reform rabbinate to a pro-Zionist stance.

Daniel Musher: Reform Jews in the main weren't interested in another country. They were Americans. They had a concept of ethical Judaism and a supernatural God that you related to on a personal basis; they didn't need any ethnic trappings at all, much less a country someplace. The Orthodox didn't accept the notion of Zionism because the Messiah would take care of the whole thing; and the Conservatives were inclined to follow the Orthodox.

My grandfather, Mordecai Kaplan, advocated the idea that Judaism is a peoplehood, a civilization as well as a religion. He was a tremendous force in moving first the Conservative movement and then others to a Zionist position.

Susan Levin Schlechter: Our rabbi at Temple Emanuel in Birmingham was one of the first Reform rabbis to speak in defense of the State of Israel. He was a Zionist from the word go. That was unusual, to say the least, in Birmingham in the 1950s. In the country, too, at that time. There were Jews who were violently opposed to involvement, in any way, with Israel. A group of people actually left our temple because of the rabbi's support.

All those cries of dual loyalty were out and about. Why would any Jews in Birmingham want to be accused of dual loyalty? They were, they had to be, Americans first. It was that feeling of being peripheral, marginal, of being not quite secure in one's own life.

Frank Rich: As I encountered organized Reform Judaism while growing up, many things rubbed me the wrong way. The religious school attempted to imitate secular school with pop quizzes and homework. Everything was framed in a secular context, so that it felt like a kind of a bush-league version of regular life without any particular spiritual content. The emphasis on Chanukah in relation to other more important Jewish holidays was one of the things that made organized Reform Judaism seem bogus to me. There was also a certain type of hypocrisy, like the ritual of people paying huge sums of money to have the best seats for the High Holy Days and then not showing up—or listening to the World Series through an earpiece. It all had a kind of canned quality; it was like a game that everyone played.

But if the liturgical aspect and the practice of Judaism were peripheral, what was not peripheral was the feeling of identification with a people who have a history, a history that always struck me as fascinating. Even though my mother did not belong to a synagogue the entire time I was growing up, she thought of herself as a Jew. She was extremely interested in all aspects of Jewish history, and she was a Zionist.

That's what I inherited. I identified with Israel. It was very important, particularly for someone who grew up in the 1950s, when the assurance that there would be an Israel was far more precarious than it is now.

Natalie Cohen Monteleone: When I was a teenager, I had this great desire to go to Israel, not so much for religious reasons as for romantic ones. I expected Paul Newman to be there waiting for me when I got off the airplane.

Jim Sleeper: Growing up as a Jew in Springfield, Massachusetts, in the 1950s, you had your parents' memories, your going to your grandparents' home for the High Holidays, and a suburban temple. That was it.

One of my mother's favorite stories was when her mother was away for a few days, and my father said, "C'mon I'm gonna cook you some bacon." My grandmother comes back unexpectedly while he's frying bacon. She has conniptions. She's shaking out the curtains. But it's all "What will the neighbors think?" It's not some deep belief. It's a *shanda,* a shame. The whole thing was held together not by some internal faith but by not wanting to lose face.

And then in 1960, right after my bar mitzvah, I won a scholarship through the synagogue to Camp Ramah, a Conservative-Zionist camp. I remember trying to fall asleep in my little bunk while the counselors and staff up in the dining hall were singing Israeli songs with a piano background. The melodies would waft down over the hill. Listening to the singing on a summer night, I felt a spirit, an excitement like nothing I had ever known. Suddenly I seemed part of an immense community that was cast up across time and space.

Then, during the summer of my junior year in high school, I actually went to Israel. And the ground shifted under my feet. I now understood that there was a physicality to my Jewishness. It wasn't just some spiritual thing. There was a national reality that I had never connected with.

At the time, Israel was a young, fledgling pioneering country. For me it was totally intoxicating, a complete revelation. This was pre-1967. The country was still only seven miles wide across the middle, and you had an overwhelming feeling of pride and admiration for this country—a sense of its vulnerability, its energy.

Mitchell Serels: During the Six-Day War, I was standing on the corner with an Israeli flag and collecting money. People were dropping in coins left and right. A woman gave me two dollars and said in an Irish brogue, "This is to help the Israelis because they beat the British."

Jason Freed: I was born in May 1967, just before the Six-Day War. My mother used to tell me how she lay in her hospital bed the days after my birth, listening to the radio, and worrying about what would be.

I grew up hearing about the military might of Israel, how the image of the brave soldier had replaced that of the meek shtetl Jew. My grandfather, who had been born in Europe, had a tremendous sense of pride in Israel's military prowess. He used to tell me how Israel had the only army in the world where the officers lead the men in battle. When he visited Israel, he kept having his picture taken with soldiers.

To me it seemed that here in America we had such safe, ordinary lives while there in Israel, our other world, all these adventures were going on. In 1973 they wheeled a television into our Sunday school classroom, and we watched the news about the Yom Kippur War. I was six years old and didn't really have a sense of what was at stake, only a small boy's excitement at the idea of battle. And then there was the rescue at Entebbe in 1976, which was more adventurous than a movie.

As I was growing up, the fact of a strong, vibrant Israel was a given. It figured in my self-definition. When I was a little kid, these two kids in Hebrew school used to pick on me a lot: David, who was big and fat; and Ira, who was very tall and thin. I wasn't into fighting, but I was able to hold my own. Once I had a fight with Ira, and David was the so-called referee.

Ira complained that I pulled his hair, which was against the rules. David, who was supposed to be neutral, hit me as kind of a punishment.

I saw the whole thing as a political metaphor. Ira was the Arabs: my main enemy. David was Russia: the big, fat superpower who was totally unfair. And I was Israel: small but brave and clever. Against all the odds, I—like Israel—was able to fight back and win.

REIGER'S

Mr. and Mrs. Sidney D. Harris

invite you to attend the Circumcision

ברית מילה

of their Son

Monday, October 25th, at 10 A. M.

at The Women's Hospital

110th Street and Amsterdam Avenue

New York City

Part Three

THE SACRED AND THE SECULAR

Making a Living

Sacred Time

Coming of Age

L'Dor Va'Dor—
From Generation to Generation

A Tenuous Balance

9

MAKING A LIVING

"Bless thee in all the work of thy hand which thou doest."

—Deuteronomy XIV:29

Shalom Goldman: As the old joke goes, being a rabbi is no job for a Jewish boy. My father was ordained but never became a rabbi because he knew he could never make enough money. Also the job brings nothing but endless tsuris. For two thousand years, the rabbis told the Jews what to do: this you can eat, this you can't eat; this person you can marry, this person you can't marry; this book you can read, this book you can't read. Then they come to the *goldeneh medina,* and all of a sudden everything is turned upside down. The Jews in America don't want to be told what to do. They want to tell the rabbi what to do. The president of the shul becomes the most important person. Or the president's wife.

Ruth Perlstein Marcus: In Europe my father was trained to be a rabbi. In this country he was trained by a doctor to be a *mohel.* He even had papers to prove it. He became one of the best-known *mohels* in all of Chicago.

One day in grammar school, we had to fill out forms asking for our parents' occupations. I wrote "*mohel.*"

The teacher read my form. "What kind of a business is this?" she asked.

"It's what my father does," I said and tried to explain the procedure of circumcision. She thought I was nuts.

I went home crying to my father.

"Next time," he said, "just write down 'clergyman.' "

Irv Kaze: My grandfather was both a *mohel* and a *shochet.* Whenever he set out on one of his rounds, I used to kid him: "Zayde, make sure you got the right knife now."

Zipporah Marans: During the Second World War, my father's congregation was in Raleigh, North Carolina. As he was a *shochet* as well as an Orthodox rabbi, he would have to go out occasionally and slaughter a cow. One Passover, when they were preparing for a seder at nearby Fort Bragg, the army brought five hundred live chickens to our house. It was a warm spring day, and the trees in the backyard were all in bloom while fifty soldiers readied the chickens for my father to slaughter. He set up an assembly line and showed the soldiers how to drain the blood, then pluck and salt the chickens. Feathers were flying all over the yard.

The soldiers would come to us for meals and long conversations, a touch of real home life. Sometimes they would have three days' leave before being shipped overseas. Their girlfriends would come down, and my father would marry them in our living room. My mother, sister, a soldier friend, and I would each hold up a corner of the *chuppa,* the wedding canopy.

Roz Starr: To get my mother out of her depression after her sister died, I talked her into becoming a matchmaker. I even created the ad she ran in the Jewish papers: "Sabbath-observing matchmaking office, Sunday to Thursday 2–9. Singles, find happiness with Mrs. Rabinowitz." She used her maiden name so they couldn't crash into our mansion.

She generally had a nice word for her male clients, and they often tried to make a pass at her. So I had to be there while she was conducting her interviews. I was the secretary sitting behind this big black Underwood typewriter in the foyer. I never said a word, only looked and listened.

As the matchmaker's daughter, I learned a lot. For example, the Germans thought they were better than the Russians. "So why are you coming to me?" my mother would ask. If a girl was very shy and ashamed of needing a *shiddach,* my mother would accommodate her by having a guy visit the girl's mother on some pretense.

I'd often hear her say to an unsuspecting client, "She's not only pretty [few were], she also has such a good heart."

"How do you know she has a good heart?" I'd ask afterwards.

"I imagined."

One woman client called up screaming, "He took out his tool and he showed it to me!"

My mother was furious. She always instructed the ladies never to let anyone into their apartment when they were alone. "What are you, an engineer that he had to show you his tool?" she said.

My mother charged five dollars down. If a couple held hands, they were engaged by the next week. That's how fast it was. Then the fee was fifty dollars each. Some of them tried to keep their engagement secret to avoid payment. My mother always found out.

She'd telephone: "I hear I have to wish you *mazel tov.*"

"Oh, I was going to send you a check."

"So send it," said my mother sweetly. She'd replace the mouthpiece in the cradle and add her favorite curse: *"Du zol vaeksen vee ah tzibeleh"*— You should grow like an onion: upside down.

Sidney Helfant: When the laundry my father worked for closed down during the Depression, he and nine other workers pooled their last few cents and bought their own. They were in hock for it the rest of their lives.

My father would pick up the dirty laundry and then deliver it wet or flat, shlepping it up as much as five flights of stairs. He never made a hell of a living.

Things got really bad after the war when washing machines came around. Then my father died. My mother had to go to work in the garment center. What could she do, an immigrant woman who went from nursing her sick mother to raising her family and taking care of a sick brother besides? She returned to the garment center, doing *"shnydern fur clyder"*— cutting material for clothes.

Morris Friedman: My father was a coffee salesman, one of two Jews in a family-owned WASP company. He never worked on Sabbaths or holidays, and his bosses respected him for it. The trunk of his car was always filled with coffee; whenever I think about riding in that car, the aroma of roasted coffee beans comes back to me.

He lived in the world of barter, and he'd always work out a deal. If he wanted to go to the Yiddish Theater, for example, he'd barter two bags of coffee for two tickets.

Let's face it: my father and his peer group were after economic survival. They had to pay fifty-five dollars a month rent, five dollars for the car in the garage. They had kids growing up, and they were busy working morning to night to secure themselves. My father was not a Mason, did not join clubs. It was out of the realm of possibility for him to attend a rally at Union Square after a full day's work.

Jim Sleeper: I think if you came of age during the Depression or the war, the necessity of keeping your nose to the grindstone was there; the futility of rebellion was there. You could not be self-indulgent.

Like many Jewish men of his generation, my father was very focused on his business. The son of a Lithuanian immigrant tailor, my father took a lot of pride in being a good provider and poured his hopes into the next generation. He didn't want me to be a businessman like him.

In college, my father had majored in Romance languages and acted in Shakespearean plays. But he knew from his older brother, if you were a schoolteacher you just barely made a pittance. So he went into the wholesale health and beauty products business instead. It was a question of economic necessity; he wanted to send his kids to college and provide.

He was always working. It wasn't the store. It was my father. His life revolved around hard work. He'd come home for dinner and afterwards would lie down on the couch with his shoes off and fall asleep for an hour while the TV was on. By the time he'd wake up, it would be my bedtime.

Moe Skoler: My father didn't talk to us much and didn't like to hear us talking much. He would come home from work, usually in an angry mood, have dinner, sit down on the couch, and read the paper. During the baseball season we weren't allowed to speak at the dinner table because he was listening to the game on the radio. But at least we experienced the Red Sox games together.

A custom peddler, my father sold clothing to people on budget programs where they paid him two or three dollars a week. He was always on the run. I'd be in the living room with one of my friends when my father would come in.

"Hello," he'd say to no one in particular as he raced up the stairs to get something he'd forgotten. A minute later, he'd rush out. "Good-bye," he'd say, again to no one in particular. My friends nicknamed him "Hello-Good-bye."

Ann Gold: My father's name was Martin Gordon, but his customers called him Mr. Martin. Many of them lived out in the country, far from stores. They were very poor people who looked to my father to solve their problems.

My father worked within a forty-mile range from our home in Auburn, Maine, selling refrigerators and pants and shoes and mattresses on the installment plan. Once a week, he would make the trip to Portland and stock up. The garage was his store. It was always packed.

His more than five hundred customers paid through the nose. But in those days before credit cards, it was the only way they could get merchandise. Through the week, my father would do his route, picking up a dollar from one, two from another, crossing the payments off his little card. He drove through storms, climbed terrible steps, worked ridiculous hours, and never missed a day of work. He was a salesman.

Menachem Katz: My father sold dry goods on the road. Once he was in a neighborhood called Hell's Kitchen where they dealt in bootleg homemade liquor. While he was making a collection, someone hid in the back of his car and tried to attack him and steal his money. Fortunately Dad was able to fend him off, but after that he began taking me along with him. Driving around with Dad and hearing him talk about business was a great education.

When I was still in my teens, Dad decided to get off the road, and he asked me what I'd like to do. I said I always enjoyed men's clothing and fashion; he said, "Fine, let's go into the men's clothing business." We found a place, a very, very small store on a side street off Quincy Square in our hometown of Quincy, Massachusetts. The many customers Dad had from his years on the road would be the basis for our business. But because it was right after the war, we had a great deal of difficulty finding someone to sell us merchandise. Our credit was good, and we had enough money to pay for it, but supplies were limited and demand was great. Finally, Abe Miller from New York City gave us our first break and sold us some suits. That's how we started out in March 1947.

Dad said to me, "*Nu* son, now you're going to learn to shave on my beard." He had put his whole life's savings into this enterprise, and I wasn't going to let it fail.

Soon after we opened, a customer came in and asked if we had any

100-percent camel's hair polo coats, double breasted with a belt. Not to let an opportunity go by, I said I'd be happy to order it for him. He was a tall slim man, size 38 long. I found a manufacturer who happened to have a coat like that in just that size. It was two hundred dollars; today it would be a thousand. I took it and let the customer know I had gotten the coat he ordered. But he never came in for it. I called and called, but he ignored me.

We always take inventory on Christmas day. As it approached that first year we were in business, I dreaded having to include this very expensive item in our inventory. Then, just before Christmas, the coach of the Abington basketball team—the man who invented the glass backboard—walked into our store. He asked whether we had a 100-percent camel's hair polo coat, double breasted with a belt. I ran downstairs, took the coat out of a zipper garment bag, and brought it upstairs. It was exactly what he wanted. He paid us the two hundred dollars and became a very good customer, and we didn't have to include the coat in our inventory.

A year and a half after we began, we got the opportunity to move to Hancock Street in Quincy center. That was a big move for us. We were still a very, very small operation. Across the street from our new location was Remick's, a large department store owned by Frank Remick, the father of the actress Lee Remick.

Opening day, a big bouquet of flowers arrived from Remick's. When I closed up that evening and noticed Frank Remick on the other side of the street, I crossed over and thanked him for the flowers and good wishes. He said to me, "I know there's plenty of room on this street for both of us to do good business."

I couldn't get over it. Here was this important businessman, and he was so gracious. He talked to me as if I were an equal.

Al Lewis: I began my performing career when I was still a teenager working as a roustabout, cleaning up after the animals at the circus that played in Brownsville before it went on to its big run at the old Madison Square Garden. From there I worked myself up to being a clown doing a slack wire and riding a trick unicycle while playing a musical saw. Once I stopped and said something. People laughed. "I must be funny," I thought.

I moved on to burlesque, which was exciting—not because of the half-naked girls but because it was so creative. There is no script in burlesque, just a basic outline. You have to create right at the moment. You take a girl in the chorus and hope and pray she's a "talking woman," a woman who besides tits and ass can dance and talk.

I spent my teens as a singer, acrobat, and strong man in vaudeville all over the country. For a while I operated my own medicine show in southern towns so small Rand McNally never put them down. I'd make the medicine the night before in a bathtub. Don't laugh. They bought it.

You go into a town in the South. They never saw you before so they hate you. You're from the North so they hate you twice. They decide you're Jewish, because that's what they think anybody they never saw before is, so they hate you three times. And you're trying to get fifty cents from them.

I'd buy fifty cents worth of used lumber, put it on the end of Main Street, the one street in the town, and set it on fire. That's my opening act. It's the biggest thing to happen in that town in twenty years. Everybody comes out. I set up my stepladder with the American flag, climb up a few rungs, and I'm selling.

I look out at the crowd. I pick the worst, most savage-looking guy, the guy who if you blink the wrong way is going to kill you, and use him as a springboard. In my mind, I say, "You son of a bitch, I'm going to get fifty cents from you. And if I get fifty cents from you, I'm going to get ten dollars from the rest 'cause those are easy."

But you had to be cunning. You had to be humorous. Guys would yell out the worst kinds of curses, and you had to use them and turn them around and get the crowd laughing against them—not too loudly though, because they could get violent. You don't know how cunning you have to be until you're on that firing line. You needed a *Yiddishe kup*. But I learned the whole spiel from an Irishman.

Doris Modell Tipograph: New York was dominated by the Irish in the 1930s and 1940s, and the Irish newspaper people, sportsmen, and politicians were all friends of my father, Henry Modell. Men like Mayor William O'Dwyer, whose campaign my dad worked on, and Mayor Jimmy Walker, were always around.

The Modell stores carried golf, tennis, and horseback-riding equipment—

the goods of the WASP sports world. Yet my father was hardly your athletic type. He was this little Jewish man with a head of prematurely white hair, a genius for promotion, and a sporting interest limited to boxing matches and the Brooklyn Dodgers. He loved the Dodgers with a passion. His other passion was his business.

He and my mother worked in our stores six and sometimes seven days a week. My father was frontstage and my mother backstage as buyer and bookkeeper. Friday nights, they'd come home exhausted. They were hard-working Jews, building a business. My brother Bill and I accepted what they did. That was all we knew.

Leon Toubin: My mother's father tended to his store in Brenham, Texas, all by himself. He ate his lunch in the store—a full lunch, usually roast chicken and gravy, and it had to be hot. Since my school was right across the street from his store, it would be my job to bring Grandpa his meal after I'd gone home for lunch. I'd pour the gravy into a paper bag, and the stuff would start to leak by the time I reached the store. But he loved his hot lunch. He also loved his Chesterfield cigarettes and the shot of whiskey, good bourbon, that he had every day.

Because Grandpa had to keep the store open on Saturdays, he did not *daven* or lead prayers in the synagogue until after he retired. While he was working, on Fridays before sundown, he would tear pieces of wrapping paper and string to prepare for the Saturday customers. He would never break the string on the Sabbath. Instead he'd give the customers the wrapping paper and string, and they'd walk through the streets trying to put their packages together.

My father came to Texas from Lithuania at the age of sixteen. First he sold ice cream in Austin. Then he tried to get a junk business going outside of San Antonio. Then he opened up a dry goods store in Smithville. But the Ku Klux Klan were big there, and they wouldn't trade with a Jew. So he moved on to Brenham.

Like most small southern towns, Brenham had a downtown square with a courthouse at the head and stores on three sides. On the east side of the square was a sixty-by-sixty emporium called the New York Store because its merchandise originally was brought in from New York City. He bought that store.

In 1934 J. C. Penney came to Brenham and drove almost all the Jewish merchants out. But not the New York Store. My father and his brother, whom he brought in with him, talked a Dallas wholesaler into selling to them direct from the manufacturer for a charge of 3 percent. In this way, they were able to get merchandise and compete with Penney's. Then they opened eight other stores in towns around Brenham. They did a lot of advertising, a lot of direct circulars. They'd move into a town and do what J. C. Penney had done in Brenham.

Before air-conditioning came in the late fifties, the store had ceiling fans and fans on top of the counters. Outside the store, there still was the post they used to tie the horses to. I started working in the store in 1942 for a quarter a day. The clerks made ten to twelve dollars a week. A good shirt was ninety-nine cents, a pair of work pants was forty-nine cents. We worked with pennies. And everybody was happy.

Is Crystal: Most of the thirty or forty Jewish-owned corner grocery stores in Duluth were of the mini-supermarket style. But Crystal's Kosher Delicatessen was more of the mom-and-pop variety. We waited on our customers one at a time. We knew them individually and helped them pick out the stuff.

Our store had a high plaster-carved ceiling and a floor made of long wooden planks. A big pendulum clock hung on the wall, and the plain light fixtures were suspended from the ceiling by long chains. Against the walls were wooden cabinets and shelves neatly lined with merchandise. Out on the floor were wooden tables stacked with cans and jars, bins and wire baskets filled with different kinds of produce and packaged foods. My dad, with a white apron over his jacket, shirt, and tie, was usually positioned behind one of the counters, which had slanted glass cases that showed off the foods.

In the back of the store, there was a kitchen-dinette where we did our homework and ate most of our meals. We hardly ate at home except on Friday nights.

We sold kosher foods, most of which came from the Sinai 48 Kosher Sausage Company in Chicago. We sold kasha in bulk and halvah that came in cones like a dunce's cap. We'd cut out pieces from the top and keep on going down. The lox we'd lay out on a slab and cut one slice, two slices, three slices, ninety-eight cents a pound. We retailed caviar. In 1924, to give you an idea, a two-ounce jar cost thirty-five cents. Jewish people like good food.

My dad carried all the Passover products, so practically the whole community used to shop in our store. Plus we used to ship to all the range towns out of Duluth, fifty and more miles away. We'd get in cones of sugar, Russian mushrooms, and dried mushrooms that came on a string from New York or Chicago. My dad would literally comb the markets for kosher and fancy foods. Figs were a big item. Also Russian *tsikarkis*, hard sugar candies filled with fruits, which we sold out of a barrel for a penny a piece. Each was individually wrapped with a picture of its fruit: raspberry, lemon, orange, strawberry, and so on.

Morris Kerness: I was twelve years old when I went to work for Issy's father in Crystal's Delicatessen. I used to get out of Washington Junior High about an hour early and go down to Crystal's, where I'd make corned beef and salami sandwiches that sold for a nickel and a dime. My mother was a real *berrieh*, a live wire who could make a seven-course meal for her nine kids out of a soup bone. But this kind of stuff I didn't get at home so I would nibble quite a bit at Crystal's.

Jacob Crystal was a wonderful man to work for. He asked you to do something, and that was it. Never bawled me out, not once. The old man trusted everyone, but Mrs. Crystal was a little sharper.

Dan Kossoff: Rachel Crystal was a very stately woman who would sit in the store and watch everyone who came in, making sure they were minding their manners and being honest. Jacob Crystal was very finicky about how things were placed on the shelves. He was a master at making incredible gift baskets of fruit and packaged foods tied up with fancy ribbons.

Crystal's was a fancy food store, probably the only one in the state of Minnesota. In the 1950s, when I was a teenager and worked there, it was the place with the best food in town. I remember the delicious dill pickles in the barrels, the corned beef they prepared themselves, the quality and size of the fruit. The work ethic impressed me the most. The family was always there, always working. Even when the elder Mr. C. was in his eighties, he was still a dynamo, moving through the store.

Dinah Crystal Kossoff: By the late 1940s and 1950s, when I was growing up, the store had become a gourmet-type operation, and there was very little kosher food except for a deli counter. Nevertheless, whenever the Chasidim came through, they would come into our store. My grandfather would give them each a dollar. How strange those men seemed with their old-fashioned black coats, their hats, sidecurls, and long beards.

Is Crystal: All his life, my father remained very religious and kept kosher, even on the road. He'd take along a kosher salami, sardines, and so forth. If he ate out, it was just a *glus tay* (glass of tea). Early every morning before work, he would put on *tefillin* and *daven* in the store.

Still he had to make accommodations to living in the *goldeneh medina*. Friday nights, my dad would close up the store at about seven o'clock and come home to have his typical Sabbath dinner. That was very important. But Saturdays, although I went to shul, my dad opened up the store and worked. He used to say, "What's to man is to man, and what's to God is to God."

Jeff Solomon: How do you make a living in America with English as your second language and having been expelled from high school in Germany? You worked. My mother worked as a bookkeeper, and my father as a butcher in a nonkosher environment. Knowing that my parents were trying to get enough money together to buy a business, my observant grandfather, who lived with us, insisted my father bring the nonkosher meats into our kosher home because it was an economic savings. We separated dairy and meat, but we ate nonkosher meat.

Ultimately my parents got enough money together to buy a luncheonette and delicatessen. At first my father worked six and a half days a week—day shifts one week, night shifts the next. We kids didn't see him. My mother would leave at eight in the morning and return home at six. Dinner was always very simple: broiled chicken or steak and some potatoes. No sauerbraten or schnitzel. After dinner, she'd do the bookkeeping. I worked long before I was of legal age. Into his eighties, my grandfather would spend Sundays in the store. It was a struggle.

Even after we moved from Washington Heights to Queens and could afford nicer things, my parents lived very modestly. But there were certain indulgences. They always had a convertible, and starting from the time I was seven, we went to Miami Beach every year. My mother had to find an excuse to do something nice for herself, and in this case, the excuse was my brother's postnasal drip.

As my parents became more successful, we kept moving north in our Miami Beach stays in an annual progression. We began at the Tides Hotel on Eleventh Street, then moved up to the Delano on Seventeenth, up and up, until finally we made it to the Fountainbleau.

David Bisno: As a young kid growing up in Kenosha, Wisconsin, my father was taken to an ophthalmologist in Milwaukee. He was absolutely blown away by the idea that one could make a living in an office seeing patients as opposed to running a store like his father. He loved electronics and was intrigued by the development of the radio and the crystal set, but he realized Jewish boys never got a job with General Electric or Westinghouse. So he decided on a career in medicine.

He went to the University of Wisconsin, where he got all A's and a scholarship to Johns Hopkins. There he was one of only two Jewish students, and both had a very tough four years. They had to deal with the snobby attitude of all the rich gentiles who were following their fathers' careers as physicians.

In 1937 my father began running the eye clinic at the Catholic hospital in St. Louis for fifty dollars a month; he also worked part time running the eye clinic at the Jewish hospital. I was born in 1939.

There were two separate Jewish worlds in St. Louis then. The Germans were heading the big companies and making the big money. The Russians had the small delicatessens and were trying to move up into the professions.

My parents joined Temple Israel, the German synagogue where they were out of their element.

We lived in a big white rented house that had a washing machine on the front porch. My father drove an old Nash. But he took whatever money he could save and sent me to the private school with the German Jews that fed into prep schools and then Ivy League colleges. I was the only Russian Jewish kid there.

When I was in the fourth grade, all the fathers came to a father-son softball game—except my dad. He was seeing patients in the operating room. That was a big afternoon in my life. It was when I realized there was a major difference between my background and that of the other children.

His practice began to grow. By the time I was a teenager, he had become one of the two best-known Jewish ophthalmologists in St. Louis. We were now living in a house in University City, a nice suburb next to the best public school in St. Louis, which I had transferred to. My parents had paid twenty-three thousand dollars for the house—cash. That was the effect of the Depression. My father had seen a house taken away from his family and was concerned with survival every day of his life. He was very uptight about putting himself in debt.

His purpose was to survive in his practice and not turn people off. He never wanted people to know how he voted. He never went to a PTA meeting for fear that an issue might come up where he would have to take a position that was different from his patients' position. He kept very much to himself.

Every Saturday we drove over to the Russian Jewish bakery in the Jewish ghetto of St. Louis, a neighborhood of tenement buildings where many of my father's patients lived and shopped. My mother would go shopping while he'd sit in the car a block away from the bakery. God forbid his patients should see him without his white coat and flashlight and Phi Beta Kappa key! In our backyard, he would grease the car, but in the front he wouldn't be seen cutting the grass.

At night my dad would sit with me and teach me about electricity, speed of light, optics, magnetism. Then he would retire to his room and talk to people across the world with a flip of a button. He never knew to whom he was speaking on his ham radio. The conversations were not personal; they amounted to absolutely nothing. I thought it was a waste of time. But my dad found an escape that way. He did not have to confront anyone; he had no visual contact.

Robert Leiter: For thirty-five years, my father was a physician in Overbrook Park, a middle-class Philadelphia neighborhood that was so overwhelmingly Jewish it was called "Little Israel." We lived in a Philadelphia row house over his office, one of eighty or ninety connected houses on a long block built in the postwar push. Being on the corner, we had a side lawn. But living above the office made it impossible for my brothers and me. If we made one sound that could disturb his patients, my mother heard about it. As a result, she put us to bed very early. I remember evenings in the summertime, crying as I watched the kids play wire ball outside in the daylight. But my father didn't want us traipsing into the house and disrupting his hours.

When I was five, we moved to a neighborhood five miles away. Economically, it was a huge jump. My father bought a three-story stone colonial house, a solid and formidable structure.

At the end of our street was City Line Avenue. You crossed it and you were into the suburbs—which, to me, was the golden land. Jews were starting to move into parts of the Main Line. I would wonder, "Why is my father so stupid? Why didn't we move there?" But my father had no need to cross that line. He didn't buy into any of that stuff.

He had decided that he was going to become successful as an American, not necessarily as a Jew. Although he wasn't the kind of guy who talked about how experiences shaped him, I got flashes of how he had to fight the Waspish medical establishment in Philadelphia, of what it had been like to be a Jew at the University of Alabama and the University of Pennsylvania Medical School. If he had been challenged, he would have fought. He never tried to pass.

He never belonged to a country club. He never gave to causes. I don't think he ever went through a liberal phase as most people did. He thought it was showing off. The entire family and people throughout the community looked up to him. My father was like a god; he answered to no one. What he did was become a collector. His objects became intermediaries between him and the WASP society. By buying them, he was buying a piece of America. This was a man whose father was a weaver.

After his office hours, my father would go downtown and make his rounds at the graduate hospital at the University of Pennsylvania. Then he would go down to Pine Street and visit his antique dealer cronies. They knew what he wanted. He collected books, art, oriental rugs, furniture, all museum quality. He also collected Orientalia—Japanese art mostly—ivory carving, jade. Our house looked like a museum.

He thought people who spent money on clothing and cars were frivolous. It was his money. He had made it. We, his family, were just encumbrances who sometimes took it away from him.

Although he came from a very devout family, my father took no solace from religion. The story, which may be apocryphal, was that my grandfather had died of a massive heart attack on his way back from shul. My father had no sentimentality about death. He never visited his mother's or father's grave. But when he got older and very anxious, he became the Medical Director of the Talmudic Yeshiva and gave the children there free medical attention. In doing so, I believe he made peace in some way with the father he had turned his back on.

Balfour Brickner: My father, Rabbi Barnett Brickner, was a great orator who could fill the old Madison Square Garden without a microphone. He was also a passionate Zionist, a committed socialist, and a humanist. My mother, Rebecca Aaronson, was the first woman Hebrew teacher in the city of New York.

Growing up in Baltimore, my mother had been encouraged to be whatever she wanted to be. She wanted to be a feminist. She attended Hebrew school under the tutelage of Dr. Samson Benderly, who came to New York in 1910 to begin the Kehila movement, which sought to modernize Jewish education and make Hebrew a living language. He convinced my grandmother to let my mother come up with him to New York, although she was only about seventeen years old. He convinced the Underwood Corporation to create a Hebrew typewriter, and she became Benderly's secretary. She would go from Barnard, where she studied, to the Educational Alliance on Lower Broadway, where she taught new immigrants. I can't tell you how many times people have come up to me and said, "Your mother taught me Hebrew."

Dad went first to medical school in New York City but couldn't stand it. Then he went to the Jewish Theological Seminary to enter the rabbinate but he had trouble with Talmud. He moved over to Columbia, where he met my mother. While there, he was urged to consider the rabbinate and the Hebrew Union College in Cincinnati, where the emphasis there was more on the Bible and less on the Talmud.

My mother went along with him and helped him out with his Hebrew. She wanted to be ordained. She knew more Bible and more Hebrew than 99 percent of the men graduating from the College in those days. They wouldn't ordain her because she was a woman, which really angered her.

I was born in 1926. The year before, Dad succeeded Rabbi Louis Wolsey, rabbi of the Euclid Avenue Temple in Cleveland, one of the earliest and most prestigious Reform temples in this country. "EAT" on Eighty-second and Euclid was to be his spiritual and physical home until the new building was built around 1957 on Fairmont Boulevard. He was in that building only until 1958, when he was tragically killed in an automobile crash in Spain.

Our Tudor house in Shaker Heights was like a mini hotel. We had at least six bedrooms and usually two people to help. Sundays we would have a seven-rib standing roast and a table filled with guests. Dad would bring people home: religious figures, political people. Seders at home would be huge. I never knew all the people at the table.

Stephen Wise would take the Twentieth Century Limited into Cleveland to give a speech, and he'd stay at our house overnight. He and Dad were close friends socially and allies politically. Zionism was their common and passionate concern.

Wise was a huge man. His face and hands were very large. He had a great big voice. I was a fat kid. Wise would put me on his knee and knead me like dough. He'd pinch me and pummel me. I didn't like it. Whenever my mother would say, "Stephen is coming for a couple of days," I'd try to eat in the kitchen.

My father's congregation really had two rabbis: him and my mother. Dad would sometimes get stuck out of town and Mom would preach. If Dad couldn't make the confirmation class, Mother would teach it. The congregation saw them as a team. They were both strong willed, but they had a relationship that was very unique. They were an institution.

Yitz Greenberg: My father was a rabbi who taught Talmud in the downstairs part of Temple Beth El in Borough Park, Brooklyn. The very term "temple" for an Orthodox shul was a statement. There was an organ in the women's section, although to my knowledge it had never been played. That would be going too far for an Orthodox synagogue.

The rabbi of Temple Beth El spoke English. My father, who never learned English, gave his class in Yiddish. His fantasy was that I would become an English-speaking rabbi, an upstairs rabbi, an American rabbi.

Until I was thirteen, I *davened* downstairs with my father. I loved that world. My father was the star. He did not so much give sermons as teach adult immigrants—the less successful so to speak, the ones who spoke Yiddish, who didn't make it or assimilate as much. They came in every night after a long day of work to study. At its height, there were thirty to forty men sitting at this long table with open volumes. My father would read and comment. They'd ask questions and argue over some point.

My father loved the stories and the humor in the Talmud. That was unusual for a Litvak, because typically they focus on the laws and skip the stories. One of his favorites was about a man who goes to this famous Roman dream interpreter to explain his dream. The interpreter says the man's vision of a tree means his child is going to die, and his image of a flying bird means the man will go bankrupt.

Then someone tells the man to go back to the dream interpreter and pay him a good fee. Now the tree means he will have ten children. Now the flying bird means his business will be a great success.

The point is the man is a fool because he doesn't understand that money gives him the answer he wants. The story also mocks dream interpretation. I don't remember any other teacher aside from my father who would tell this story and laugh with it, finding in it the humor and humanity of the Talmud.

My father had been orphaned as a boy and grew up in a yeshiva. He never had pals or a father who played ball with him. So it was hard for him to play with us. He expressed himself to his children through his learning. His religious and emotional expressions were the same; the line between the sacred and the secular blurred.

My father was also a *shochet*. He had to get up at four in the morning to go to the market. The work was hard and bloody, and the crews and owners of the markets were vulgar and ignorant, tough men. My father dreaded their language. It was an agony for him to be there. But it was America, and he had to make a living.

At noon he would come home quite beaten and tired. His clothes, which were past the point of being worn-out, would be splattered with blood.

Then he would wash up and change into something simple and clean, come out, sit down and find his place in the *Gemara*. And suddenly he was bathed in light.

If he had been demeaned in the morning, in the afternoon he was transformed. It was like the old story about the peddlers in East New York. All week long, they were spat upon. But on Shabbos they were kings.

10

SACRED TIME

*"These are the appointed seasons of the Lord
which ye shall proclaim to be holy convocations."*

—*Leviticus XXIII:37*

Shalom Goldman: My early years were spent in a cocoon that was rosy and very Jewish. All of that Jewishness was mother's milk to me, very deeply imbued. You don't realize how deeply until you become secularized.

Our Young Israel in Hartford was an old white clapboard house that had been converted into a shul sometime in the 1940s. It was totally unpretentious, Old World, smelling of herring. The services were held in the living room with a *machitza* separating the men from the women in the back.

My most vivid memories are of the men gathering in the synagogue. It was *haimish*—cozy and unpretentious—and very much a male society. On Mondays and Thursdays, only the men came to read the Torah. Then they'd have a shot of schnapps. Friday nights, the women stayed home cooking the Shabbat dinner while the men attended services. They didn't hurry up. They lingered. I was seven or eight, and my brother Ari was five or six. We would hold hands with my father as we walked home from synagogue. It was all very sweet. My father was somewhat distant, but religion was where we got together. It forged our relationship, for a while.

Caroline Katz Mount: Time was divided into the ordinary and the sacred. Our seasonal calendar was punctuated by holidays, our weekly calendar by Saturdays.

Each holiday was distinctive for its food. For Chanukah, my mother made potato *latkes* and *kreplach* with pot cheese. On Shavuoth we had *verenykes* filled with sour cherries or blueberries or, better yet, buttered bread crumbs—for some reason, my grandmother called these *"foile"* (lazy) *verenykes*. For the High Holy days, my mother made *perishkes,* pointed little pastries stuffed with apples and flavored with cinnamon.

The holidays were preceded by anticipation—a busyness of shopping for food, cleaning the house, buying new clothes, getting ready.

Marnie Bernstein: Before the High Holy Days, my father would go to Quincy, where much of his family lived, to visit his father's grave. Those were the only times we were ever separated overnight. I remember the long nights, the hollow feeling while he was away. I missed him terribly.

One year he returned with a story about his younger brother, my uncle

◀ *(top)* Grandfather reading the Haggadah. *(bottom left)* Shabbat services—bar mitzvah boy with elders before the Torahs. *(bottom right)* Giving the final touches to the seder table.

Saul, who made a solitary visit to the cemetery on a Sunday afternoon that fall. The cloudy sky and yellowed leaves falling from the trees put him in a reverential and nostalgic mood. Thinking of his beloved father, of his last illness, and of how much he had suffered before he died at a young age, he sang the "El Moley Rachomim" with great feeling, pouring his emotions out into the ancient melody of the Hebrew prayer.

As he finished, he was startled out of his reverie by a gentle tap on the shoulder. A little man had evidently been listening to him pray. "That was beautiful," the little man said. "You have such a good voice, just like an opera singer. Would you sing the 'El Moley' over my parents' grave?"

"I'm sorry," said my uncle, "I'm not a cantor or a rabbi."

"It doesn't matter," the man insisted. "Please. You will be doing me a great *mitzvah*."

My uncle couldn't get out of it. He followed the man along the winding paths of the old cemetery until they came to two weathered tombstones, where Uncle Saul once again sang the prayer. When he finished, he turned and found that a little crowd had gathered.

A woman stepped forward. "That was beautiful. Would you mind saying the prayer over my parents' grave?"

My uncle ended up spending an entire afternoon in the cemetery singing the "El Moley" over at least a dozen graves. "From now on," he told my father, "I'll sing it to myself."

Is Crystal: The High Holy Days, the Days of Awe, were very intense times. You knew you had to stay out of school. You got your new suit and were dressed prim and proper.

Natalie Cohen Monteleone: Rosh Hashanah was the big one for me. My *bubby* had a tiny row house in Baltimore, and we all piled in there. All the leaves were put into the dining room table so it stretched out into the living room. The adults sat there, and the kids sat at their own little bridge table.

We'd walk to shul. I had no comprehension of what was going on. It was all in Hebrew. I sat with my aunts, who were always pointing out, "Look, there's Uncle Abie" or "There's Stevie, oh boy!"

Children's services in, adults services out. We were out and in, in and out of services all day. Outside on the sidewalk, we kids threw chestnuts at each other or whatever it was that was falling from the trees.

Alex Rosin: We used to drive from Arcadia, Florida, down to Beth Shalom Synagogue in Sarasota for the High Holy Days. It was a fifty-eight-mile, two-and-a-half-hour hard drive. The roads were what we called nine feet wide. You had half the road, and the facing car had half the road. Most of it was potholes and washed out. The weather was so hot and sticky. Thank God, the synagogue was air-conditioned.

Brenda Robinson Wolchok: September in Savannah could be ninety-five degrees. It didn't matter. You'd have to wear the new wool outfits you bought for the High Holy Days.

Terry Drucker Rosin: The observant families used to take hotel rooms in downtown Savannah so they could walk to services. Some of them came to shul all dressed in white, down to their shoes.

Elliot Colchamiro: On the High Holidays, my family went to the Greek shul up on the second floor of an existing synagogue in Bensonhurst, Brooklyn. We were not Sephardim but Romanoites, Jews whose ancestors in the Greek town of Ioannina dated back to before Jesus' birth.

I knew I was a little different from the rest. My father would eat sheep's heads. My grandfather would brew gallon jugs of *raki,* something like anisette with much more of a kick. When my *theas* (aunts) got together, they would pass around a jar of sweet jelly with a little teaspoon and speak in the musical tones of Greek so we children would not understand what they were saying.

The musical tones of our synagogue were different, too. When we sang "Shema Yisrael, Adonai Elohenu, Adonai Ehad," it sounded like a *muezzin* calling the faithful to the mosque.

The first thing I'd do when I got to shul was find my grandmother, who was always sitting behind the curtain with the other women. I'd kiss her and then I'd watch how the *shammes* kept count of the hundred or more people at services and their donations with those little Delaney cards, like the ones teachers used to take attendance.

Linda Katz Ephraim: My mother didn't go to shul. I went with my father to the little Orthodox synagogue a few blocks from our home. I loved sitting beside him in the men's section; I loved the way his after-shave lotion smelled; I loved to play with the fringes on his *tallit*.

Sylvia Skoler Portnoy: The times I sat beside my father in shul on Rosh Hashanah and Yom Kippur were among the few times I felt any real intimacy with him. Because I was a girl, I didn't go to Hebrew school and therefore didn't understand what was going on. Still, when they came around with the Torah, it was thrilling. I would kiss the tips of my fingers and lightly tap them against the satiny cover as they carried it by.

Caroline Katz Mount: My mother sat behind the curtain with the other women, but I was beside my father in the men's section of our little shul. He would be showing me off to all his friends and telling me about all the different prayers and how in Russia, the peasants would stand outside the shul, listening to the beautiful singing.

The last two years of my mother's mother's life, when she was sick and forgetful, my father spent the afternoons of Rosh Hashanah with her. They'd sit together by her bedroom window, where for so many years she had spent Saturday afternoons reading her *Siddur*. Now he read aloud to her the prayer that asks God not to forget you in your old age. My grandmother understood very little by that time, but nevertheless she wept.

Is Crystal: The day before Yom Kippur, the *shammes* used to come to the house early in the morning when we were still in our underwear. He would take a live chicken out of a gunnysack, hold it by the legs, and swing it in circles over our heads. That was the custom of *shlogn kapores*. Supposedly your sins were taken away from you and given to the chicken.

Ansie Sokoloff: In Eldorado, Arkansas, I had to stay home from school on the High Holy Days and walk around with a dress and a hat and gloves. The next day, when my friends asked where I was, I'd tell them I was sick. The holidays did not mean much to me. We did not even fast on Yom Kippur.

But I do remember *erev* Yom Kippur. The Jews of Eldorado would gather. My father would read the services. Then he'd put down the book, pick up his violin, and play the haunting and plaintive melody of *Kol Nidre*.

Is Crystal: The men went to shul first. The women would come later. They wanted the time alone at home to read some prayers and cry a little bit, to speak to God. They didn't want the men around the house.

Marnie Bernstein: Yom Kippur morning we awoke with a vague sense of trepidation. It was not the fasting. We were too young to fast and couldn't wait until we were old enough to go without eating for an entire day. No, what we dreaded was the prospect of *Yizkor*, the memorial prayer, looming ahead.

Our little shul was exceedingly modest but comfortable and familiar. Its walls were decorated with big round murals of lions in desert settings. There was an amber quality to the place, like sunlight at the end of a day. People were not so decorous there; they gossiped as much as they prayed. Children ran in and out freely.

Except for the time of *Yizkor*. Around noon, all of a sudden, the mood would turn very serious. It was as if the Indian summer day had abruptly become cold.

The children would be hurried out while people in the neighborhood who otherwise never came to shul would arrive, and they would be let in. It got so crowded in the little shul that people pushed forward as if they were in a subway car and the double doors were closing.

We children were left outside. We'd hang around beside the bolted doors aimlessly. No one felt like playing. No one talked. Ten or fifteen minutes would pass. It seemed like hours.

Finally the doors would open and all the grown-ups would come out—

silent, red-eyed, holding handkerchiefs in front of their faces. "What went on in there?" we wondered. But no one asked, and no one told.

Brenda Robinson Wolchok: B'nai B'rith Jacob, the Orthodox synagogue of Savannah, was a three-story building with two cupolas on top. The men sat on the ground floor and the women on the second- and third-floor balconies that ringed the rim of the sanctuary. On Yom Kippur, the congregants brought ammonia and smelling salts along with them to keep from fainting from the combination of hunger and the heat. I remember being up in the balcony looking directly down to the men praying below, hearing the whir of the ceiling fans, and feeling overcome from the heat and the smell of ammonia.

Karl Bernstein: At the end of Yom Kippur, my cousin Bill and I had the job of picking up Grandma Libby at the synagogue. We spotted her easily up in the balcony where the women sat, a chubby little figure in a hat with a veil. Usually she was in the center of a small group of women, helping them find their place in the prayer book.

Brenda Robinson Wolchok: During a break in services, we'd walk on Broughton Street in downtown Savannah. Many of the stores were owned by Jewish people, and nearly all were shut with signs announcing, "Closed for the Jewish holidays."

Murray Polner: In Brownsville, *erev* Yom Kippur and Yom Kippur itself, every store was shut. There were no automobiles in the streets. The neighborhood was like a deserted town. The little shuls were ubiquitous, and Orthodoxy reigned supreme.

Is Crystal: On Succoth, the *shammes* came back to the house and this time he brought the *lulav* and the *estrog,* the branches and lemon that symbolize this harvest holiday. He would *bentsh* the *estrog* and *lulav,* take out the cider and recite the prayer, shake the *lulav,* and go on to the next house.
    It was Indian summer in Duluth, such a nice time of the year. I used

to watch our neighbors put up *succahs* in their backyards. We never had one of our own because we spent most of our time at the store.

Mel Loewenstein: Our small congregation in St. Louis had a *succah* built in the foyer of the synagogue. You walked through it in order to get to the sanctuary. At the end of the service, everybody got a big red apple.

Later in the fall, the four Reform congregations would join together for a Union Thanksgiving service. It was an opportunity for the Jews of the community to get together on Thanksgiving morning in a Jewish patriotic way, so to speak, and celebrate the freedoms and blessings of America.

Helen Fried Goldstein: One year when Succoth came late in the fall, Mom decided to combine it with Thanksgiving. After all, she reasoned, both are harvest holidays. We were more than thirty people, so one of my aunts suggested they invite Leibel, a landsman who did the cooking at some of the finer Catskill hotels. As expected, Leibel accepted on the condition he design the menu and prepare the dinner.

Like many chefs, Leibel was temperamental and stubborn, but tolerated because of his culinary gifts. Now he said, "Of course we'll have turkey and also Yorkshire pudding."

"Yorkshire pudding?" cried my mother and aunts. "The kids won't like it." But Leibel insisted.

The day of our dinner was mild Indian summer, perfect for outdoor dining. The afternoon sunlight streamed through the latticed top of our *succah,* and the hanging fruits and vegetables cast shadows on the long table that stretched out beyond the bamboo walls onto the backyard lawn.

Leibel presided over the kitchen wearing his chef's hat and a long white apron. He dished the turkey and a good-sized portion of Yorkshire pudding onto each plate, and my mother and aunts served.

Luckily, Leibel remained in the kitchen preparing dessert and did not notice that the Yorkshire pudding went untouched. After everyone finished their turkey, a paper bag was passed around, into which each portion of pudding was deposited. Then the plates were returned to the kitchen.

Leibel looked at the stack of puddingless plates. "What did I tell you," he said with evident satisfaction. "I knew the Yorkshire pudding was going to be a hit."

As soon as Succoth began, I started counting the days to Simchat Torah, the joyous holiday marking the Torah's "new year." It was such a tumultuous time in our synagogue. Even grown-ups who were usually sedate acted a little crazy, marching around the synagogue with Torahs, some getting a little tipsy. It was bedlam. I heard that Mark Twain once came into a synagogue on Simchat Torah, saw and heard all the commotion, and said, "These Jewish people must be crazy."

Even as a young child, I understood there were two kinds of sacred time: the happy festivals like Succoth and Simchat Torah and the serious, introspective holidays like the Days of Awe and fast days. Naturally, I loved the festivals. As soon as Simchat Torah was over, I began looking forward to Chanukah.

Karl Bernstein: Chanukah was a very modest holiday when I was a kid. We'd all gather at my great-aunt's house, where someone had sewn little cloth purses for all the children. We'd line up and go from one adult to another, and they would drop *Chanukah gelt* into the purses. Usually it was a nickel or dime. A quarter was a big deal.

Murray Polner: There was very little hoopla over Chanukah. Once my Uncle Willie gave me fifty cents, and my father bought me a paper suitcase.

Marnie Bernstein: Purim came around the time of St. Patrick's Day. Aside from the *hamantashen* my mother made—little pastries with *"muin,"* poppy-seed filling—it was most important because it heralded the next big holiday: Passover.

Shalom Goldman: I spent hours on the Lower East Side hanging out where they were selling all the stuff for Pesach. Once before Pesach, I got an after-school job corking bottles in the wine factory around the corner from Ratner's on Delancey Street.

I visited the matzoh factories. There were two kinds: the regular and the handmade or *shmura* matzoh. You'd walk into a *shmura* factory and be transplanted back 150 years into the Pale somewhere. There'd be all the screaming: "Yes!" "This!" "Now!" "No!" "Do it!" "Now!" "Quick!" The atmosphere was volatile, yet everything ran with incredible precision and finesse because the whole process, from the time they mix the flour with the water until they take the finished matzoh out of the oven, must be completed in exactly eighteen minutes. There are all these rabbinical rules about matzoh that are incredibly complex. They had it down to a science.

Marnie Bernstein: Somehow, somewhere in our little apartment, my mother managed to store a whole kitchenful of Passover items: dishes, flatware, pots and pans, even table linens. Little by little in the weeks before the holiday, these would be taken down from closets, off the top shelves of cupboards, out of boxes stored behind doors and under beds, washed and dried and set aside for the holiday. The grocery order would arrive: boxes of matzohs, packages of multicolored sugar-coated jellies, sacks of walnuts and pecans in their shells, tins of Barton's chocolate miniatures (kosher for Passover), bottles of Manischewitz Malaga wine. Cartons of food stood silently in the foyer, waiting like props of a play in the wings for opening night.

The morning of the seder, I'd walk into the kitchen and the old iron *chaynik* with the spiral handle, the one they brought along from Europe, would be on the stove in place of the modern teakettle that usually stood there. A new drainboard would be on the sink; a metal plaque would be covering the stove's surface. On the table the glasses filled with orange juice were not the ones we used all year. These were tall with a barrel-shaped rim, around which red camels followed one another. We were moving into special time, transported back to the desert of the Exodus. The show was about to begin.

Irv Saposnik: The seder was a kind of litmus test of the family status: who came, who didn't, how much Hebrew was used, how long it lasted. Every year I would look around the table and see my uncles, my cousins, my mother. It was a time of great warmth and tenderness.

I ran the gamut from being the youngest child who asked the Four Questions to, after years of yeshiva, virtually conducting the entire seder.

We never stopped to analyze the *Haggadah*; we took it on faith and raced through it.

Roz Starr: Our seders stopped either at the halfway point or after we spilled wine all over everything. We never finished. Once we left the wine outside the apartment for Elijah, and some guy came by and drank it all up. There was nothing for Elijah—or for us.

Gail Eiseman Bernstein: My grandfather sat on an armchair surrounded by colored cushions. Beside him was a big china pitcher and basin, which he used to wash his hands. He would intone the whole service from beginning to end without leaving one word out. We'd be dying. "Come on, Pop, let's go," everyone would cry. But the little man kept right on.

Elliot Colchamiro: Greek seders had a special twist. The meal began with hard-boiled eggs and lemon juice. Then we had pies made of spinach, beef, onions, and sage with a matzoh crust. Instead of matzoh ball soup, we had a chicken broth enriched with a lemon and egg mixture. Our *charoses,* a mixture of nuts and raisins, was less sweet than the Ashkenazi type. We dipped celery into vinegar for the bitter herb. And we ate a lot of rice.

Artie Allen: My grandmother was very emphatic about our reading the entire Haggadah. She did the cooking, and one of her Isle-of-Rhodes specialties was eggs that she boiled in coffee grinds and onions. The eggs would turn totally brown inside and out and have a sweet taste. My grandfather would eat the eggs, drink the ouzo, and get totally smashed.

Shalom Goldman: After four cups of wine, I was drunk of course. I remember going outside, looking up at the stars, reeling and laughing.

Caroline Katz Mount: Even though my parents had drifted away from the religious lifestyle of their European childhoods and were not truly Sabbath observers, Friday nights and Saturdays were set apart from the rest of the week. My father gave up his work clothes and dressed up in a suit, a white shirt, and a tie. My mother didn't write or smoke.

Friday mornings, my mother washed and waxed the linoleum floor in the kitchen and long hallway. At sunset she'd light the candles and set out the *challah*.

Karl Bernstein: Grandma Libby would put a dishtowel over her head, light two candles, cover her face with her hands, and cry. "Grandma," I would ask, "why are you crying?"

"I'm crying for the troubles of the world," she'd say in a heavy Yiddish accent. I used to think that as you got older, you started to speak that way.

Marc Angel: My grandmother lit oil lamps for Shabbat in the old Sephardic style. She'd fill a glass bowl with water and add a little layer of oil on top. Then she'd float a steel device in the liquid with places for wicks. We'd break small pieces of straw off a broom and wrap them in cardboard. These became the wicks. We'd put them in the holders, and my grandmother would light them.

Roz Starr: If my mother made it, you wouldn't eat it. My father was the cook. Thursday night, he'd prepare the Shabbat dinner: koshering the chicken, making his own horseradish and gefilte fish. Sometimes he'd make a soup out of a beef bone.

Shabbos was very warm. The candles were lit. We'd have the big dinner with all the accompaniments: the chopped liver with a nice pat of fat on it, the *grivenes* (chicken fat with fried onions), rye bread smeared with garlic, *kishka*. Afterwards it was time for music, the Yiddish songs. My brother played the piano. My father played the violin. Sometimes my mother played the piano. Her left hand was so loud that you had to cover your ears.

Jason Freed: The Fridays of my childhood held a powerful attraction. All week long I looked forward to coming home from school on Friday afternoon, getting in the car, and riding from Long Island to my grandparents' house in Brooklyn.

Grandpa would always be waiting for us out in the street, reserving a parking spot for my mother. Although he didn't own a car and hadn't driven one in maybe twenty-five years, he would be making all these motions like a traffic cop, directing my mother to park.

We'd get out of the car, and he'd gather us together with hugs and kisses. He'd take us up in the elevator, open the door to the apartment, and call out to my grandma in Yiddish, "Gussie, come quick! We have guests!"

He was keeping up a tradition, my mother told me. When he was a little boy, they'd send him to visit his grandparents at their inn way out in the Ukrainian countryside. He'd arrive in a horsedrawn wagon, not a car, but his grandfather would be waiting for him just the same. He'd take him down, bring him up to the house, and call out to his wife, "Toby, come quick! We have a guest!"

I wondered whether his Grandma waited in the kitchen for him like my Grandma did. We'd come into the apartment, and Grandma would light the candles, and then we'd sit around the kitchen table and have chicken soup and *challah* and little minute steaks, which I loved—that was before I became a vegetarian. After dinner we'd pull out the toys Grandma kept for us in a big stack behind the bedroom door and play or watch television on their black-and-white set.

When we left, Grandma and Grandpa would stand at the window, waving as we walked down the long court to the street. We'd lean back and yell out, "Bye Grandma, bye Grandpa" over and over until they were out of sight.

May Thaler Abrams: We did nothing on Shabbos except go to shul, read, and eat. Our *Shabbos goy,* the Italian kid from next door, would come in and turn on the stove for us.

My grandmother, Esther Sarah Lerner, was the matriarch. She ruled the roost. Most of the time her hair was covered with a scarf. But every Friday night, *erev* Shabbos, she took out her black wig and brushed it till it shone. Saturday morning, she'd put on her wig and a beautiful dress and go to shul carrying nothing. Even her handkerchief was tied around her wrist.

Shalom Goldman: On Shabbat, everything was run by clocks. My grandparents had a *blech* (Russian for kiln) and kept the pilot on the stove going with a tin of "cholent," a kind of vegetable casserole which lays heavy.

Caroline Katz Mount: When I was in sixth grade, my parents enrolled me in the first Hebrew school for girls in our neighborhood. The rabbi encouraged us to attend services on Saturday mornings. This act came to be the only thing I did all by myself. I'd get up early and walk the five or six blocks to the synagogue. I felt very spiritual. I believed in God; I took the prayers literally and would sit through the entire service, luxuriating in my solitary time.

Daniel Musher: From the late 1940s on, I can recall Shabbat mornings, walking uptown along Central Park West from Seventy-first Street to Eighty-sixth Street. Along the way, we would pass people walking downtown to the Spanish and Portuguese Synagogue, and we would nod to each other. It seemed all of the Upper West Side of Manhattan was closed down for Shabbat.

My grandfather, Mordecai Kaplan, was the senior rabbi at our synagogue. He was a very famous and distinguished theologian, an imposing-looking man who stood perfectly erect and had a beautiful sonorous voice.

As the senior rabbi, my grandfather sat on one side of the *bimah*; my uncle, who was the active rabbi, sat on the other side. My father's parents sat on the left side in the second row, and I sat beside them every single Sabbath of my growing-up years.

Addi Friedman: After Shabbat services, we'd come home, and my mother would read the *Chumash*. My father would go over it with her, and the two of them would discuss the Commentaries with my sister and me.

Every summer, when we traveled by car to places like New England, Halifax, Nova Scotia, and the southern states, we'd always try to find a synagogue so we could attend services on Shabbat. If we did, we would rent cabins within walking distance. If no synagogue was nearby, we would *daven* in our cabin and spend the rest of the day quietly.

Marc Angel: Every Shabbat after shul, we would have lunch and then walk to my grandparents' house on Fifteenth Avenue in Seattle. It was a re-creation of their homes in Turkey. The floors were covered with oriental rugs of vivid colors. The furniture was old-fashioned, sturdy, and comfortable.

There were always a lot of children and grandchildren and few toys. But because Grandmother Romey was so creative, we were never bored. She'd have us guess what she was hiding—but it had to be something green, like a book or a plant. Since we couldn't watch television on Shabbat, she invented "Shabbat Television": looking at pictures of France, Italy, and Greece through her Viewmaster. That gave me my first experience of the world. She would also tell us long stories about the old country, which seemed a place very far away but also very similar to our own.

When Shabbat was over, my grandmother would send us out to gather the rue, a special fragrant herb that Sephardic Jews love. It grew wild in our yards in Seattle. We would use that for *Havdalah*, the ceremony marking the end of Shabbat, when you're supposed to smell something with a beautiful aroma.

Marnie Bernstein: All I knew of the *Havdalah* ritual was my mother's European memory. She would tell us how my grandmother would gather all the children around the single twisted candle and have them smell the spices in the box. She would take a vegetable and break it in half, saying, "This is for Shabbos, and this is for the rest of the week." They would treasure the last waning minutes of the special sanctified time Shabbat was before they descended into the ordinary, everyday workweek.

When my mother described this scene, it was with a tenderness, a wistfulness that made me think she sometimes longed for the life of observance and piety she had left behind so many years ago.

Max Wechsler: My family was definitely not religious. While some lip service was paid to the ritual and trappings of being Jewish, my parents rarely set foot in the synagogue and never made a seder. At Passover we had our choice of matzoh or bread.

Nevertheless, for about half a dozen years, Saturdays were a special Jewish time in my life. That was when I would go with my mother to the tenement walk-up apartment on the Lower East Side to visit her mother.

As we arrived for lunch, we were greeted by the smells of Europe—

usually chicken soup and chopped liver, and at times chopped eggplant. After lunch I'd get busy with my job.

The candlesticks that were smudged with wax droppings from the Shabbos candles had to be cleaned up and polished. And while my mother and grandmother spoke in one room, I'd sit down with the candlesticks and a can of Noxon, a couple of rags, and a little spoon. I'd use the spoon handle to scrape off all the excess wax, making sure to get into all the corners. I'd take a rag and shine up the brass with the Noxon. Then I'd take another rag and rub and rub till the golden glow of those old Romanian candlesticks almost lit up the room.

I wasn't allowed to go to my grandmother's funeral. I guess they felt children should be protected from such events. But I did go back to her little apartment one last time. Now, instead of onions and chicken soup, the apartment smelled of camphor balls and alcohol. It had always been such a warm place, but now it was cold. Cartons and boxes were stacked on the floor and tables. The closets were empty of clothing; only the hangers hung lopsided. The kitchen shelves, where the flowery dishes had once been neatly stacked, now just showed off a lining of dingy oilcloth.

My mother told me we were there to put things in order and give the place a once-over. While she got busy, I noticed the candlesticks standing on a shelf near the dumbwaiter. They looked a lot different. I hadn't been to the apartment for quite a while, hadn't had a chance to do my cleaning work with my little spoon or my special polishing job that always brought out the golden glow I loved to see.

"Ma, can I take care of the candlesticks again?" I asked. "They don't look too good."

"Just leave them alone."

"Why?"

"Because I told you. Just leave them alone."

I never again had the experience of polishing my grandmother's candlesticks. But the memories of those Saturday afternoons in that tiny apartment near Delancey Street are my strongest growing-up memories of feeling Jewish. Whenever I carefully rubbed and held those candlesticks, I was in a kind of sacred time.

11

COMING OF AGE

*"Let your father and your mother be glad,
and let her who bore you rejoice."*

—Proverbs XXIII:25

Shalom Goldman: Why do American Jews make big bar mitzvahs? To celebrate the end of the religious life of the child. But in orthodoxy it's the beginning of the religious life. It's like the first day of school.

In America of the 1950s, there were no glitzy bar mitzvahs in orthodoxy. It was simply what had been in Europe. There were no bat mitzvahs. Rabbi Mordecai Kaplan made that up. He had daughters.

Is Crystal: The congregation of Tifereth Israel in Duluth originally met in a little house, but in 1922 they built a proper synagogue. My bar mitzvah was the next year, one of the first at the Fifth Street Shul, as it was known.

It was hardly like the ones today, strictly religiously oriented. Saturday morning I read my portion, davened. After, there was a little *Kiddush* with herring, wine, and whiskey supplied by my dad. Sunday my mother had twenty friends and relatives to the house for a chicken dinner. I stood up on a chair and gave a little talk in Yiddish. I wasn't too fluent in English then. But that was just as well. The people there wouldn't have understood the English anyway. Then I went outside and played with the kids and let the adults do whatever they wanted.

Sol Breibart: I was bar mitzvahed in the little shul in Charleston in 1927. My family had some friends over to the house and served wine and that was that.

Arthur Cantor: The seders in my family were long, too long. My father was a stickler for doing the whole thing. My bar mitzvah was even longer than the seder. I could write a book about it, a long book. I was trained in Hebrew school and also by a bar mitzvah consultant with bad breath. They all had bad breath.

I chanted the *Haftorah* and made three speeches: one in Hebrew, one in English, and one in Yiddish. Very few kids could memorize three speeches at that time. I enjoyed it. Getting through all the prayers was like solving a puzzle.

The party was in the ballroom of the synagogue. My father took the gift money. I was delighted that he did. He had no money. Times were very tough. This was during the Depression when you could get a small Hershey

◀ (*top*) Bar mitzvah boy at prayer, c. 1980. (*bottom left*) Bar mitzvah boy at celebration, 1985. (*bottom right*) Bouquets after confirmation ceremony, 1955.

bar for a penny, a monster-sized bar for a nickel. That I helped him pay for this ceremony which meant so much to him was great. I would have hocked the fountain pens I got to help him. I got too many of them as it was, although the fact that they all disappeared was upsetting. I lost them through the years in many fell swoops.

Norman Tipograph: People were kind of broke when I was bar mitzvahed in 1937. Even so, I got quite a few fountain pens.

Since my mother had no money to make an expensive affair, she took over an empty apartment on the fifth floor of our building in the Bronx. There were plenty of empty apartments in those days. She took an old door, put it across two wooden horses, covered it with a cloth, and that became our banquet table. She cooked a big dinner and invited my aunts and uncles.

Karl Bernstein: While we were at shul the morning of my bar mitzvah, the caterers came and took all the furniture out of our house. I never figured out where they put everything. They brought in big tables decorated with beautiful ice sculptures. The whole house had been done over. As my grandma Yetta used to say, the painter came all the way from Williamsburg. He painted the walls forest green, which was the hot color in those days.

Murray Polner: In honor of my grandfather, I was bar mitzvahed in the shul he attended on Hopkinson Avenue in Brownsville instead of my father's shul on Bristol Street. All the people I loved were there.

Into the Haftorah, my voice broke. I began it as a thirteen-year-old soprano, and halfway through I turned into Andy Devine. Afterwards my grandfather came up and kissed me and said it was the best bar mitzvah *Haftorah* he'd ever heard. Of course it wasn't true.

Cal Abrams: My voice hadn't changed at the time of my bar mitzvah; I sang soprano. But I did well, having been prepared by Rabbi Albert, a little hunchbacked man with a long gray beard and hair creeping out the sides of his black hat. We paid him twenty-five cents a week. It was kind of a crash course. He taught me the alphabet in one day; from that point on, he gave me a half a sentence and then a sentence a day. He timed me with a clock. The idea was to see how fast I could read without making mistakes.

Bless the man, at first he didn't want to take me on. I was twelve and a half years old when I started, and he said it was impossible to teach anyone in that short a period of time. We weren't religious in my family. We didn't realize it takes more than six months to prepare for a bar mitzvah.

The rabbi gave me a beautiful ivory-covered Bible as a gift. He showed me how to put on *tefillin*. I did it for a couple of weeks, but then it became too much of a chore. I'd rather go out and play ball with my friends.

Alan Lelchuk: My father personally prepared me for my bar mitzvah. It was the only really bad experience I had being Jewish. My father had a good voice; I didn't, and he punished me for it. He was a rough teacher, would grab me and call me a *narr* (fool). And add his favorite curse: "You'll grow up to be a goy and a truckdriver."

Leon Toubin: My friends would be out in the fields playing ball, and I would be stuck in this hot little apartment preparing for my bar mitzvah.

There weren't enough Jewish families in Brenham, Texas, for us to have a regular Hebrew school, so my father got this rabbi, installed him in a little apartment above a store downtown, and supported him. He looked like someone out of *Fiddler on the Roof* in his white knickers and the big black hat trimmed with fur that he put on whenever he davened. It was so hot, I don't know how he could stand it.

Alex Rosin: I was prepared for my bar mitzvah by an elderly gentleman in Sarasota named Elihu Edelson. He taught me the alphabet and how to read and gave me some old black records to learn the prayers from. I'd leave public school—where I was one of four Jews—get on my bicycle, and pedal five miles for Hebrew instruction. Then I'd pedal another five miles back home. I'd do my homework, go to sleep, and next morning go to school again. Sometimes I would wonder, what am I doing this for? But it was ingrained in me that this is what you do to be a Jew.

My bar mitzvah was a strange event. Sarasota had no rabbi so we rented one from Tampa. I was four feet nine, ninety-two pounds. They had to stand me on two concrete blocks so I could see the fifty or so people in the congregation. Outside the synagogue, a crowd of nuns were peering in through the windows, listening in on the services. This was my mother's connection. She had been raised in Savannah, the daughter of tailors whose biggest customers were priests. In exchange for making the habits, all the kids in their family got a free Catholic education. My mother became close to the nuns and kept up with them even in Sarasota.

By the time my younger brothers were getting ready for their bar mitzvahs, Mr. Edelson had died. There was no rabbi or teacher around, so once again my mother turned to the nuns. They taught Michael and Simon their Hebrew.

For Simon's bar mitzvah, my mother hired this guy who used to travel around the countryside in a trailer performing bar mitzvahs. He claimed to be a rabbi. Later we heard he was really a Presbyterian minister.

Karl Bernstein: The reason my parents gave for not sending me to Hebrew school was that I was involved in scouting and piano lessons and had enough to do. But also, I think my father was left with a bad taste from his own experiences. They used to call him the rabbi killer. Whoever taught him died.

I was schooled by Mr. Cantor, who came to the house. He was very Orthodox and had bad breath. But I learned more Hebrew in two years than all my friends who went to Talmud Torah for five years.

Neil Postman: My parents were not religious in an organized sense, although they went to shul on the High Holidays. But they sent me to Hebrew school from the age of five because the teacher, who lived in our building, was very poor. It was a good deed, a form of *tzedaka*.

When I was bar mitzvahed on March 11, 1944, you didn't have to read your portion on a Saturday; you could read it on a Thursday. For a lot of boys that was it, followed by a *Kiddush:* herring, wine, honey and sponge cake. But my bar mitzvah was on a Saturday and was followed by a party at a place on the Lower East Side called the French Romanian Restaurant. They served tenderloin steak and julienne potatoes—kosher style.

My mother was something of a writer. She liked to write speeches that she delivered at the various organizations she belonged to. For my bar mitzvah, she wrote three speeches for me to deliver—memorized.

I gave the first one Saturday morning at the Young Israel of Flatbush in Brooklyn. It was an Orthodox shul of course. Everything was Orthodox in those days. The second one was at the French Romanian Restaurant. This was the big speech. I stood behind a table that had two photographs, one of each of my brothers who were away in the army at that time. Although I didn't know it then, my brother Jack was on the Queen Mary on Fifty-seventh Street at that very moment, getting ready to ship out to England.

I had to begin the speech, "Mom, Dad, sister Ruth," and then I had to look at Jack's picture and say, "brother Jack," and at Sol's picture, "brother Sol. . . ." My mother had said, "If you don't look at each of the pictures, the whole effect will be ruined."

Both speeches went off splendidly. The third was scheduled for the Monday after my bar mitzvah at the women's auxiliary of the Knights of Pythias, one of my mother's organizations. But when I got up to deliver my speech, I looked out at the crowd of women and blanked out. I couldn't remember a word. There I was standing before twenty Jewish ladies—you know how they look—and I knew I had to say something.

During the previous year's baseball season, I had learned the word *extemporaneous* from Red Barber. I decided this was the occasion to use it. "I had prepared a speech to give this morning," I said, "but I think it would be better if I just spoke extemporaneously. I just want to say that I appreciate the gift that you gave me and the fact that you all came here in my honor." (That wasn't really true. It was a regularly scheduled meeting.) I sat down. They were all delighted.

But my mother was furious. Driving home she kept saying, "Extemporaneous, extemporaneous. I'll give you an extemporaneous."

My Aunt Alice from Somerville, New Jersey, also had something to say to me after my bar mitzvah because of an item that appeared in *The Postbox*. This was a family newspaper I composed during the war years and mailed out to all the relatives at home and to the boys—there were forty of them—in the army and navy. It was mostly family gossip, although I did include an item designed to give culture to the family. Someone had given me a book of a hundred novels condensed into one page for each book. In each issue of *The Postbox,* I condensed one of the condensed novels.

At my bar mitzvah, there had been a bottle of Scotch and rye on each table, a typical setup for those days. Jews are not such big drinkers, and the guests took only one or two drinks from each bottle. But at the end of my bar mitzvah, I noticed that Aunt Alice collected four nearly full bottles, put them in a big bag, and took them home.

The next issue of *The Postbox* included the following item: "What person from Somerville was seen at Neil Postman's bar mitzvah stealing four bottles of Scotch?" Coming on the heels of the "extemporaneous" issue, I had a lot to answer to in the weeks following my bar mitzvah.

Norman Tipograph: I was a very shy kid and terrified of the idea of having to make a speech, but my Uncle Bernie wrote one for me. He was a buyer of boys' clothing, a suave and outgoing kind of guy and did a good job with it. I was so nervous, I would have forgotten the whole thing if I hadn't had it in front of me.

Robert Leiter: My maternal grandfather was a socialist, communist-oriented. He thought the religious rituals were ridiculous. The morning of my bar mitzvah, I was up on the *bimah* when he and my grandmother entered the synagogue. I saw one of the ushers chasing my grandfather around trying to get him to put on a yarmulke. He refused to wear one. I was so embarrassed, but that's the way he was. My father was furious.

Herb Kalisman: When my brother and I each turned twelve, my father asked if we wished to study with a rabbi and be bar mitzvahed. We did not. My mother did not like the idea, but she felt the children should have the freedom to choose.

My father said to me, "You need some Jewish background. I may be an atheist, but I'm a Jewish atheist." He sent me to a Sholem Aleichem school where I studied Santayana, the Jewish philosophers, and ancient history—all in Yiddish.

The Sholem Aleichem and also the Workmen's Circle schools taught Yiddish, general world history, and Jewish history with a socialist slant. They were a uniquely Jewish-American phenomenon; there was nothing quite like them in Europe.

Alan Lelchuk: Instead of sending me to the Talmud Torah schools with all my friends, my father found a Sholem Aleichem school on Topscott Street in East New York, Brooklyn, for me. It was created from an offshoot of the Socialist Bundt. I went there every day after school from the time I was seven until my bar mitzvah. In terms of my Jewishness, the Sholem Aleichem school was the most important influence upon me.

In each grade there were about ten or twelve kids, boys and girls. We wore no yarmulkes. It was liberal and progressive, secular rather than religious, more Yiddish than Hebrew. We read the Bible as literature and as the history of the Jewish people.

We had a great Yiddish *lehrer* or teacher, a Polish immigrant named Israel Goichberg. My father was friendly with Goichberg. He respected him, and there were few people my father respected. Goichberg taught high school uptown where he lived. After school, he traveled an hour down to Brooklyn to teach and transmit Yiddish culture to kids. Only in later years did I learn that he was a Yiddish poet. He never once told us.

A college friend of his became president of the University of Oklahoma and offered him a position. "Come out and teach Jewish studies," the friend had said.

Goichberg was crazy about his old buddy, but he just couldn't accept because his mission was teaching Yiddish culture to children.

It was such a magical time for a boy to grow up under the guidance of this man. He was of a different quality and different nature from the Talmud Torah teachers that my friends had. As a boy in that school, I read all the Jewish writers in Yiddish. We read this *Kinderjournal* that had stories for children by Sholem Aleichem, the Singer brothers, Peretz, and Mendele. We gave oral reports on the stories in Yiddish.

Goichberg put on plays in Yiddish in a public auditorium, and when I was about ten, I started acting in them. Increasingly, I took bigger parts. I'd spend a month or so with the help of my father rehearsing a part. I had become immersed in a Yiddish life without it being a religious life.

My father and I were mocked because I attended this "Commie school."

But it was a literary, social *Yiddishkeit* that you got sitting in Goichberg's class. He never was interested in transmitting any politics to us. It was all about Jewishness. Yet he imparted a very strong sense that Jewishness meant social justice and progressive thinking. He did this in a whole variety of ways but mainly through the stories that we read—those of Sholem Aleichem, say. Through Yiddish stories, Goichberg taught us about right and wrong and how Jews should behave.

He was a vigorous man in his late forties, close to six feet tall, firmly built, and with wonderful white hair. And he could fly into a red-faced rage when you were being a pest, as I could be. Our school was in the basement of a two-family house, and periodically we would be taunted by a group of Italian kids who came to the windows, threw rocks, made fun. It was mainly a nuisance thing. Goichberg would run out into the street and chase them, and I would follow him.

I was a kid who liked mischief. But he knew how to handle me. Sometimes he had to sit down and talk with me to get me to fulfill myself as a serious student. Sometimes he would grab hold of me and shake me hard. But I took it from him because I knew we had a trust and that I deserved it. He was the best motivator I ever had.

Helen Fried Goldstein: When I was growing up, the general belief was that girls don't have to learn Hebrew and how to *daven*. Some people had their daughters tutored privately, but we could not afford that.

My brother started Hebrew school in the only synagogue in Port Chester, New York. I was dying to go. I'd trail along with him and try to sneak in, but the Orthodox rabbi would always get ahold of me and say, "Out you go." I was tenacious; I tried it over and over again, but I was always kicked out.

One day my father came home from work—he was a junk peddler, today he'd be called an antique dealer—and my mother said, "Yussel, you've got to sell Nellie (the horse), we've got to sell the house, and we have to move to Brooklyn. The boys in Port Chester are dating the richer girls from Mamaroneck and New Rochelle. Our girls will never find fellas here."

I think she had a hidden agenda; her family lived in Brooklyn. But it was a wonderful move for me, not only because of the Jewish boys I met, but because I got to teach Sunday school in my grandfather's synagogue. I didn't know Hebrew, but I did know Bible stories well enough to teach them.

My mother's father, Isaac Boehm, was a very important figure in the synagogue and in the Conservative movement. His house was a kind of salon. Students from the Jewish Theological Seminary boarded with him, professors were always visiting. I'd overhear their conversations, never knowing how important these people were. Living in that environment, my intellectual interest in Judaism developed. Grandpa was observant but flexible in his attitude to religion. He took note of my interest and encouraged it by giving me books to read. Nevertheless, because I was a girl I never had that formal Jewish education. I have regretted it all my life.

Gail Eiseman Bernstein: None of the girls I knew were bat mitzvahed. I never even heard the term until the early 1960s.

Dinah Crystal Kossoff: Thirty-one years after Dad's bar mitzvah, I was one of the first girls to be bat mitzvahed in Tifereth Israel in Duluth. My grandparents were founders of the shul—my grandmother had actually sold her jewelry to have the synagogue built—so it was very meaningful to me.

At a Friday night service, with my parents and both sets of grandparents present, I read the *Haftorah*, delivered a sermon, and led the congregation in "Ein Keiloheinu" and "Yigdal."

Marc Angel: My bar mitzvah straddled both the old and new worlds of Seattle's Sephardic community. In the mid-1950s, the old neighborhood, the place of my childhood, started to decline. Ezra Bessaroth, the congregation from the Isle of Rhodes, saw the future. They bought property in Seward Park, where many of the Jews were moving, and built a new synagogue. Traditionalists continued to hold the fort, my mother being one of them. She was absolutely in love with our house. Her parents and all her sisters lived nearby. But there was more noise, more crime. Ultimately she gave in.

We moved to Seward Park when I was fourteen. The Saturday of my bar mitzvah, we attended the Turkish synagogue in the old neighborhood where we still lived. The next day, I put on *tefillin* as the first bar mitzvah in the new Seward Park synagogue. The party was the Saturday night in between at the Norway Center, the only place in Seattle that had kosher catering at that time. There was Turkish dancing, but there was American dancing as well. We moved to the Seward Park neighborhood one block away from Ezra Bessaroth in the fall of 1959.

Elliot Colchamiro: Aside from the standard Jewish-American food at my bar mitzvah, the affair was like something out of Greece. People spoke in Greek, the music was all Greek and so was the dancing. Everyone stood in a line, the leader twirled a handkerchief, and the rest followed along.

The time I liked best was the in-between time—after the services in the morning and before the party at night—when everybody crowded into our house, and my father took home movies.

Abraham Peck: Only a couple of my mother's nephews had survived the war, and they came up with their families from New York City to our home in Waterbury for my bar mitzvah. There were also some friends and a few Holocaust survivors who were part of the community. My bar mitzvah was distinctive for its lack of family.

The party took place in the house we had moved into the year before. My mother made everything except for the baked goods. As a young man in Poland, my father had owned his own bakery; he was a master baker and cake decorator. Like many survivors, he had developed a spot on his lung and could no longer work in an environment with a lot of flour. But he could still do the baking at home for my bar mitzvah, and he created all kinds of wonderful European pastries.

No one talked about the Holocaust. The rabbi's sermon did not allude to the subject. Nevertheless it was a very muted bar mitzvah compared to those of the time. There was no theme of Yankee Stadium or skiing.

Jeff Solomon: My parents, who had gotten out of Germany in the 1930s and worked very hard to establish themselves in this country, indulged themselves in a Cecil B. DeMille spectacular. Big time. This was my mother's opportunity, and she did a bar mitzvah *extraordinaire.* Sunday afternoon,

1958. One hundred and twenty people. The Sherry Netherlands Hotel in Manhattan. Hot and cold running hors d'oeuvres. My parents were in the food business and saw to it that the caterer did it right.

Six years later, my brother's bar mitzvah was Saturday night and formal. We hadn't made it to the tuxedo point in time for mine.

Robert Leiter: My bar mitzvah party was a Jewish-American extravaganza at the Barclay Hotel on Rittenhouse Square, Philadelphia, an old Waspy area filled with beautiful town houses. No *Yiddishkeit*. My father would not have allowed it.

Before the dinner, we marched into the ballroom as the bandleader made the introductions. "Here comes Dr. and Mrs. Leiter, the parents of the bar mitzvah boy." Then the siblings. And finally, "Here he is, the bar mitzvah boy!" Everybody stood up and applauded. A grand production.

It wasn't even a matter of my being on display; I was inconsequential to the whole thing. My bar mitzvah was not for me and my friends. It was for my father and his friends. Aside from one table of older *Yiddishkeit* people who didn't have any money, it was an elaborate party for a crowd of elegant, well-dressed Jewish-Americans who had made it.

Once my bar mitzvah was over, I was not encouraged to continue my Jewish education. It had nothing to do with education. It was a ticket that enabled my father to stage a massive party that would prove to his peers that he had arrived.

Phyllis Taylor: With my parents' approval, my brother stopped religious school the day after his bar mitzvah. But I decided to continue and went on for confirmation and postconfirmation—twelve years in all. I learned Hebrew, history, and culture, but I have absolutely no recollection of our ever talking about God.

Robert Leiter: It was my father who insisted that my brothers and I be bar mitzvahed. My mother would rather have had us attend the Ethical Culture school. When it came to my sister being bat mitzvahed, she drew the line.

Frank Rich: My bar mitzvah was not lavish. My mother was totally against all that. She was deeply Jewish but did not belong to a synagogue because of the social stuff that was attached: the country club, the expensive seats for the holidays, and the like.

I was bar mitzvahed at a Reform temple in Washington, D.C. The party was all my junior high school friends dancing. We decided it would not be something that turned into a social occasion for the neighborhood or my family.

Jim Sleeper: The bar mitzvahs were all the same. Mine was in that brand-new synagogue, the standard cookie-cutter thing. You hired a band; Gluck-stern Caterers would come and hand out the prime ribs and the chicken; all your friends would come and bring gifts.

You learned the *Haftorahs* from teachers who did not speak English well. We didn't like them; they didn't like us. It was all gobbledygook, part of what I thought being Jewish was—stuff you had to memorize. I didn't want to have a bar mitzvah.

Shalom Goldman: My parents couldn't agree on anything, so I ended up having two bar mitzvahs and resented each one. But the nice thing about the one my father did in Hartford was that there was no glitz or pretension at all. I read from the Torah, the guys came around and drank some schnapps, and that was it. My Jackson Heights bar mitzvah was only slightly bigger. I did the thing in shul on Saturday, and Sunday morning we had lox and bagels.

Eric Portnoy: I hated the guy who taught me Hebrew at our little Reform synagogue in Barrington, Rhode Island. Granted I wasn't the best student and wasn't studying, but he was just mean and nasty. He ended up being discharged.

They replaced him with Rabbi Shankerman. He was the rabbi from Hawaii who had converted Sammy Davis, Jr. and he was a little like Sammy, with the beard, the rings on all the fingers, the silky shirts with two or three buttons unbuttoned. A real 1970s, swinging kind of guy.

Once he had to get some repairs done on his car. He took us along when he went to drop it off, and we wound up practicing our *Haftorahs* at the Dunkin' Donuts counter. We'd practice anywhere—on the little island in the middle of a highway, out in his backyard beside the above-ground swimming pool. He was cool.

About sixty people came to my bar mitzvah. My parents had just gotten divorced. My dad was up there being uncomfortable. I got up there and did my thing. It was fun being the center of attention. Rabbi Shankerman was very supportive; I was the first of his students to get bar mitzvahed, and it was very important to him. I had never put a lot of thought into this special Jewish thing. But because of Rabbi Shankerman, a lot of the ethics and history came through to me.

Robert Yaffe: I was a troublemaker in Hebrew school at Beth El, Omaha's Conservative synagogue. I just could not get into it. But when I began preparing for my bar mitzvah, Rabbi Alex Katz—who trained me—turned me around. What did it was the singing. I had one of the better voices and took the preparation very seriously because I wanted to perform. The melodies of the synagogue had a big effect on me. I can still sing them.

Julie Sussman: I was doing my bat mitzvah because everyone else was, and also because I wanted to get the presents. I did not think of it in any deep, symbolic way. I enjoyed the scholarly part but didn't really internalize it.

What I did get into was the singing. I loved the melodies of the prayers and the particular way you had to chant the *Haftorah*. There were all these symbols, little codes on top of the Hebrew letters, that stood for the inflection you're supposed to use.

At our Far Rockaway synagogue, we went to Talmud Torah school in the big old house that had been the sanctuary before the new one was built. But to prepare our *Haftorahs*, we had private lessons with the cantor at his home. He seemed to me to be an old man, and he lived in a poorer section of the neighborhood in a kind of tumbledown house. But he was very gentle and kind, especially to me because he liked the fact that I had a good voice and was interested in singing.

My bat mitzvah was at a late Friday-night service, the day after

Thanksgiving 1977. Outside was dark and rainy, but the sanctuary was rosy and glowing as if it were lit with candles. The altar was decorated with baskets of gigantic pink and yellow chrysanthemums, and I was dressed in this Victorian-looking ivory-colored outfit with lace trim at the collar and cuffs and tiny pearl buttons down the front. Everyone was there in the sanctuary except for my grandfather, who had died about a year before— we still felt his absence terribly. And everyone turned to look as I walked down the aisle in between the cantor and the rabbi, whom I also liked a lot, while the cantor sang, "How goodly are your tents O Jacob, your sanctuaries, O Israel."

Avrohom Hecht: My father prepared my twin brother and me just as he had prepared hundreds and hundreds before us. I had known the *berachahs* since I was five years old, having sat in while my father taught them to boys in Burlington, Vermont, where we used to live.

The morning of our bar mitzvah, he was up on the *bimah* with us in his shul in Richmond Hill, Queens. We picked a double portion: I did the first, and my brother the second. We split the *Haftorah* in half.

To me, the bar mitzvah was the letter and the spirit—not a showy event, but a sacred time. I don't know if my brother and I had the feeling then that we would become rabbis like our father. I did feel that I had reached a milestone: I could be part of a *minyan,* I could lead services and put on *tefillin.* I was an active player in the Jewish community.

Our reception was not your typical affair. We did it all ourselves. The night before we set up the tables. We served the bagels, salads, whatever to a crowd of several hundred people. It was held at the Rabbinical Seminary of America in Forest Hills, Queens, where my father had been ordained years before. My brother and I each delivered a speech in Yiddish.

Artie Allen: My 1977 bar mitzvah was typical for Montgomery, Alabama. There were no caterers. All the women got together and cooked. Even the *meshgiach*—the person who made sure everything was kosher—was a volunteer. You'd call her up and set up the time. She'd come over and watch to see all the ladies were doing what they were supposed to do. To make things look nice, they draped the tables with these long green skirts.

David Landau: Most of the bar and bat mitzvahs I went to in the affluent Long Island suburb where I grew up were competitions among the parents. Each one tried to outdo the other in staging a bigger and more elaborate extravaganza.

The biggest extravaganza I witnessed was in 1985, the same year I was bar mitzvahed. The incredibly oversized invitations did not come in the mail; they were hand-delivered to each person's home by a uniformed chauffeur who drove up in a Rolls Royce.

The affair had all the usual gimmicks and more. Airplane lights flooded the nighttime sky, and strobe lights flooded the dance floor. Showstopper Dancers came around and pulled you up to dance with them. When the twelve-piece band took a break, a deejay took over who let you sing over a record. There was a Benihana chef with a big hat and lightning-fast hands, a sushi bar, and a pasta bar—all kosher, of course.

The affair went on till three or four in the morning. Then they served brunch—bagels, lox, herring, cakes, tea and coffee and cocoa—and a copy of the Sunday *New York Times* to take home.

But what I remember most about this bar mitzvah was the *motzi*, the blessing said over the *challah*. This takes place after the smorgasbord, when everyone has been seated for the dinner. Usually there is a drum roll and the bandleader calls up the kid's grandfather to perform this honor. This time, I took a look and there was this big black guy coming out with a yarmulke stuck on top of his Afro. This can't be the grandfather, I thought.

Then the bandleader announced, "Mookie Wilson will make the *motzi*"—and sure enough, the center fielder for the New York Mets picked up the knife and cut the *challah*. After, Mookie took Polaroid pictures with each kid and personally autographed each photo. Mine is still sitting on my dresser.

12

L'DOR VA'DOR—
FROM GENERATION TO GENERATION

"And these are the generations of Isaac . . ."

—*Genesis XXV:19*

Frank Rich: The stories I heard about my father's side of the family were stories of how long we had been in America. My father's German-Jewish ancestors came over before the Civil War and settled in Washington, D.C. A relative of mine fought in the Union Army. Another was in Ford's Theater the night Lincoln was shot.

My mother's story is more conventional. Her Russian-Jewish ancestors came over toward the end of the nineteenth century and settled on the Lower East Side. In 1933 her family moved from New York to Washington, where my parents met.

Moe Skoler: Our favorite family story goes back to the early part of this century, when my mother's father and his brother owned a bathhouse. Their biggest expense was soap. It would sink to the bottom of the pool, and they'd have to scoop it out with a fishing net.

As he had been a chemist in Europe, my grandfather began fooling around in his basement until he came up with a formula for making a soap that could float. Somehow Procter and Gamble heard about this guy in Dorchester, Massachusetts, and sent a railroad car to Boston to pick him up and bring him to New York City. He sold his process to them for twenty-five thousand dollars, ten thousand of which he donated to build the Beth El Synagogue in Dorchester—which is now a black gospel house—and fifteen thousand of which he used to buy houses for himself and his brothers. If only he had collected royalties, we would have been among the wealthiest families in the United States. Instead we have to settle for the story that my grandfather invented a product named Ivory Soap.

Neil Postman: We were interested in roots and origins. "Did you know your grandfather?" we asked our parents. "What did he do for a living?" "Did the family experience any pogroms?" But we didn't get anything near an accurate account. They would say, "We're in America now. What happened then, happened then. There's no sense going over it."

They didn't even want to talk much about their turn-of-the-century childhood on the Lower East Side, when survival was a preoccupation. In this country you learn English, you go into business, you make sure your children get an education, you become American. But things come out.

◀ (*top and middle*) European grandparents with their American descendants. (*left*) two Jewish literary lights: Sholem Aleichem and his granddaughter, Bel Kaufman. (*bottom right*) Nearly half a century after emigration, a couple enjoy a bit of old world bucolic pleasure, 1949.

Not long ago, I mentioned someone named Harriet to my Aunt Molly. And she said, "You know, that's my name."

I said, "What do you mean, that's your name? Your name isn't Harriet. It's Molly."

She said, "No, Molly's not my name."

She told me that her oldest sister, my Aunt Alice, was six years older than the next one, my mother. Since their parents did not speak English in the early years, it was Alice's job to register the girls in school.

Alice didn't like their names, so she made up new ones. She registered my mother under the name Berdie. How many Berdies do you know? Then she registered a Daisy, a Rika (if you asked me how to spell it I wouldn't know how), a Molly, and a Rose.

I asked Molly, "What's everyone's real name?"

So she started telling me. "Your mother's name is Rifka, so Alice called her Berdie. And my name is Harriet, so she called me Molly." And so on.

Bel Kaufman: It was the name of my grandfather, Sholem Aleichem, that brought us to America. We had been caught in the Russian Revolution. I remember standing in line for the bread made of the green shells of peas, stepping over dead bodies frozen into grotesque postures. My father was a doctor and therefore a bourgeois; many of his colleagues were shot.

But even in an anti-Semitic country, amidst the chaos of all the different governments, Sholem Aleichem was loved and admired. And so, on the ruse that Sholem Aleichem's daughter and her family were going to visit her widowed mother in America, we were able to leave Russia for Riga in a private train. From there we took a Cunard White Star Line ship. It was the ship on which Stanislavsky came to America for the first time. We arrived in 1924 when I was twelve years old, and moved into my grandmother's apartment on Southern Boulevard in the Bronx.

Until I went to a Sholem Aleichem school in the Bronx where Yiddish was taught, I had read my grandfather's works only in Russian. He had begun writing in Hebrew, then in Russian, and only afterwards in Yiddish, which is when he took the name Sholem Aleichem.

I must have been thirteen when I saw my first Sholem Aleichem play, *Shver Zu Zein ah Yid*—"It's Hard to be a Jew"—in the Yiddish theater. It was an occasion; people were all dressed up. I was introduced: "I want you to meet Sholem Aleichem's granddaughter." That was both a pride and a problem. Who was I? A frightened child in a strange country. I was so alien looking, tall and famine-skinny, with long corkscrew curls and a velvet dress with a little collar. I was so envious of the American girls with their bobbed hair, their saddle shoes with little bells on the laces, their skirts and sweaters. I just didn't belong. I began to appreciate, however, how my grandfather belonged to the great Jewish family of the world.

The last time I saw him, I was about three years old. It was the summer of 1914, and we were at a resort in Germany. My cousin Tamara and I were playing in the sand with our little shovels.

All of a sudden we became persona non grata. We couldn't use our rubles. There was chaos. The whole family was at the railroad station. We returned to Odessa. My grandparents came to New York. Sholem Aleichem died two years later, at the age of fifty-seven, in a shabby little apartment on Kelly Street in the Bronx. He once wrote that the angel of death never asks if the shroud is ready.

I remember he was a bit of a dandy: the velvet vest, the longish blond hair and goatee, the twinkle in his eye. I remember his playfulness, his delight in pranks of all types. With children, he was like a child himself.

His humor was thumbing the nose in the face of disaster, thumbing the nose at adversity. Once when we were in a zoological garden, he stopped before a monkey on a tree. He took a piece of paper, rolled it into a cone, filled it with water from a nearby fountain, and offered it to the monkey. The monkey refused. My grandfather said, "That's a spoiled monkey," and drank himself very thirstily. Later, I learned he was already suffering from diabetes. But even of that, he made a joke: "I'll never die of hunger. I'll die of thirst."

My Uncle Norman reminded me of my grandfather. When he returned from Mexico with a stomach problem, he said, "They don't give you food in Mexico; they lend it to you."

Once we were waiting at a red light to cross the street. The light changed to "Walk," and my uncle hesitated. A woman behind tapped him on the shoulder and said: "It says *walk*." Uncle Norman turned with a courtly bow. "Madam, it's a suggestion, not a command."

In his will, my grandfather stipulated: Take care of grandmother. Preserve your *Yiddishkeit*. I don't want any monuments. If people read my books, that will be my best monument. Read one of my merriest stories aloud in whatever language is most convenient.

The anniversary of his death is May 13. He was superstitious. He always numbered page 13 as page 12a. Since he died, every "May 12a" has been observed according to his will.

The first year I was here, my grandmother was nervous. Will there be enough cookies? Will there be enough chairs? All the family came and many friends; we were as many as thirty people.

In later years, people like Herman Wouk have read my grandfather's will with great feeling. That first year, the well-known Yiddish poet Nochum Yud raced through it. But he slowed down when he came to the line, "Take good care of your mother. Sweeten her bitter life." And I saw the tears in my grandmother's eyes.

Barbara Kreiger: When my great-grandmother died, my great-grandfather Abraham Kreiger asked us to move in with him in his big house, which he had built himself. He was the patriarch, the founder of the family business, yet he was very unauthoritarian. I remember him rolling out dough on the kitchen table, helping my mother make pies for the holidays, and letting us climb up into bed with him. He was a quiet, warm presence.

Every Saturday, my mother would take us to Stamford, Connecticut, to see her side of the family. Her father, Sam, was a very unambitious man in the best sense of the word. All he wanted to do was read and study. His tiny hardware store was down a dark and dingy street. It had one narrow aisle, with things piled up so high on either side that you could barely move. At the end of the aisle was his big oversized desk; and there he'd be, his Hebrew books open all around him.

The store was open seven days a week. One Sunday, the police came into the store and said, "It's the Sabbath, and you're not allowed to stay open."

He looked at them. "I don't even close on my own Sabbath," he said. "You expect me to close on yours?"

All the stores on his block were owned by elderly Jews. He would take us up to see old Molly, who owned the candy store, and she would scare the daylights out of us. He had told her, "Mother, look around. They say the world is round and it's spinning." She looked around and looked around. Finally, she looked back at him. "You know, Sam. It's your head that's round, and it's spinning."

Young blacks lived in the apartments over the stores. My grandfather felt perfectly safe living among them. He would have never left the location. It was urban renewal that finally closed him down in the early 1970s.

He would take me down a few alleys and up a few flights of rickety stairs to an apartment in a kind of tenement where his father, my great-grandfather Mendel, lived. An old woman, who I think was his third wife, answered the door and ushered us in. The moment I saw my great-grandfather, my elderly grandfather turned into a young man.

Mendel was a bit frail by that time. He was Orthodox but nonjudgmental. When he heard I was going to have a bat mitzvah, he found it very strange. "Is that what they do in America?" he asked.

My grandfather Sam considered himself to be very ignorant, having only gone as far as the fifth grade. More importantly, he only knew half of the Torah by heart, whereas his father Mendel knew the entire Torah. When I was assigned "Noah" as my bat mitzvah portion, I said to my grandfather, "I want to test you." I opened the book, and from memory he recited the entire thing. He did know quite a bit. But he was a simple man, and that's what I loved in him.

He was actually antireligious; yet he was a Jew to the core. He believed in books. He believed in reading. To him, Judaism was history, story, the life of his people. He spoke Yiddish, of course, but preferred Hebrew. "I'm going to teach you Hebrew because it's the language of free Jews," he would say to me. He was a man of Hebrew not Yiddish culture, a real Zionist.

My grandmother Gert was the daughter of a horse trainer who came from Russia and got a farm in Norwalk. It was said they were the first family in Norwalk to have indoor plumbing. My great-grandfather was killed in a train crash out West on a horse-buying trip; he left ten children behind. I still have this image of his wife, my great-grandmother, sitting in a rocker by a grape arbor.

We would have many overnights at Sam's and Gert's, a big frame two-story house with a mysterious two-level yard out back. No matter how many things we broke or spilled, all my grandmother did was hug us and smile. "Accidents will happen," she'd say.

Except for Sam, all my grandparents were born in this country. That's what made me feel closest to Sam—some immigrant connection that had a lot to do with my own inexplicable feeling about being Jewish.

Herb Kalisman: The first thing my father told my mother when she came to America was, "Libby, I'm a totally changed person. In Europe I was beginning to doubt religion. Now I am an atheist. I don't go to synagogue. But you can do what you wish."

She kept a kosher home; she lit candles on Friday nights. When she prayed an exuberant calmness, a glow would come over my mother that I never saw at any other time. Her eyes would be blazing; her cheeks would seem fuller, and she had full cheeks. It was as if she had a direct link to God.

Karl Bernstein: Grandma Libby was superstitious. If someone complimented us, she'd say "poo-poo" to ward off the evil eye. If I stepped over my cousin, I had to step right back or he wouldn't grow any more. I would go to her to interpret my dreams. They always had a wonderful meaning: something good for the Jews or a long and happy life for the dreamer.

Herb Kalisman: As a bread baker, my father was in very high demand; he was never unemployed, even in the depths of the Depression. They made rolls and *challah* by hand then, beautiful creations. For my nephew's *bris,* my father made a *challah* that was about sixteen feet long. They had to send a truck to bring it. But at home, it was my mother who was the master baker: *challah,* apple cake, strudel—every one a work of art. It was a constant frustration to my father that whatever he baked at home didn't come out right. He claimed the oven was different.

He had sort of a wry—no pun intended—sense of humor. He'd tell us, half jokingly, that the best inheritance he could give us was that he was going to die a poor man. We'd stay together because we would not have money to fight over.

Karl Bernstein: My father's parents were divorced when he was very young, and he was raised by his grandmother. I had heard about Krona from the time I was a little boy. She was a mythical figure, an optimist who ran her family of twelve children and all their spouses and children with great organization and energy. Over a period of twenty-eight years, she helped arrange the passage of her extended brood to America, giving them a home and support until they were ready to go out on their own.

When my father brought my mother to meet her, Krona was very disapproving because my mother was a *Galitziana,* from the Galicia region of Poland. But then she found out my mother had graduated from Teacher's College, Columbia University. A college degree cancelled the *Galitziana* part out.

In the old country, Krona and her husband, Itzhak Hirsch, had owned a little store. Krona was the businesswoman, taking care of the merchandise and keeping the accounts. Itzhak Hirsch was a scholar. He'd sit out front beside the barrels filled with grain and produce, reading a Talmudic tract. When customers came by, his head remained buried in the book. *"Nem, nem,"* he'd say. "Take, take."

I remember Itzhak Hirsch as an old man with a beard, a long coat, and derby hat. He was a cantor in a shul on the Lower East Side and would walk there and back across the Williamsburg Bridge. On November 12, 1938, he crossed the bridge, went to the ritual baths, crossed back, and went to bed. The next morning, they discovered he had died in his sleep. He was nearly a hundred years old.

Irv Kaze: On the High Holy Days, my grandfather, Azriel Siff, walked down Romaine Avenue to the Cottage Street Shul in Jersey City. He was a distinguished figure with his long white beard, his top hat, and Prince Albert cutaway. All of the gentiles would say "Happy New Year, Mr. Siff." And he would acknowledge them.

Every Friday night and Saturday I went to shul with him. We'd come back on a nice fall day, and I would be standing at the window watching my friends play. As often as not he would come up to me and tap me on the shoulder. "Yitzhak," he'd say, *"gai shpiel"*—go play. I didn't wait for him to think about it a second time. I was out the door.

In the summertime, all the kids would be out playing. We'd cool off by sucking ice and drinking Cokes. I'd look up and through the dining room window, I'd see my grandfather at the table, studying Talmud and drinking hot tea from a tall glass. Little beads of perspiration would be on his brow.

"Zayde," I'd ask him later, "How can you drink hot tea in the summer?"

"I feel very cool," he'd say.

He was the coolest cat around. He really was.

Artie Allen: My father's father came to New York from the Isle of Rhodes in 1910. After getting married, he and his wife moved to Montgomery, Alabama, where there was a long-established Sephardic community. Along the way he changed his name from Nace Alhadeff to Nace Allen.

A gambler who made money going from place to place looking for a card game, my grandfather was a strong man with tremendous muscles. When he wasn't making enough money from his gambling, he did all kinds of physical labor.

He owned a billiards parlor that had glass doors on the street and saloon-type doors inside. These led into a big room with about ten pool tables. The place smelled of smoke, the air was thick as fog. In the back was another room where the illegal domino games were played. Some of the men were Jewish, and some were not. But they all got along. Just in case, however, my grandfather carried a little one-shooter in his pocket. He believed in having protection. Once, he said, he shot someone who was stealing money in a billiards game.

When we went to my grandparents for Sunday dinner, my parents were always complaining, "Why is there so much pepper?" My father hated spicy Sephardic food because that was all he had when he was growing up. As a kid, he had always begged my grandfather for hamburgers.

My parents didn't appreciate what a great cook my grandfather was. For a while he cooked for George Wallace at the governor's mansion. When he went to synagogue, it wasn't to *daven* but to cook, especially on Wednesday nights when they had the big spaghetti dinners at Etz Chaim, Montgomery's Sephardic synagogue.

Marc Angel: My grandmother made a tremendous amount of great and colorful foods of the kind they would have eaten in Turkey. Among my favorites were *rosca*, big round sweet rolls with sesame seeds. We'd spread butter on them; they were wonderful. Because she didn't want to be caught without anything to serve if people came to visit, my grandmother would make five times as much as was needed. But leftovers were never thrown out. She'd toast rolls and slice them in strips, and they'd last a long time. She called these *parmak*. They were so delicious with butter or jam or dipped in coffee. We liked them better than the real thing.

There were always the inviting smells of food coming from the kitchen, and sometimes my grandmother would burn orange peel on the stove. Its fragrance would fill the whole house.

We are named after the living. I am named for my grandfather, Mordecai Romey. I was very close to him. He was a strong, silent type with a wonderful mastery of his children. My mother told me when they were little, whenever anyone did anything wrong, he lined up all seven of them and spanked them all. They would ask why. His answer was, "You're all responsible for each other."

Grandfather Romey had come to Seattle from the Turkish city of Kekirdag, with no formal education whatsoever. He had no skills, no trade, nothing. He started off as a longshoreman, but the work was too hard and he made little money, so he went to night school, learned to become a barber, and opened up his own shop. That was a very classy trade in those days. It was a clean profession; you didn't have to break your back. But my grandfather had to raise a family of seven kids, and it was tough.

Grandfather Romey was a strong-willed man, a fine speaker and charismatic personality. He became expert at raising funds to help the old community whenever there were fires or earthquakes in Turkey. On Shabbat he'd be dressed like a prince in a suit, shirt, and tie. But on Sunday, when we would go for a drive, he'd wear a flowery shirt, baggy pants, and a baseball cap turned to the side.

My grandfather was very tradition-oriented. In those days, many of the first generation in America had to work on Shabbat. Many stopped keeping kosher. But my grandfather, God bless his soul, wanted all his children to live as Jews, marry Jews, keep Shabbat, keep kosher homes. He wanted to be able to eat in everyone's house.

By external standards, my grandfather might be considered a failure. He didn't have much education, never made much money. But in his own eyes he was an aristocrat, and he carried himself with great dignity. There's a tradition among Sephardic Jews that when the Temple in Jerusalem was destroyed, the aristocracy moved on to Spain. He believed that's what he came out of, that he was a descendant of the tribe of Judah. His nobility stemmed from the heights of Jewish tradition.

Moe Skoler: In Russia our grandfather had been a big shot. Here in America he was just another immigrant trying to make a living out of a little dry-goods store. Perhaps that was why he was so cold and controlling. We never saw Zayde smile.

He retained the demeanor of an aristocrat, saw himself as a country squire. Every day he exercised and dressed up in a suit with a white shirt and a silk tie.

Bubby was the opposite of him: affectionate and full of fun. She had to sneak us our Chanukah gelt so my grandfather shouldn't know. She'd play an old Russian card game with us, cheat on purpose, and laugh when she got caught. I don't know how she tolerated Zayde. He'd come to the kitchen table, sit down with a knife and fork, and wait to be served. My father got that from him. If the soup was not warm enough, he'd push it aside without a word. My mother would take it and warm it up.

Sylvia Skoler Portnoy: Zayde's tiny dry-goods store was near the shipyards in Quincy Point. During the war he did very well, but he wasn't satisfied. His younger brother did even better selling goods to the government. My granduncle was as cold as my grandfather; he never spoke to me.

A whole branch of our family lived in New York, and whenever they visited we were showered with affection. I came to the conclusion that the New England family was cold, and the New York family was warm. My father was very close to his cousin Abe from New York, a very expressive and demonstrative man. I thought it was so unusual to see qualities like that in a man of my father's generation.

I also found it hard to believe that Aunt Feiga was my grandfather's sister. She'd come up on the bus from New York City, laden down with bundles and packages. We'd hear her high-pitched, sing-song voice and come running. She had little money and a large family of her own, yet Aunt Feiga always had presents for us. She gave me my first doll. My father did not believe in giving us toys.

Moe Skoler: My father seemed so angry all the time. I guess that had something to do with coming out of the immigrant experience with four children and a wife to take care of. But also I think it was because he was the only son of a despotic father.

There was a rift between my grandfather and a cousin that translated into a big family *broigus* (feud). My father would not dare defy his father by speaking to anyone in this forbidden family. It was a terrible thing. We were part of a Jewish community in a small city where many were related by birth or marriage and came from the same area in Russia. For years and years on the High Holy Days, my grandfather, father, and this cousin all sat next to each other in the front row of shul. And they never spoke to each other.

Sylvia Skoler Portnoy: My mother was forbidden to speak to the cousin's wife, who had been a very dear friend. She obeyed that injunction for the rest of her life, even though I know it made her suffer. My poor mother. She was so lonely. She kept so much bottled up.

Jim Sleeper: Typically, the women of that time suppressed their own yearnings. My mother got accepted to Simmons College and really wanted to go. But her mother wouldn't allow her to attend college, partly because her father had died and she had to help support the family.

Missing out on a college education was a lifelong frustration of hers. I remember her most for her love of books and learning; it was part of that frustrated college thing. She read incessantly.

Arthur Cantor: I meet a lot of people who are my mother. I never met a Jewish woman of my mother's generation who was not exactly like my mother, with all the good points and some of the less-desirable ones as well. My mother was quick to anger. She could characterize someone very quickly and usually unfavorably, always in Yiddish. She ran the home. She ran the family. But she didn't make the living. She was frustrated.

My mother had cooking facilities in the cellar. The fumes were redolent. She had it in for gentile food. Couldn't understand when I went to New York how I could eat sausage. Much of what she cooked was indigestible, but at least it was Jewish.

Roz Starr: My mother's name was Beatrice Rabinowitz Goldstein. Her notes to my teachers always ended with, "By doing so, you will oblige— Mrs. Beatrice Rabinowitz Goldstein." Her philosophy was, if you're Orthodox and you're singing and you're eating well, it's a very comfortable life. God will see you through everything.

I was two years old when I got polio. The doctors put me in a glass box called a "death case" and told my mother to go home. Instead she went to the rabbi and prayed. When she came back, I was better.

My mother had two handicapped children. Other people would have had anger. She taught us to have hope. She bought me a lovely dress and put me on a chair in front of the building. "People are looking at you not because of your braces but because your dress is so nice."

I was so comfortable I didn't even know I was handicapped. After one of my brothers came home from the store with french fries on a nonkosher plate, my mother decided I would have to do the shopping. I shlepped six tomatoes, a hard head of lettuce, six oranges, three lemons, and a nice pineapple—all on crutches. I climbed monkey bars with my polio. My mother taught me how to dance.

Her hat, shoes, dress—they all came from Ohrbach's, but everything matched. She had four kids. All of them laid on one leg. She'd put her good leg up, and all the men would come over. They were always flirting with her. After my father died, she got forty proposals.

Ours was a bilingual home. "*Nem* the milk and put it in the refrigerator," my mother would say, or "*Famacht* the door on your way out." She believed in *kineahora* to ward off the evil eye and always remembered how the day before I came down with polio, a woman remarked what a happy child I was. But she also believed you could transfer good luck. Every Saturday night, we'd go into the brassiere store across the street to buy something. That guaranteed the owner customers for the whole week. The guy who owned the delicatessen down the block wanted a piece of the action. So my mother or I became his first post-Shabbat customer. It was very interesting. They started to believe that we brought them luck, and so we brought them luck.

If my mother was the cockeyed optimist, my father was the pessimist. For him it was black Monday, Tuesday, Wednesday. . . . He was also fifty-fifty: Orthodox only when my mother was around. He was a shoe cutter and a paintbrush maker. With four children, he needed two trades.

My parents were very jealous of each other. They used to have fights and throw chairs through the windows. The police would have to come separate them. An hour later they'd be hugging each other, so in love.

Alicia Devora: My parents were the renegades of the family. My father had been married once before. My mother had been married twice before, and one of the guys wasn't Jewish. Those were pretty scandalous things.

They were a gorgeous young couple—dashing, flamboyant, great ballroom dancers. Driving around Miami in their cream-colored convertible, they led what they thought was an all-American and not a Jewish existence. Aside from the Yiddish that permeated their humor, they had all but dropped their history and background. My father was a fireman, bodybuilder, and skin diver—the hot catch on the beach—until he decided that a family man had to do something more stable and settled in with an insurance company.

When relatives from New York came down to visit, I was given to understand that I was part of some Jewish family thing. I went to some relative's bar mitzvah when I was about seven or eight. But to me it was just like my backyard birthday parties. No different. I remember the occasional seders, but I have just as strong a memory of Christmas in Miami, hanging around in pajamas with the Catholic kids.

My mother was miserable in Florida, hated the weather. In the 1940s, when she was young, wild, and single, she had lived in Los Angeles. Now she pined for Southern California. So my father got a transfer, and off they went to L.A., fabulous L.A., with their kid who grew up fast.

This was 1967. I was eleven years old. My mother took me to a production of *Hair,* and my eyes opened up. I was no longer a kid playing with dolls. I had to get out on the streets. You know what was going on on the West Coast then.

All my traces of Jewishness were pretty much gone. But there were people I hung around with who went wild in the streets all year long and then went back to their mothers' houses for seders. I would hear about this, and a distant bell would be triggered. Oh yeah, I think I remember that stuff.

When I was fourteen and decided to become a vegetarian, my mother came home with a stack of books about protein and meat. She threatened to stop cooking for me. I said, "Fine, I will cook for myself."

That was how I found out about her mother, Anna Kramer, who had died soon after I was born. Not only was my grandmother a vegetarian, she wouldn't even eat food cooked in pots that had been used to cook meat. She was a milliner, which is one of the things I do. She believed in the evil eye and was forever throwing salt over her shoulder or knocking on wood. To my mother that was a bunch of bunk. But not to me.

As I grew towards adulthood, my mother began to see all these similarities between her mother and me. I have her coloring, acted like her, spoke in the same way she did. My mother felt like she was caught between the same woman in two different bodies: mother and daughter.

Not long ago, I came across a photo of my grandmother taken in Russia around 1910. She's wearing a hat with an enormous brim and a dress with a long train, and standing with one arm resting on a chair and the other on her hip. I compared it to a photo of me taken in L.A. maybe sixty years later. I'm wearing a "flower child" kind of jumpsuit, standing with one arm resting on a pickup truck and the other on my hip. The stances are re- markably similar. I believe that my grandmother entered me when she died, and somehow all that Jewishness, that Russian-ness that I didn't get from my parents came to me from her.

At the same time, I also have my mother's non-Jewishness and her desire to go your own way. She was the one in her family who went out on a limb, married whom she wanted, did what she wanted to do for a living. The rest of her family didn't like it, but in a way she lived out their dreams and fantasies. I took to the streets as a hippie when I was barely in my teens and have been a free spirit ever since.

Marnie Bernstein: For a number of years, my father's mother lived with us. It was a difficult situation. We were very crowded, and she was a terrible busybody, always interrupting, interfering, giving unasked-for advice. My mother used to say the only place she could read the newspaper without being disturbed was in the bathroom.

Looking back on it now, her living with us seems unjust. My father's brothers and sister had homes of their own, and we a little one-bedroom apartment. And yet, claustrophobic as they were, I am glad for the times she was with us. Not because she was good, although she was a model of family devotion. Not because of the lessons she taught, although she was certainly honest. But because of the example she set of competency, cleverness, and supreme self-confidence. Would that I could reach her mark.

My father used to say that when other women cleaned a chicken the water dripped from their elbows, but when my grandmother cleaned a chicken her fingernails were dry. When she drained a pot of noodles, she turned the pot upside-down, holding the lid open just enough for the water to run out. A colander was beneath her dignity. Once her hold slipped, and all the noodles fell into the sink. She couldn't get over it. It wasn't the waste or the mess; it was a matter of personal pride. "To me such a thing should happen?" she said again and again.

Bubby would have had no use for a calculator. She'd check the grocery checkout slips, totaling a column of two-digit numbers in seconds. Sometimes we'd check her math. Of course she was always right. She'd smile at her own good sense, a glimpse of gold teeth shining like flashes of sensible logic.

Bubby was a master of characterization, particularly of figures she saw on television. Alistair Cooke would appear on the screen, and she'd say *"Ach, er iz shoin doo, der nudnik shammes"*—which roughly translates as "Ah, he's here already, the annoying, cloying sexton." Her name for Louie Armstrong was *der hazerike forts*—"the hoarse fart." Although she'd deny it to the last, she was mesmerized by wrestling. Staring intently at the screen without missing a bear hug or drop kick, she'd keep up a steady stream of commentary in Yiddish: *"Feh, paskidna"* (awful, disgusting).

Bubby would listen to the radio and understand enough of the English to get a rough idea of what was going on. As soon as my father came home from work, she'd present him with the latest on the McCarthy hearings, the news from Israel. And whatever she didn't quite understand, she invented.

Sometimes, when she interfered, my father would fly into a rage and scream at her. Later my mother would ask "*Shviger*—mother-in-law—why do you mix in?"

And she'd reply, "Ah, if only the fool were not mine."

Her youngest son was my Uncle Saul, the only easygoing, lighthearted member of a very intense, dramatic family. Living in the Boston area, Uncle Saul seemed to be more Irish than the Irish he hobnobbed with. He had that gift of gab, that charm, and a beautiful tenor voice. He was always singing.

Linda Katz Ephraim: My father sang in the car; he sang at parties; he put me to sleep singing, "When I go to sleep/I never count sheep/I count all the charms about Linda." He'd sing the Russian folk songs he'd learned as a child and the pioneer Zionist songs of his youth.

Privately, my father told each of his three children he loved him or her best—but not to tell the others. I was the only girl, though, so I've always felt in my case he really meant it.

Although he had a terrible temper—he could turn red, yell, and scream—he mostly let things run off him. If a customer couldn't pay, he understood. If my mother spent two hours trying on shoes while he waited in the car, he understood. People would tell him he was the only Jew they liked, and he had to put up with that too.

Fridays, he did his collections in bars. It was more or less an Irish thing, not a Jewish one, but he fit in so easily they thought he was one of them. He was everyone's buddy. He'd hang around, have some drinks—of course my mother never liked that, but it was part of the job.

His job was selling dry goods and home furnishings. But what he really sold was himself.

Marnie Bernstein: In spite of his great personal charm and no small amount of ability, my father never made it here in America. He alone in his family remained a working man. Why, I often wondered. Was it fear, was it my mother's passivity, was it his overwhelming sense of responsibility to others—hardly the prescription for a successful businessman—that prevented him from taking the chance and going into business like the others did?

For more than fifty years, he was a furrier. His working life combined anxiety over making a living with the deadening effects of a dreary routine. Every working day, year after year, he walked the six blocks from his modest apartment to and from the subway, made the forty-minute trip to Seventh Avenue, and sat at a machine in a dim shop sewing together the skins of Alaskan seals.

Not only did he fail to live out his destiny, he failed to even try. Some unknown thing held him back. In Russia his education had been interrupted before high school; here he never went to school. Yet he read my college books—he completed Franz Werfel's *The Forty Days of Musga Dagh* overnight—and *The New York Times* every day. When a neighbor's son was struggling with a calculus problem, my father solved it with the most elementary mathematical knowledge. It took forty-five minutes and left him with a ferocious headache. But he was glad he did it, proud of himself.

He exuded confidence, was sure of his good looks, his immaculate appearance, his unworkmanlike, manicured hands, the gleaming white shirt and perfectly knotted tie he wore on weekends, the stiff crease in his trousers, the exact tilt of his fedora whose brim he touched when a lady passed by.

Because he was so outgoing, so vital in public, people thought he was a happy man. Only we knew his dark side. Each spring he agonized through the long months of the slack season. Each summer he suffered through the heat and humidity of New York City. The fall rejuvenated him—the prospect of overtime at work and the promise of winter ahead. It was the Russian in him. He'd stand outside our apartment house on snowy nights drinking in the cold silence.

He was so much a man of feeling, and the excesses of his moods ruled his life and ours as well. His depression and anger terrified and defeated us. But oh, there were the times—when we did well in school; when I sang for him; when he heard music that moved him; when he was telling a story, clinching a point, recalling the successes of his briefest youth—that his blue-blue eyes were lit with joy, and we were blinded by his radiance.

Addi Friedman: My father was chief financial officer of Schenley's. He had gotten his Ph.D. from Columbia at age twenty-three, and although he was a loving father, he also exerted pressure. He wanted us to succeed and was a very severe critic of our academic progress.

He opened his tremendous library to me and did not forbid my reading anything. At the age of twelve, I was reading Guy de Maupassant, whose works were considered very questionable for a young girl as they dealt with themes of infidelity and adultery. I studied piano for a dozen years. Five days a week, my sister and I went to an Orthodox Talmud Torah. Two afternoons a week a young man came to the house and gave us private Hebrew lessons.

Our household was very European, very private and proper, perhaps Germanic in that respect. My parents, sister, and I formed a tight-knit nuclear family. Occasionally my mother would invite her friends from Europe, her brothers and their wives, or her cousins to visit us. But my father was not that gregarious; he liked his privacy.

My mother lived through my sister and me. She wanted us to be devout. Being devout was much more than form for her; she believed with her whole heart. Her behavior exemplified her beliefs. She would say things like, "Wait for someone to say something nice about your own. Don't be the first to say it." Or, "Your reputation is like a white handkerchief. If it gets a spot, everybody can see it, and it's hard to take out." These all come from rabbinic sources.

We lived in an apartment on Riverside Drive that was as large as a house. Ours was a lovely, lovely world—like an Edith Wharton story, a protected, nonthreatening environment. On the one hand, we were treated like little adults. But on the other hand, our parents tried to hide frightening news from us. They watched us, didn't let us go too far from home. I always felt guilty if I stayed out too late and didn't call.

We had Christian help who would go home for Christmas, and when they came back, they brought with them the smell of ginger. Christmas was seductive: the lights, the coaches, the singing. I'm sure we wanted something like that for ourselves, but it never became an issue. It was not ours.

We were made very aware of the Christian world in the summers when we traveled. We often saw restricted signs that meant no dogs, blacks, or Jews. There was a lot of that in West Virginia, in remote villages in Canada. The amazing thing is that my father had the courage to go into these places.

We could have passed very easily, but we refused to go in except as Jews. My mother would say, "Why can't we go to a nice hotel in the Catskills?" But my father said, "The children have to learn to travel and see everything."

When it came time for us to go to college, we knew it was not possible for us to go away because the Jewish life we lived did not exist on an out-of-town campus. But that was no problem. Neither my sister nor I had the desire to leave our world, our magic garden.

Frank Rich: My grandparents and parents passed on a Jewish heritage that gave me a sense of who the Jewish people were and where I fit into that history. That heritage was enhanced by literature—the earliest Philip Roth and Bernard Malamud—and by musical figures like Leonard Bernstein.

Karl Bernstein: I grew up in a home pervaded by secular, cultural Jewishness. My mother would put me to sleep playing Chopin on the piano.

Herb Kalisman: Every one of my four sisters played the piano. As each got to take her piano with her when she got married, we had to keep getting new ones. My brother played the violin.

When I was in sixth grade I brought home a Jew's harp I'd found in school. My father picked it up and started to play beautifully—*boing, boing, boing*—all kinds of Polish folk tunes. "I played this as a kid on the farm," he said. "I still remember."

Marcia Lee Goldberg: Music was all around me as I was growing up. According to my father, my first words were "turn it"—meaning "Turn on the radio, I want to hear some music." My uncle was the principal flutist of the Pittsburgh Symphony. My father taught music and began a small music store, which became a big operation.

I wanted to be a singer and could sing "Ave Maria" or "O Holy Night" with as much soul and passion as I would sing a Jewish song. But Jewish music was there as well, from poignant cantorial prayers to my brother's favorite, the Mickey Katz record of "Don't Let the Lox Get in Your Socks."

David Sager: Though I couldn't understand a word, I loved listening to Grandmother Dorfman's Mickey Katz records, especially the hilarious take-off on "Tico Tico."

She was a professional musician; her third husband was a violinist. She had a collection of sheet music that had all these *fraylich* melodies. They were always playing them. My feel for Jewishness came from my grandmother and her music, from people like George Gershwin and Harold Arlen, Al Jolson and Eddie Cantor.

Frank Rich: When I was a kid, the media images of families were *Ozzie and Harriet* and *Leave It to Beaver*. They were not Jewish. But there was also a whole strain of popular entertainment that even if I couldn't pinpoint it as Jewish, was so ethnic to me, had such a Jewish feel: Jack Benny, Burns and Allen, Phil Silvers. I always enjoyed that grittier kind of humor. I recognized a kind of voice and tongue. Even "The Honeymooners," who weren't Jewish, had that ethnic thing.

Natalie Cohen Monteleone: My grandmother listened to the Yiddish programs, that wushy-wushy talking I couldn't understand. I thought her radio was different from everyone else's. My mother would entertain with stream-of-consciousness stories in different dialects and sing in the kitchen with a towel over her shoulder like she was Sophie Tucker.

David Sager: One time both sides of the family gathered at my grandmother's apartment for Rosh Hashanah. There were lots of great-aunts and -uncles and my other grandmother, who was very Old World and much older than Grandmother Dorfman.

In the middle of dinner, one of the parakeets Grandma Dorfman trained piped up, *"Gut yuntif, cocker-pisher"*—"Happy holiday, shitter-pisser."

My Old-World grandmother dropped her fork. "Who talks like this?" she asked in Yiddish.

Like her parakeets, Grandma Dorfman performed spontaneously at gatherings, in auditoriums, wherever. She did her version of the Fanny Brice parody of "Swan Lake," told bawdy jokes, and sang songs like *"Shayn Vee di Levanah"* ("Beautiful as the Moon") in several versions: straight, in a southern accent, Al Jolson–style, and as a stutterer using a whistle to break the stutter. For her finale, she combined all the versions. Talk about politically incorrect!

Marc Angel: The people in my family were real. Some were intellectuals and others not very bright. Some were passionate and opinionated, others passive and bland. Some were gifted and others handicapped. But all belonged.

Neil Postman: There were over two hundred people in our extended family. Only one was psychotic, but everyone else was neurotic—very introspective in the sense of "Why am I doing this?"

There were always fights within the family, usually as a result of someone going into business with someone else or making an investment with someone else. Or because someone lost eight dollars in one of the gin games my uncles were always playing. The only rational one in the game was Uncle Carl, the Republican.

Like all the Jewish families I knew, ours wanted to have one representative from every known profession. And it wasn't good enough to have a physician; there had to be a dermatologist, an internist, an ophthalmologist, a gynecologist, an allergist. Then they wanted a dentist, a lawyer, and an accountant. I don't think they cared that much about engineers, and oddly enough there wasn't much talk about professors.

Someone in the family married a non-Jewish woman. At first she couldn't get used to his family. It seemed they were always arguing with each other, talking loud to each other, not waiting for someone to finish a whole sentence. But what happens in such situations is if all of this does not become completely detestable to you, you begin to become like that yourself—especially if you live in New York. In the end, this woman changed. She stopped waiting for the other person to finish a sentence. Her reason: "Why should I wait if I know what he's going to say?"

Marc Angel: My mother used to say if you want to know about human society, human nature, all you have to do is look at your family. If you understand your family, you understand humanity.

13

A TENUOUS BALANCE

"Behold, thou shalt call a nation that thou knowest not,
And a nation that knew not thee shall run unto thee."

—Isaiah LV:5

Jim Sleeper: I think a lot of people are profoundly ambivalent about their ethnicity. They don't want to ignore the tragic, but on the other hand they don't want to *rah-rah-rah*. It's a very complicated thing. Every ethnic identity has a deep mix of pride and shame, and no one talks about the shame.

Roger Harris: In 1944, when I was seven years old, my father decided it would be better if we were out of the big city and moved us from Brooklyn to Putnam County, north of Westchester. I doubt if he realized it at the time, but the town we moved to was a hotbed of pro-German sentiment, and we were one of the first Jewish families to live there.

School began. I entered the second grade, and my brother started kindergarten. Since it was a rural community, we got picked up by a school bus. The first day on the bus, a couple of the bigger boys got ahold of my brother and me, took us on their laps, and said, "So, you're a little fucking Jew bastard, aren't you?" That was all they did. They didn't hit us or shove us, but I felt very threatened nevertheless.

When I came home, I asked my mother, "What's a fucking bastard?" and told her what had happened.

"Oh my, oh my," she said. "We will have to do something about this. I'm going to have to speak to those parents."

That was the end of it. She didn't explain what the words meant, or tell me what she said to the boys' parents, or whether in fact she ever did speak to them. So I was left with this vague, disturbing feeling.

My mother was a fearful woman. Many years later, I learned that when she had become pregnant with my brother, she did not want to have the baby because of what was happening to the Jews in Germany. She went around to all the gentile neighbors, asking them to take in and protect her children if Hitler should win the war. I'm certain she transmitted such fears to me. Maybe that explains why I found it so upsetting when Israel became a state in 1948. Why, I wondered, should all the Jews get together in one place where it would be so much easier to kill them off?

Having a name like Harris and being a regular kind of kid, I don't know how anyone knew I was Jewish, but the word got around. Every so often, I'd be standing at the urinal in the boys' room, and a kid would look over my shoulder to see what a circumcised penis looked like. Once a little girl

◀ *(top)* Jewish-American boy scouts in Duluth, Minnesota, c. 1955. The range of the Jewish-American experience: *(bottom left)* With Santa Claus at Filene's, Boston, c. 1968—"Christmas was a time to get toys." *(bottom right)* Chassidic father making a point.

raised her hand in class and asked, "Why do Jews always have so much money?" and I could feel my face turning hot and red.

In fifth grade we began studying ancient civilizations. I was browsing through the textbook, looking at chapters on the Byzantine Era, the Greek era, the Roman era. Then, all of a sudden, I noticed—Chapter 5, page 132—it was about the Jews. Again I felt my face turn red. Oh-oh, I thought, at some point, a couple of months down the road, we're going to start talking about the Jews. I started planning excuses for being absent on those days.

After a while, I began denying being Jewish. If someone asked me, I'd say, "I'm not a Jew; I'm Catholic." Then it dawned on me that people who are liked don't get harassed. Nobody notices they're different. And what better way to be liked than to be funny? So I became the class clown. I'd sit around telling jokes, fooling around, cracking everyone up. It worked. Sometimes I wonder whether that's why there are so many Jewish comedians.

It wasn't that I rejected my Jewishness as much as I didn't want to appear different. At home we were not observant; there was not much of a Jewish identity in the family. The time that should have been my bar mitzvah was a secular birthday party. But being identified as a "fucking Jew bastard" as a seven-year-old was traumatic.

Years later, I learned that one of the boys who harassed us on the school bus fell in love with a Jewish girl and married her. When I found out, my reaction was: I hope the circumcision hurt.

Marc Angel: I was in the tenth grade in a Seattle high school when my literature teacher approached me.

"We're going to read *The Merchant of Venice*," she said. "Do you have any objection?"

I was fifteen years old. I had never heard of *The Merchant of Venice*. "Who wrote it?" I asked.

"Shakespeare."

"Shakespeare is a fine writer. Why should I have any objections?"

For six weeks we studied the play, and for six weeks I didn't open my mouth in class. It was absolute terror. There were three or four Jews in the class, and reading the play gave us such a sense of isolation that none of us even spoke to each other about it. You know when you're a teenager and you have a pimple, you think you look different. Here I was in a class reading a play that chastised my whole people.

I felt Shakespeare should rot in hell just for that play. The sin that he committed against humanity by creating Shylock, the suffering that he caused people, knowingly or unknowingly, is unforgivable. Reading that play made me vow to graduate really high in the class. I wanted to show them that Jews are really okay.

Barbara Kreiger: The teacher said: "Now Barbara will tell us about the Jewish Christmas." My brother had done a Chanukah presentation, so I used his report. But I was very ambivalent about it. The kids would ask, "Why do the Jews have to have their own Christmas? Why can't they just have ours?" And then they'd say things like, "You Jews are so smart because you eat so much fish." I guess that came from seeing my mother at the fish market.

Jim Sleeper: In the fourth grade, I was one of two Jewish kids at the Center Street School in Longmeadow, Massachusetts, a real Yankee town. My teacher, Florence Smith, was a real Yankee schoolmarm. A week before Christmas, she asked me and the other Jewish kid to stand. "I want to tell you children that these are Jewish boys," Miss Smith announced to the class. "They don't celebrate Christmas. But I want you to treat them with respect because not everybody celebrates Christmas."

Everything on television was Christmas. Every store was decorated for Christmas. And Christmas day, they were all closed. A Jewish kid had nothing to do but sit at home. It was like twenty-four hours in a bunker.

Your attitude toward your own tradition at this time was ambivalent. There was a sense of deep pride but also a muted shame. The goyim had it all: the splendid cathedrals, the lights, the carols, the opulent presents, the thunderous triumphant music. By comparison, we were the little people with our second-rate holiday, our Chanukah.

Marnie Bernstein: In a kind of schizophrenic way, we participated in Christmas publicly, although never privately. My mother used to take us to

Macy's, where we'd wait for hours in this long line for the chance to sit on Santa's lap and tell him what we'd like for Christmas even though we knew we weren't getting anything. We went to see the Christmas tree at Rockefeller Center and the show at Radio City Music Hall. We saw *The Nutcracker* a couple of times with all its gorgeous Christmas imagery.

These experiences were wonderful and exciting, but they reinforced my sense of being on the outside. They reminded me of how I felt looking out the bedroom window at a group of children playing in the courtyard and not being invited to join.

Alan Lelchuk: When I was about seven years old, I went to Rock Creek, a little town in southern Ohio where my mother's father had moved with his new wife. He had a small farm and haberdashery there. Though I was treated well by the townsfolk, I had the distinct sense that this world, unlike the one at home, was not Jewish. I seem to remember someone saying—casually, not with malice—"You're the grandson of the Jew."

Linda Katz Ephraim: I'd go with my friend to visit her aunt. Only I would stand on the sidewalk, waiting patiently until my friend came out again. I knew I was not allowed into the yard because I was Jewish. Yet, like a fool, I went and waited many, many times.

Barbara Kreiger: My great-grandfather had built the house we lived in way before many of my friends' parents came to Shelton, Connecticut. So why, I'd wonder, should I feel like the outsider? But I often did.

I recall my friends saying to another kid, "Watch what you say because Barbara's Jewish." Once at a Girl Scout meeting, one of the girls started making derogatory comments about Jews. I just sat quietly. Then she turned around and said, "I hope there are no Jews here." And I casually said, "I am." She looked at me with total disbelief, thinking I had the greatest sense of humor making such wild jokes. All my life people didn't believe me. I wasn't supposed to look Jewish or act Jewish—whatever that meant.

Terry Drucker Rosin: My parents were American-born, had no foreign accents. Both my brother and I had blue eyes and didn't look Jewish, I guess.

My mother dressed me beautifully, and I had these long Shirley Temple curls that everyone was forever pulling to see if they were real. When Jewish salesmen came into our store in Westminster, they'd tease my father that my mom was a shiksa.

But a lot of priests and ministers would come into the store, too. I'd overhear them debating religion with my father. Though he never seemed uncomfortable, he would always warn me not to discuss politics or religion.

Jim Sleeper: My uncle's name was Samuel Sleeper. He had an M.A. in English from Columbia and cut a nice figure. He got a job teaching in Munson Academy, a fancy private school in Massachusetts where all the kids were Waspy boys. Had they known he was Jewish, they would never have hired him.

There was a tremendous assimilation thrust in our family and a lot of the other Jewish families in the Springfield area. You wanted to pass, not because you wanted to deny you were Jewish but because you wanted to be on a good footing with the rest of the world. You wanted to speak the king's English. I will make no bones about it: my father and his brothers passed. They passed.

Sylvia Skoler Portnoy: I was blonde and blue-eyed, and the name Skoler sounded Swedish. When people said, "Oh, you don't look Jewish," I was pleased. It meant it was possible for me to pass.

Phyllis Taylor: My father became I. W. Brody—*I* for Irving, an Americanization of Isaac, and *W* for Wolfe, after Thomas Wolfe, whom he read in college—because he learned Americans had middle names. But everyone knew him as Steve Brody, a nickname he selected for himself after a man who had jumped off the Brooklyn Bridge. My uncle went from A. B. Danowitz to A. Robert Van Dyne. My father's sister thought the family name was really Schuster, although their father maintained it was Brody. We'll never know.

Yitz Greenberg: My name touches on the classic problem of growing up Jewish in America. I'm named after my great-grandfather Yitzhak. We do not think of the patriarchs as Abraham, Irving, and Jacob. So why is the name on my birth certificate Irving?

The answer obviously is my parents. Even though they were Orthodox Jews, the Americanization thrust was so powerful that in the crunch, when it came to naming a child, they did not want to stigmatize me with a name like Yitzhak, which would be hopelessly un-American. So they looked around for the most WASP name they could get that began with the letter *I*. To the outside world, I was Irving; at home, though, I was Yitzhak. My parents spoke Yiddish, but we answered them in English. They wanted to learn English so as to become Americanized.

Irv Saposnik: Our parents and their friends seemed disconnected from the world we were moving toward. Their language was Yiddish, or at best a hybrid "Yinglish" spoken with gesture and inflection that evolved as they moved farther away from their roots. While in school we were being taught to avoid speaking with our hands, to speak with the bell-like tones we heard on the radio, to restrain ourselves from raising our voices or swaying back and forth when we should be standing still.

Phyllis Taylor: Although all four grandparents were around, we were not allowed to mix languages. If unknowingly I'd say a Yiddish word, my parents would correct me.

David Elcott: The rules in my family were clear: you do not want to be like the loud Eastern European Jews. You don't speak Yiddish, the *mama-loshen*. You speak softly in restaurants and other public places. You don't wear a *kipah* publicly—ever.

Robert Leiter: I wanted to wear a *mezuzah* around my neck. I begged for one. My mother was appalled and let me know that was not the kind of thing I should want to wear.

Nicki Tanner: We were hardly observant. We did not belong to a temple; our home was not kosher. For Christmas, we'd have a two-story tree in our two-story living room. My friends would be invited to help trim the tree, and we'd gather around it singing "O Tannenbaum," a song my father loved as he adored his German-speaking mother. There was this German connection to the tree, the wintertime, the Christmas season.

I went to Ferry Hall, a private girls' school near our home in Lake Forest, Illinois. I was the only Jewish girl in Lake Forest and the only Jewish girl in that Episcopalian-inclined institution, where it was *de rigueur* to attend chapel. To this day, I can sing the words to all the Christian hymns.

Yet my father insisted I attend Sunday school, not to learn about Judaism but to meet Jewish boys. He was concerned I marry a Jewish man. I think he felt they made better husbands.

Phyllis Taylor: Mother never lit Shabbat candles. The Jewish delicacies we ate were made by our black housekeeper, southern style. My parents were very charitable, but they had little interest in religion.

Lucille Brody Noonan: I wanted Phyllis and her brother to have some sort of Jewish education because I think I missed it in my Ethical Culture upbringing, so we joined the Reform temple in Lawrence, Long Island, where they went through religious school. When the rabbi objected to our having a Christmas tree, we replaced it with an imaginary tree, under which we'd lay all the Christmas presents.

Phyllis Taylor: Our temple was a physically beautiful place. People dressed up for the holidays. The competition was how many pairs of shoes you have, how many cashmere sweaters you have. Our parents never went to temple with my brother and me.

I was dating Larry, a Jewish guy, when I met the Christian man who became my husband. I called home and said I was in love with Dick, and my mother said, "No dear, it's Larry." We went to talk to my grandparents, who had given up Judaism for Ethical Culture years before. My grandmother cried as she made an omelette. "Marriage is hard enough. How can you marry a non-Jewish person?"

Yitz Greenberg: For every Jewish-American boy, the ideal was the blue-eyed blonde girl. A *shiksa* would be too far a stretch for me, but a Jewish girl who looked like that.

Mike Lecar: I had a blonde *shiksa* as a teenager. She lived in Bay Ridge. If you wanted sex, you either joined the Young Communists or Socialists in Greenwich Village or you found a blonde *shiksa*. I did both.

Eric Portnoy: There lay the appeal of Woody Allen. Just the fact that there was this not-good-looking, nebbishy person whom I identified with, who was very funny, very New York, making great movies and bedding these beautiful *shiksas*. It was great that somebody Jewish could be doing these things.

Yitz Greenberg: I grew up in the pre-Chasidic era in Borough Park, Brooklyn, in an Orthodox family. By every standard that is American we came out on the most religious end of Judaism, but we were very different from the Chasidim who came over after World War II—in groups and not as individuals. They were less intimidated than my generation.

Neil Postman: It was many, many years before there was a Jewish mayor in New York City. But that was all right with everyone. We didn't want a Jewish mayor. Who knows what the repercussions might be? This way we'll get along with the Italian mayors, the Irish mayors. We got a good thing here.

In my day, you would never deny that you were Jewish, but there was the sort of attitude that the outside world doesn't have to know. You don't have to make a big deal over it. You're at school to do what the teacher says, to become an American. You don't have to talk about Shabbos, Chanukah. That's our business.

Phyllis Taylor: There was that preoccupation over any Jew who might have committed a crime or reinforced the stereotype of wealthy, selfish Jews. We'd meet someone we weren't sure of, and my mother or I would say, "Do you think that person's an M.O.T.?"—that is, a member of the tribe.

Marnie Bernstein: Although he was against their being executed, my father was enraged over the Rosenbergs' apparent treason—terribly, terribly ashamed they were Jews. He used the deeply ironic expression, "They *beshankt der mishpocheh*," which means literally "light up the family" or "cast honor on the family."

Morris Friedman: The *shanda* was a powerful operative. We didn't want any Jew to bring shame upon the Jewish people. We took great pride in a Jonas Salk: it was as if not he alone but all the Jewish people had made his great discovery.

Caroline Katz Mount: Our father retained the immigrant's mistrust of the goyish world. If you get close enough, the anti-Semitism will always come out. If you intermarry, the husband you think adores you will one day turn on you.

Yet, at the same time, he was able to cross the bridge—I guess because he was such a natural extrovert. Living in an Italian-Jewish neighborhood, it was inevitable that he become friends with the Italian men.

He had no car, so he relied on his friend Steve to drive him to the nursing home to visit my grandmother. Every so often he'd tell him, "Steve, when you die and go to the gates of heaven, Gabriel will bar the way. He'll say, 'Why should we let you in? Were you always true to your wife? Were you always honest in business? Did you stay away from the horses and the poker games? Sorry, Steve, you can't come in. You have to go to the other place.' "

Then my father would add, "But Gabriel will stop for a minute to think it over. And he'll say, 'Wait a minute. There was that Jew-boy, Abe Katz. When he needed to go to the nursing home to see his mother, when he needed to go to his doctor, you always drove him in your car. You never let him take the bus. Okay—because you were there for Abe Katz, we're going to let you in.' "

Irv Kaze: My friends were Gerard Ahearn and Mickey Kelly. We played ball all the time. When they went to St. Aedan's for confession, I'd go along and wait outside. Father Maloney, the priest with the wonderful Irish brogue, would come out. "Hello, Irving, how are you?"

"Fine, Father," I'd say, and then I'd ask, "How come they're in there so long? We were all very good this week."

He'd smile, we'd chat for a while. How was I to know my friends were at the end of a long line waiting to make confession?

Yitz Greenberg: It was a non-Jewish world, and the highest goal was to succeed in it. We were taught not to challenge America but to make concessions to it. You had to excel not just in Jewish studies but in general studies as well.

My brother and I went to yeshiva. My sisters went to public school. That partly had to do with the notion that there was less pressure for a girl's education, but also it was a conceding to America, where the place to be educated was the public school.

Jim Sleeper: It was articulated to me to be an excellent student. But that stemmed from an assimilationist drive as much as from a Jewish one. It meant sublimating your Jewish tradition into a kind of secular vein.

Nicki Tanner: My father was an admitted agnostic, indifferent—even hostile—to orthodoxy in any form. He was romantically attached to universalism and talked about Esperanto, the universal language. Yet his essence was Jewish—his work ethic and his value of education. His intellectual expectations for me were very high.

Jeff Solomon: In my family, there was very much the appreciation of hard work and success. One of the ironies was the oft-repeated message that you have to work hard in school so you can wind up in a profession where you don't have to work so hard. No matter how well I was doing in school, it was always a case of I could do better. If I got a 99 on a test, my parents wanted to know where the extra point was. If I got 100, it was an easy test.

Mike Lecar: My father made it clear that he wanted me to be an intellectual. He had a lot of books around the house. He read *The New York*

Times and we discussed it. My parents admired intellectual stuff, and I knew in my fiber, from the atmosphere, that was what you wanted to do.

Yet, when it came time for me to go to MIT, my mother became very anxious. "You don't need engineering. You don't need to go into this goyish world and finally face anti-Semitism." In my Brooklyn neighborhood, Jews were the majority. The only gentile in our apartment house was the superintendent. My mother really believed that in Cambridge, I would be thrust into a Vilna or Moscow, besieged by goyim with sticks, running away from pogroms, hiding in basements.

Actually I was quite at home at MIT with a bunch of bright guys who liked science. A fellow from my apartment house who also went to MIT was worried enough to change his name from Bernstein to Burns. They were smart enough at MIT to figure that one out.

My father was extraordinarily proud of America. He felt it was a country where a Jew could live freely and do whatever he wanted. But although he never expressed any desire to go to Palestine, his heart was in Zionism. We had the conflict of my wanting to be American and his wanting me to be part of his Zionist heritage.

I became an American Boy Scout. To my father, it was a very American thing. He wanted me to join the Zionist Boy Scouts. He didn't want me to desert this Zionism that was so important to his life. Ultimately I won him over, and he became a committeeman for the American Boy Scouts.

At a big ceremony held at the Jewish Community Center in Brooklyn, my father was sworn in and had to say a few words. Usually he was a marvelous public speaker: I had heard him inspire thousands of people when he spoke at the Zionist family camps we went to in the summer. But here he was nervous. He was embarrassed to speak to a group of strangers in his heavy Jewish-Russian accent. He did nevertheless, and he did well.

It was a very big deal for him to get involved in what he called a *goyisha meshugas*, "gentile craziness." But it was a recognition that we're here, and Mike is doing what American boys do. I was very proud.

Yitz Greenberg: To my father, everything but learning was a waste of time. Socializing, emotions, idle talk. But he never fought with me over baseball. For the yeshiva boys, baseball was a religion. We studied and followed the game till we knew all the records, all the personalities, every statistic. It was not *narrishkeit*. It was American.

There was this tremendous pull of America, assimilation, Americanism. In those days, even Young Israel had mixed dancing for teenagers to attract the youth. The American way was mixed dancing.

Murray Polner: For the young, their eyes were on the prize, as they say. They had a lot of dreaming to do, a lot of education to get, an America to conquer. The Judaic notion of reverence for family remained powerful; I never heard a single word from any of the people I knew that was critical of their parents. But there were terrible battles between the generations.

Irv Saposnik: Ironically, the more my parents pushed me to be educated, the more they were pushing me away from them. They sent me to Yeshiva Toras Chaim on Jerome Avenue in East New York where the texts were in Hebrew for the Jewish subjects, the language of instruction was Yiddish, and the teachers were European rabbinic types.

But I began to worship those who taught the secular subjects, mainly teachers from the public Thomas Jefferson High School nearby. They came from a background similar to mine, and they had made it by virtue of being educated. Their very presence seemed to say, "Look, I've done it. There's a chance for you."

At the same time I was attending the yeshiva, I was drawing away from all it represented into the secularized world. I made some pretentious noises of moving to Greenwich Village and becoming a playwright. It created a great storm and tearful nights.

Mike Lecar: My mother was very religious. She had all of these things she brought over from Russia, a chain of beliefs about how God will punish you if you don't obey this or that law. To my mind that meant superstitions.

I questioned Judaism from the very beginning and sort of stopped believing in God when I was six or seven. I went to Hebrew school reluctantly to study for my bar mitzvah.

My uncle, who was a rabbi, had one of these gadgets that turned the lights on automatically. I always felt it was cheating. I used to say, "You can't fool God like that. You think he can't figure out that you want to read so you set that little dial?"

And my uncle would say, "In Judaism it's the letter of the law and not the spirit. The rabbis have decided that what I'm doing is allowed, and I want to read."

I never did like that, the fact that you could obey the law to the letter but destroy the spirit. It didn't make sense to me.

Phyllis Taylor: I did not rebel. I was a loving and dutiful daughter who grew up in a loving home with tremendous privilege. I always had beautiful clothes. I went to summer camp from the time I was eight. My parents took me to the theater often, always first or second row center. We drove around in a new Cadillac.

Then, the summer I was sixteen, I worked at the *Herald Tribune* Fresh Air Fund as a counselor and realized the incredible poverty that existed in the world. My goal became to have less. That became a source of tension with my parents, who wanted to give me things.

I went on Freedom Rides. My mother was frightened but proud. My father was frightened and appalled. He threatened not to pay my college tuition if I continued.

Julie Sussman: As I was growing up in Far Rockaway, it seemed to me that my being Jewish had something to do with my being more interesting. I thought my Christian friends and their families were like the people I saw on TV: all-American, friendly, normal. The kids played with conventional toys, whereas I made up games. The grandparents were just like older parents, whereas mine were from Europe, and they seemed deeper, less superficial.

Then, when I was fifteen, we moved to this affluent suburb on Long Island, and my feelings about being Jewish completely changed. I went from a mixed neighborhood where there were black kids in our class from kindergarten on and we all played together to a nearly all-white, nearly all-Jewish neighborhood where there were only three black kids in the whole high school.

And yet here, people were so much more prejudiced. They made racist comments all the time. In my old neighborhood, all the kids kind of hung out together. Here everyone was segregated into groups: the jocks, the greasers, the nerds, the JAPs. I didn't fit anywhere.

It was then that I began associating being Jewish with being Jappy and snobbish. Jappy meant you had a nose job; there was a special gym class in my high school for girls who had just had their noses done. It meant you wore a lot of jewelry. It meant you had a self-important, self-involved attitude.

Although my parents tried to tell me this had nothing to do with being Jewish, it was what I saw all around me and therefore what I believed.

Jim Sleeper: As part of the Woodstock generation, I went through a terrific period of rebellion. I didn't talk to my parents for two years. It seemed to me that the whole world was collapsing with the war and that my Jewish upbringing was somewhat irrelevant. I felt that some of my Jewish identity had been an easy out for me, that I had sought a kind of refuge in this posture of Jewish pride and defiance instead of engaging my American peers on their own terms.

So I went through an assimilationist stage. Forget about Camp Ramah, about Israel, about what's good for the Jews. I just wanted to go off into this new American experiment that was launched in the sixties with rock and roll and political activism.

Shalom Goldman: At the age of seventeen, I left the whole world of orthodoxy. I gave it all up. I lived in this commune in the Village with this renegade psychoanalyst. Then I went to live in Israel. I didn't go to college until I was twenty-seven. I was a total child of the sixties.

David Elcott: My mid-sixties rebellion took the form of my becoming more observant. Judaism and radicalism became all wrapped up for me. I fit into the counterculture with my long hair and beard. But I also kept kosher and celebrated Shabbat. I put on *tefillin,* secretly at first. I didn't want my parents to see. They wouldn't have stopped me, but they would have thought it was weird.

My parents had passed on to me the feeling that we were authentic

Americans. The only time in my life that I felt an outsider was when I applied to Harvard and went to this old WASP-wealth enclave in Pasadena for an interview. Here I was, this radical kid, very obviously Jewish. We started talking and I suddenly thought, forget it, this is never going to work. We were just two other worlds.

On the one hand, I had my fantasies of having blond hair and blue eyes, of being six feet tall and being able to throw a football with a perfect spiral. I was very pulled to this Disneyland American model. But on the other hand I wasn't, and part of my rebellion, my self-affirmation, was to be very powerfully Jewish.

I grew up believing in both the American dream and the Jewish renewal dream. I never knew of anything but an open world of possibility, both as an American and as a Jew. By my time, overcoming was no longer an issue. This country was already open for us to make it and be successful.

The message I incorporated was that Judaism has an incredible contribution to make to America. Our role is to improve this world. If our Jewishness is only internal, we will have no impact on the rest of the world. If we give up our Jewishness, we became part of the majority, complacent. We are playing with that tension all the time.

(*top left*) "When my grandfather visited Israel, he kept having his picture taken with soldiers."

(*top right and middle left*) Photos of the family in Israel dressed in sundresses and shorts. "Where Europe had seemed to me a place of perpetual winter, Israel was eternal summer."

(*left*) A Jewish-American flower child in fabulous L.A.

(*bottom*) "Driving around Miami in their cream-colored convertible, my parents led what they thought was an American and not a Jewish existence."

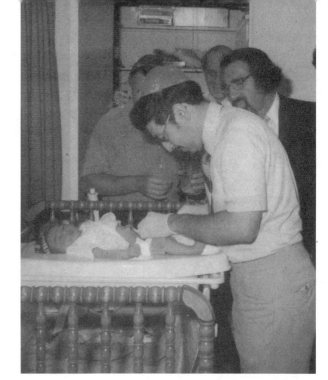

Sacred ceremony: bris in Sarasota, Florida, 1971.

Purim frolics: a contingent of Queen Esthers
with accompanying royalty.

Harvest fruits overflowing in a temple
succah as children celebrate Succoth.

THE PURITY AND SANCTITY
OF SACRED OCCASIONS:

(top) Shabbat. *(middle right)*
Erev Rosh Hashanah. *(middle
left and bottom)* Passover.

Consecration ceremony, Temple Israel, Lawrence, New York.

SACRED PLACES:

(*right top*) Synagogue in Trinidad, Colorado.

(*right middle*) The former Montefiore Temple of Salt Lake City, Utah (1882–1915), presently the Mormon Genealogical Society.

(*right bottom*) Ahavath Israel, Boise, Idaho.

Why do Americans make big bar/bat mitzvahs?

Mr. and Mrs. Charles H. Bernstein
request the honour of your presence
at the Bar-Mitzvah of their son

Ivan

Saturday morning, the twenty-seventh of November
Nineteen hundred and fifty-four
at nine o'clock
Jewish Center of Kings Highway
Avenue P at East Twelfth Street
Brooklyn, N. Y.

Open House from 3 p.m. on
at 1791 East 7th Street
Brooklyn, N. Y.

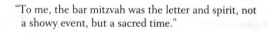

"To me, the bar mitzvah was the letter and spirit, not
a showy event, but a sacred time."

A 1980s bar mitzvah extravaganza.

Nicole Frances Bernstein

Jacquelin Bernstein
cordially invites you to share her happiness
when her daughter
Nicole
will become a Bat Mitzvah
on Saturday, the twenty-ninth of August,
Nineteen hundred and eighty-seven
at eleven o'clock in the morning
Temple Beth David
6100 Hefley Street
Westminster, California

Please join us for Kiddush immediately
following the services

"I loved the melodies of the prayers and the particular way
you had to chant the *Haftorah*."

"Part of my rebellion, my self-affirmation,
was to be very powerfully Jewish."

CONSIDERED REFLECTIONS

Marnie Bernstein: In the late 1980s, for the first time in many years, our group of formerly close, first-generation-American first cousins came together for the bar mitzvah of a cousin's son. Most of us were married by now. All were college graduates, professionals, or in business, living across the country, moving into middle age.

When we entered the temple, my cousin's wife was up on the *bimah*, reading an interfaith-sounding prayer. She had converted years before to please my aunt but remained the quintessential pure blond *shiksa*, and the children looked just like her.

We took our seats in the ultramodern sanctuary, a soaring cedar-walled and skylit A-frame, waved to one another, embraced those nearby, and turned to the printed pamphlet that contained the services. Unlike those of my childhood, they were in English, eminently rational and easy to follow. Yet my mind wandered.

I kept imagining my father, his older and younger brothers, and their sister, the youngest of all, hovering like angels in the rafters, looking down on their American progeny. That foursome with their fierce loves and relentless hatreds, their instinctive sense of theater and terrible pride—what did they think of their seemingly calm and decorous descendants in this temple that could just as easily have been a Unitarian church? What did they make of the intermarriages and divorces among us, of the ones who "dropped out" and "did their own thing," of the divisions and directions that rent a once-intimate family into so many separate parts?

Did they wonder if we remembered the legends they raised us on, of a Russia where the cherries were big as plums and the snow as high as a house, of their grandfather who could dance the kazatsky as well as the Ukrainian peasants he lived among, of the peasants who affectionately called them "our Jews" but could turn violent without pretext or regret, of their tall and handsome father whom we never saw, who died too young, whom they loved too much and mourned the rest of their lives?

Had we disappointed them? Did they lament our failure to sustain their passion and intensity? Or did they understand this is what happens in America?

Julie Sussman: All through my childhood, I felt sad that the generation of my grandparents, my grandaunts and granduncles—the whole European connection—was dying out. I had the thought that my children would know nothing about that experience except secondhand, and after them, the memory would entirely disappear. My children would never know relatives who had lived through wars and revolutions, who had gone through immigration, who had led such remarkable lives. They might be able to study Yiddish in some university, but they would never hear it as I did, moving in and out of conversations. Something important that set us apart was being lost.

Neil Postman: Some say the children of the children of the children feel less connected to their Jewishness. Some say we're expunging, we're eliminating ourselves. I don't agree.

There's always enough anti-Semitism around, and that's been a binding factor for Jews. I also don't think Jewishness is so superficial that it can be wiped out, even when I look at some of these people whose connection with Jewishness is so trivial, when their whole thing is running some sort of bazaar at the shul.

You have many cases now of intermarriage, where the children are being raised as Jews. There is also the revival of Orthodox Jewry. When I grew up, only Williamsburg was very Orthodox. Now they are many Orthodox communities, many more Chasidim, and they're much more vocal about being Jewish.

Blu Greenberg: It was deeply ingrained in me that being an Orthodox Jew was a great gift. It was never a burden for me. I had a sense of this coming down through a long line. It wasn't something of which I could say, "This doesn't count."

Al Lewis: My mother knew I wouldn't be observant, kosher. The only thing she asked of me was that wherever I am, I say *Yizkor* for her. I'm in my eighties, and I still do that.

Robert Leiter: My wife's family had always celebrated Christmas, so we put up an artificial tree. When we were dismantling it, I said to my wife, "I can't do this any more. We should be celebrating Chanukah." I thought that would be the start of our first fight, but she said, "You know, you're absolutely right."

We never looked back. My wife has been the one instrumental in our keeping kosher, lighting the candles on Friday night, going to the synagogue on Saturday. Both sides of the family think we blasted our way back into the Stone Age. But we try.

Mel Loewenstein: We had Christmas trees for our son and daughter through the years, with no religiosity connected. Until one year I said to my wife, "I think it's time for the kids to know which side of the street they're walking on. Let's not have a tree this year."

A few weeks before Christmas, my four-year-old son and I were in a crowded checkout line of a big store.

"Aren't we going to have a tree this year, Dad?" he asked.

"No, we're not, Todd."

"Why not?"

Before I could answer, he added, "Is it because we're Jewish?"

"Yes, Todd."

"But Dad," he asked, "weren't we Jewish last year?"

Neil Postman: Being Jewish is sort of what it is being a New Yorker to me. Jewish culture, history, Jewish neuroses, Jewish food, whatever—it's very rich stuff that gives texture to your life.

Alan Lelchuk: My own feeling of Jewishness coincides with my feelings of being a writer. It gives me a certain solidity in who I am as well as a freedom to be critical of our culture. It formed a major component of my rebellious identity, which is why I've never been comfortable with Jewish congregations, or organizations, or with contemporary attempts at institutionalizing. There is this double component: the positive side of the Jewishness and the positive side of the outsider. They suit me well, I think.

Neil Postman: Even in America, being Jewish means you're somewhat of an outsider. There's nothing more useful for someone who likes ideas than to be a little bit of an outsider, to say no when everyone else is saying yes, or to be able to step away and look at your own culture.

Al Lewis: People don't understand about Jews. It's not genetic; it's not that there's any more gray matter. It's that whether they are religious or not, Jews are encouraged to question. There's no such thing as you do this and this and this and don't question. The commentaries of two thousand sages say two thousand different things. Like the philosopher once said, "If they give you ruled paper, write the other way."

GLOSSARY OF
YIDDISH AND HEBREW TERMS
AND ABBREVIATIONS

aliyah—the honor of being called up to recite the blessings before and after the reading of a section of the Torah in the synagogue; the act of moving from the Diaspora to Israel

Ashkenazi (pl.: Ashkenazim)—a Jew from Germany and Eastern Europe as distinguished from a Sephardi who is of Spanish or Portuguese descent.

bar mitzvah—boy's coming-of-age ceremony

bat mitzvah—girl's coming-of-age ceremony

bentsh—to bless

berachah—blessing

beroigus—angry, a feud

berrieh—woman of remarkable energy and competence; an exemplary housekeeper

bimah—altar with Ark containing Torah scrolls

borscht—beet soup

bris—ritual circumcision

bubby—affectionate term for grandmother

chachmas—tactics

chai—life; Hebrew letter whose numerical equivalent is 18

challah—braided white bread used on Sabbath

Chanukah—eight-day winter holiday commemorating the victory of the Macabees over the Syrian Greeks 165 BCE

Chanukah gelt—money given as Chanukah gifts

charoses—mixture usually of apples, nuts, and wine used in the seder to represent mortar employed by Hebrew slaves in Egypt

Chasidim—Jews who belong to a sect that is distinguished by Old World dress, devotion to a rebbe, and emotional religious observances.

chazzen—cantor, trained professional singer who assists the rabbi in religious services

chrane—horseradish

Chumash—Bible

chuppa—wedding canopy under which bride and groom take their vows

daven—to pray

derma—stuffing in a casing

"El Moley Rachamim"—memorial prayer recited at cemetery

erev—the time commencing with sundown the night before Shabbat or a holiday, signifying the start of sacred time

estrog—fragrant citron, lemonlike fruit used with lulav on Succoth *flayshedig*—meat, poultry, or food made with animal fat, which, according to Kosher laws, may not be eaten or prepared with dairy foods

The *Forward*—longtime Yiddish newspaper, now an English as well as Yiddish weekly

fraylich—happy, also a dance

Galitziana—someone from Galicia, Poland

glus tay—glass of tea

goldeneh medina—America, the golden land

Gemara—an elaboration and commentary on the Mishnah, a compilation of oral laws made at the close of the second century A.D. Together they form the Talmud.

goy, pl. goyim—colloquial for gentile

greena—new immigrant

gut yuntif—happy holiday

Haftorah—a prophetic passage read in the synagogue on holidays and the Sabbath that is thematically linked to the Torah portion proscribed for that day

Haggadah—lit. "telling," the narrative of the Exodus read at the Passover seder with prayers, songs, and directions for observances

haimish—homelike; unpretentious

hamantashen—triangular pastries eaten on Purim, named after hat worn by villain Haman

Havdalah—ceremony at close of Sabbath

High Holidays, High Holy Days, Days of Awe—Rosh Hashanah and Yom Kippur

Kaddish—memorial prayer recited every day for a year following an intimate family member's death, on the yearly anniversary of the death, and as part of Yizkor *kibbitzer*—joker, teaser

Kiddush—prayers and ceremony that sanctifies Sabbath, Holy days, and events, usually made over wine

kineahora—protection against the evil eye

kipah—skull cap (also yarmulke)

kishka—see derma

Kol Nidre—prayer in the form of a legal formula which initiates Yom Kippur and releases the individual from all unfulfilled vows made to God over the past year

kreplach—dumplings filled with meat or cheese

landsman, landsleit (pl.)—person who comes from the same area in Europe

latkes—pancakes

lehrer—teacher

Lubavitcher—member of a Chasidic sect

lulav—a combination of palm branch, willow, and myrtle twigs used with estrog on Succoth

machitza—curtain in an Orthodox synagogue that separates the women's section from the men

mama-loshen—the "mother tongue," Yiddish as differentiated from Loshen-Koidesh—the sacred language, Hebrew

matzoh—unleavened bread eaten during Passover

mazel tov—congratulations

mensch—a person of character and humanity

meshgiach—person who certifies that food, its preparation and service, is Kosher

Meshiach—Messiah

meshuga—crazy

mezuzah—little oblong-shaped object affixed to a doorpost or hung around the neck which contains verses from Deuteronomy printed on a tiny scroll

minyan—group of ten required for public prayer

mishpocheh—extended family

mitzvah—divine commandment; colloq.: blessing, good deed

mohel—ritual circumciser

motzi—blessing over bread to be recited at each meal

narr—fool

narrishkeit—foolishness

nu—"Well?"

Palmah—mobilized force of the Haganah which operated from 1941 through 1948

payess—earlocks worn by Chasidic males

Pesach—Passover

pishke—little box for coins collected for charity

Purim—holiday in March celebrating Queen Esther's rescue of the Jews from the villain Haman

rebbe—leader of Chasidic sect

Rosh Hashanah—Festival of the New Year; along with Yom Kippur part of the Days of Awe, High Holy Days

Satmar—a Chasidic sect

schav—sorrel soup

seder—ritual ceremony and meal on Passover

Sephardi (pl.: Sephardim)—Jews of Spanish and Portuguese descent

Shabbos, Shabbat—Sabbath

Shabbos goy—gentile who performs acts on Shabbat for an observant Jew that she or he is prohibited from doing

shammes—sexton

shanda—shame

Shema—prayer that affirms belief in monotheism. It begins: "Hear, oh Israel, the Lord our God, the Lord is one."

Shevuoth—commemoration of the Revelation at Mt. Sinai and the festival of the first fruits of the harvest

shiddach—arranged marriage

shiksa—gentile girl

shivah—mourning period

shlep—drag

shmura matzoh—handmade matzoh

Shoah—Holocaust

shochet—ritual slaughterer

shofar—ram's horn blown on Rosh Hashanah and at the conclusion of Yom Kippur

shtetl—little Jewish village in Eastern Europe

shul—synagogue

shviger—mother-in-law

Siddur—prayer book

simcha—celebration

Simchat Torah—Festival of rejoicing over the Torah

succah—outdoor booth where family dines during Succoth, which serves as a reminder of the temporary housing lived in during the period of the Exodus

Succoth—Feast of Tabernacles, seven- or eight-day harvest festival

tallit—prayer shawl

Talmud—a religious and legal code that explicates the Torah

Talmud Torah—Hebrew school held after regular school hours

tefillin—phylacteries: two boxes containing portions of the Torah affixed to the head and left arm with leather straps in a prescribed manner

tikkun olam—"repair of the world"

Torah—a handwritten scroll containing the five books of Moses: Genesis, Exodus, Leviticus, Numbers, and Deuteronomy

trayf—not kosher

tsuris—troubles

tzedaka—charity

tzitzit—ritual fringes affixed to tallit and a short, jacketlike garment worn by Orthodox males

verenykes—Russian-style dumplings

yahrtzeit—yearly anniversary of a family member's death

yarmulke—skullcap; see also kipah

yeshiva—school where both religious and secular subjects are taught

Yidden—Jews

Yiddishkeit—the ethos of Eastern European Jewish culture

Yiddishe kup—lit.: Jewish head; colloq.: clever

Yizkor—memorial service held in the synagogue on Yom Kippur and the final day of Passover, Shevuoth, and Succoth

Yom Kippur—The Day of Atonement, the most sacred day in the calendar, devoted to fasting and prayer; along with Rosh Hashanah, one of the High Holy Days or Days of Awe

yuntif—holiday

zayde—affectionate term for grandfather

BIBLIOGRAPHY

Ausubel, Nathan. *The Book of Jewish Knowledge*. New York: Crown Publishers, 1964.

Dimont, Max I. *The Jews in America*. New York: Touchstone, Simon & Schuster, 1978.

Lipman, Eugene J. *The Mishnah: Oral Traditions of Judaism*. New York: Schocken Books, 1974.

Riemer, Jack, and Stampfer, Nathaniel, eds. *Ethical Wills: A Modern Jewish Treasury*. New York: Schocken Books, 1983.

Rosten, Leo. *The Joys of Yiddish*. New York: McGraw-Hill, 1968.

Shamir, Ilana, and Shlomo Shavits, eds. *Encyclopedia of Jewish History*. New York: Facts on File, 1986.

PHOTO CREDITS

collection *(bottom right)* Marc Angel. PAGES 102–103, LEFT TO RIGHT: *(top)* Archive photo; Frommer collection; Solomon Aidelson/Temple Hillel, North Woodmere, New York *(middle)* Frommer collection; Brooks Susman/Temple Israel, Lawrence, New York; Linda Katz Ephraim *(bottom)* American Jewish Archives/Leo Baeck Institute; Brooks Susman/Temple Israel, Lawrence, New York. PAGE 104: *(top)* American Jewish Archives *(bottom)* Brooks Susman/Temple Israel, Lawrence, New York. PAGE 114: *(top)* American Jewish Archives/Abraham Peck collection *(bottom)* American Jewish Archives/Leo Baeck Institute. PAGE 131: American Jewish Archives/ Abraham Peck collection. PAGE 132: *(top)* Archive photo *(bottom left)* Frommer collection *(bottom right)* Linda Katz Ephraim. PAGE 145: Linda Katz Ephraim. PAGES 146–147, LEFT TO RIGHT: *(top)* Barbara Kreiger; Frommer collection; Frommer collection *(middle)* Frommer collection; Frommer collection; Dan Kossoff; Helen Fried Goldstein; Frommer collection *(bottom)* Roger Harris; Brooks Susman/Temple Israel, Lawrence, New York; Dan Kossoff. PAGE 148: *(top)* Frommer collection *(bottom)* Ansie Sokoloff. PAGE 167: Is Crystal. PAGE 168: *(top)* Gail Eiseman Bernstein *(bottom left)* Brooks Susman/Temple Israel, Lawrence, New York *(bottom right)* Helen Fried Goldstein. PAGE 184: *(top)* Karl Bernstein *(bottom left)* Frommer collection *(bottom right)* Alex and Terry Rosin. PAGE 200: *(top and middle)* Frommer collection *(bottom left)* Bel Kaufman *(bottom right)* Barbara Kreiger. PAGE 222: *(top)* Dan Kossoff *(bottom left)* Jeff Rubin *(bottom right)* Archive photo. CREDITS FOR INSERT FOLLOWING PAGE 237: PAGE 1: *(top left and middle)* Frommer collection *(top right)* Linda Katz Ephraim *(bottom left)* Eileen Ewing *(bottom right)* Alicia Devora. PAGE 2: *(top)* Dan Kossoff *(middle left)* Gail Eiseman Bernstein *(middle right)* Linda Katz Ephraim *(bottom)* Frommer collection. PAGE 3: *(top)* Alex and Terry Rosin *(middle and bottom)* Brooks Susman/Temple Israel, Lawrence, New York. PAGE 4: *(left)* Brooks Susman/Temple Israel, Lawrence, New York *(top, middle, and bottom right)* Kenny Allisberg. PAGE 5: *(top, middle, and bottom left)* Frommer collection *(top right)* Dan Kossoff *(middle right)* Karl Bernstein. PAGE 6: *(top and right)* Frommer collection *(middle)* Karl Bernstein *(bottom)* Dan Kossoff. PAGE 7: *(top and bottom)* New York Metropolitan Region, United Synagogue of Conservative Judaism *(middle)* Solomon Aidelson/Temple Hillel, North Woodmere, New York.

ACKNOWLEDGMENTS

This—our third oral history—depended, like the first two, on an extraordinary group of individuals who generously shared their memories and reflections. Our thanks to them all.

Leonard Goldstein and Sidney Helfant not only participated in this work but lent also their expertise to the transliteration and usage of Yiddish and Hebrew terms—a most challenging task. We are most appreciative.

We are often asked how we choose our subjects. Many times they come to us through the recommendation of someone who knows someone with a great story. For leads that immeasurably enhanced this book we thank Karl Bernstein, Aaron Bisno, David Bisno, Fred Frommer, Caroline Katz Mount, Mel Loewenstein, Abraham Peck, Roz Starr, Brooks Susman, Nicki Tanner, Doris Modell Tipograph, and Harold Wolchok.

For the visual component, we are grateful to all those interviewees who lent us their precious family photographs and memorabilia. In addition, we thank Solomon Aidelson, Kenny Allisberg, Bruce Greenfield, Harriet Lesser, Kevin Proffitt, and Brooks Susman for supplying us with photographs.

Thanks to our agent, Don Congdon, who was there for us throughout, and to Candace Hodges and Maggie DeMaegd at Harcourt Brace for their patience and encouragement. Thanks also to Lydia D'moch and Vaughn Andrews for their vision. Finally, we thank our editor, John Radziewicz. This book was his idea—even though he didn't "grow up Jewish in America"— and it profits from his wit, guidance, and unerring taste.

INDEX

NOTE: *Page numbers in italics indicate speakers in this oral history*

Detroit, Michigan, 67
Devora, Alicia, xv, *213–14*
Diary of Anne Frank, The, 124
Divorce, 239
Doctors, 160–63
Dorchester, Massachusetts, 37–39
Dressner, Rabbi Samuel, 30
Drucker Rosin, Terry, xv, *45–47*, *171*,
     226–27
Duluth, Minnesota, 70–76, 157–59, 174–75,
     185, 193

E

Eban, Abba, 137
Education:
     college, 35–36, 58–59, 76, 161, 207, 211,
          219, 233, 237
     importance of, 30, 35, 48, 137, 218,
          232–33, 234
     night school, 71
     private schools, 94, 95, 161, 229
     religious, *see* Religious education
     secular, 7, 9–10, 15–16, 17, 34, 61,
          68–69, 72, 88, 89–90, 94, 232
Eichmann, Adolf, trial of, 131
Eiseman Bernstein, Gail, xv, *90*, *94–96*, *178*,
     193
Elcott, David, xv, *65*, *129–30*, *228*, *236–37*
Entebbe, rescue at, 143
Ephraim, Linda Katz, *see* Katz Ephraim,
     Linda
Ethical Culturists, 94, 195, 229
Exodus (Uris), 124

F

Family, reverence for, 234
Family roots, stories about, 201–22, 240
Farming, 59, 63
Fixer, The (Malamud), 12
Flu epidemic of 1918, 14
Food, 26–27, 35, 36, 63, 67, 70, 83, 108,
     206, 208–9, 212
     delicatessens, 67, 70, 83, 88, 157–60
     holiday, 15, 36, 46, 78, 108, 158, 169,
          175–76, 177, 178, 179
     kiddush, 185, 188
     kosher, *see* Kosher, keeping
     in New York City, 70, 83–84, 88, 96, 98
     Sabbath, 15, 42, 159, 183
     trayf, 74

Forward, The, 47, 73, 106, 107, 136
Fraternities, 69
Freed, Jason, xv, *143–44*, *179–80*
Freehof, Solomon B., 69
Fried Goldstein, Helen, xv, *175–76*, *192–93*
Friedman, Addi, xv, *116–17*, *118–19*, *135*,
     181, *217–19*
Friedman, Morris, xv, *85*, *93–94*, *151*, *231*
Furriers, 217

G

Galiziana, 25, 207
Gambling, 66, 67–68, 208
Gangs, 7, 58
Gangsters, 66–67, 84–85
Garfield, John, 86
Garment center workers, 151
Gemara, 166
Gershwin, George, 220
Girick, Jack, 14, 15
Glossary of Yiddish and Hebrew terms and
     abbreviations, 243–50
Goichberg, Israel, 191–92
Gold, Ann, xv, *152–53*
Goldberg, Marcia Lee, xv, *123*, *219*
Goldman, Shalom, xv, *25–26*, *87*, *97–99*,
     149, *169*, *175–76*, *178*, *180*, *185*,
     196, *236*
Goldstein, Helen Fried, *see* Fried Goldstein,
     Helen
Goldstein, Leonard, xvi, *65–66*
Goodbye, Columbus, 28
Goodman, Percival, 30
Gottsegen, Dorothy, *117–18*
"Greena," 12, 71
Greenberg, Blu, xvi, *76–79*, *117*, *241*
Greenberg, Irving (Yitz), xvi, *112*, *120–21*,
     122–23, *135*, *165–66*, *227–28*, *230*,
     232, *233–34*

H

Haftorah, 185, 186, 193, 196, 197, 198
Haggadah, 178
Harris, Roger, xvi, *223–24*
Harvard College, 35–36, 41, 237
Havdalah, 182
Hebrew Immigrant Aid Society, 10, 58, 70
Hebrew language, 2, 205
     glossary of Yiddish and Hebrew terms and
          abbreviations, 243–50

O

O'Dwyer, William, 155
Old age homes, 98
Omaha, Nebraska, 60–61
Orphans, 14–17, 121
Orthodox Jews, 66, 72, 79, 87, 95, 141, 230, 241
   practices of, 26, 31, 57
   revival of Orthodox Jewry, 240
   see also Synagogues, Orthodox
Ostentation, avoidance of, 28, 61
Outsider, sense of being, *see* Minority group, sense of being part of

P

Packer Collegiate Institute, 95
Palestine, *see* Israel
Passing, 10, 162, 219, 227
Passover, 176–78
   dishes for, 177–78
   food for, 46, 108, 158, 177, 178
   seder, 58, 60, 164, 177–78, 213
Payess, 27
Peck, Abraham, xviii, *127–30, 132, 133, 194*
Peddlers, 10, 59, 62, 63, 72, 73, 76, 152
Performers, 154–55
   see also Yiddish theater
Perlstein Marcus, Ruth, xviii, *120, 149*
Pesach, *see* Passover
Philadelphia, Pennsylvania, 162, 195
Physicians, 160–63
Picon, Molly, 85
Pishkes, 105–6, 117, 139
Pittsburgh, Pennsylvania, 67–70
   Squirrel Hill section, 67, 68–69
Polio, 212
Politics, 106–13
Polner, Murray, xix, *83, 84, 86, 88, 106, 107, 110, 111, 112, 174, 175, 186, 234*
Popkin, Sam, xix, 66–67
Portnoy, Eric, xix, 32, *196–97, 230*
Portnoy, Sylvia Skoler, *see* Skoler Portnoy, Sylvia
Postman, Neil, xix, *83, 84, 88–89, 90, 91–92, 111–12, 117, 188–90, 201–2, 221, 230, 240, 241, 242*
Professionals, 61, 160–63, 221
Proselytizing by Christians, 47
Prospect Club, 92

Pueblo, Colorado, 63–65
Purim, 38, 176
Pushcarts, 29, 98

Q

Queens, New York, 198
   Far Rockaway, 93, 235
   Flushing, 89
   Ridgewood, 117–18
Quincy, Massachusetts, 32–33, 210

R

Rabbis, 7, 9, 30, 69, 77, 87, 92–93, 98, 139, 164–66, 187
   attacks on, 38
   ordination of women as, 164
   role of, 149
   Zionism and, 141, 142
Ranchers, 43–44
Rebelliousness, 236, 237, 242
Reflections, 239–42
Reform Judaism, 59, 69, 140–41
   see also Synagogues, Reform
Religious education, 7, 9, 35, 38, 44, 46, 48, 78, 163–64, 181, 190–92, 195, 218
   for bar mitzvah, 186–88, 196–97, 198, 234
   Christian, 44, 46, 47
   for girls, 192, 193
   in New York City, 93–94
   studying the Talmud, 164, 165, 207, 208
   yeshivas, 93, 97–99, 232, 234
Religious services, 15, 18, 29–30, 37, 60, 87, 159, 180, 181, 207, 241
   on High Holy Days, 170–74, 207
   minyan for, 62, 76, 91, 95, 198
   on Sunday, 46
Rellis, Abe, 84
Republicans, 111–12
Reuther, Walter, 67
Rich, Frank, xix, *124, 125, 141–42, 196, 201, 219, 220*
Ridgewood, Queens, 117–18
Robinson, Jackie, 86
Robinson Wolchok, Brenda, xix, *50, 51, 171, 174*
Romanoites, 171
Roosevelt, Franklin D., 110, 112–13, 118

Rosenbergs, 231
Rosh Hashanah, *see* High Holy Days
Rosin, Alex, xix, *42–44, 50, 171, 187–88*
Rosin, Terry Drucker, *see* Drucker Rosin, Terry
Roth, Philip, 219
Rubin, Jeff, xix, 25, *37–39*
Ruppert, Jack, 12–13

S

Sabbath, 15, 31, 44, 159, 169, 178–83, 209–10, 236
   food, 15, 42, 159, 183
   lighting of candles, 44, 179, 180, 183, 206, 241
Sager, David, xix, *220–21*
St. John, George, 10
St. Louis, Missouri, 10–11, 141, 160–61, 175
Salesman, 25, 151, 153, 216
Salk, Jonas, 231
Salvation Army, 21–22
Saposnik, Irv, xix, *86–87, 106, 139, 177–78, 228, 234*
Sarasota, Florida, 44, 50, 187–88
Satmar Chasidim, 87
Savannah, Georgia, 47–48, 51, 171, 174
Schecter, Solomon, 93
Schein movie theaters, 21
Schenectady, New York, 11
Schlecter, Susan Levin, *see* Levin Schlecter, Susan
Schwartz, Fred, 69
Seattle, Washington, 76–80, 181–82, 193–94
Sephardic Jews, 28, 77–78, 79, 87, 181–82, 193–94, 208, 210
Serels, Mitchell, xix, *94, 144*
Services, *see* Religious services
Shabbat, *see* Sabbath
Shabbos goy, 180
Shammes, 91–92, *172, 174–75*
Shankerman, Rabbi, 196–97
Sharlitt, Michael, 16
Shavuoth, 169
Shelton, Connecticut, 28–29, 226
Shiddach, 150
Shiksa, 75, 230
Shivah, 42
Shlogn kapores, 172

Shoah, 108, 115–33, 136, 194
Shochet, 7, 83, 124, 149–50, 166
Shofar, 31, 69
Sholem Aleichem schools, 190–91, 202
Shul, *see* Synagogues
Silver, Abba Hillel, 119, 141
Simchat Torah, 176
Singer, Isaac Bashevis, 25, 191
Six-Day War, 144
Skoler, Moe, xix, *33, 34, 35, 36, 152, 201, 210, 211*
Skoler Portnoy, Sylvia, xx, *32–33, 34–35, 36, 172, 210–11, 227*
Skolnik, Menashe, 85
Sleeper, Jim, xx, *26, 30–31, 122, 131, 142–43, 152, 196, 211, 223, 225, 227, 232, 236*
Social life, 57–58, 59
   dating, 74
   exclusion from sororities, 51–52
   with other Jewish children, 45, 48, 51–52, 74
Socialism, 106–7, 110, 111, 119, 190
Sokoloff, Ansie, xx, *41–42, 52, 54–55, 173*
Solender, Samuel Solomon, 121
Solender, Stephen, xx, *121–22, 133, 135*
Solomon, Jeff, xx, *122, 132, 159–60, 194–95, 232*
Sororities, 51–52, 70
South Carolina, 45–47, 185
South Dakota, 59–60
Southerners, 41–53
Springfield, Massachusetts, 30–31
Squirrel Hill section, Pittsburgh, 67, 68–69
Starr, Roz, xx, *85, 150–51, 178, 179, 212–13*
Stein, Marv, xx, *63–65*
Stickball, 91
Storekeepers and store owners, 7, 8, 11, 22, 28, 29, 36–37, 41–45, 49, 59, 62, 63, 70, 72, 76, 117, 153–54, 204–5, 207, 210
Straus, Pittsburgh Phil, 84
Succahs, 175
Succoth, 174–76
Summer camp, 47, 235
Superior, Wisconsin, 70
Superstitions, 206, 212–13, 214, 234
Susman, Brooks, xx, *67–68, 69–70, 122, 132*
Sussman, Julie, xx, *197–98, 235–36, 240*

Synagogues, 46, 60, 92–93, 160
    Ashkenazic, 77, 78
    Conservative, 29, 30, 38, 47, 65, 66
    Orthodox, 29, 31, 47, 48, 57, 62, 66, 73,
        95, 165, 169, 170–71, 174, 189
    Reform, 32, 47, 48, 69, 73, 94–95, 164,
        175, 229
    Sephardic, 78, 87, 208
    ultramodern, 239

T

Tallit, 69, 172
Tanner, Nicki, xx, 228–29, 232
Taylor, Estelle, 20, 21
Taylor, Phyllis, xxi, *125*, *132*, *195*, *227*, *228*,
    229, *230*, 235
Tefillin, 65, 159, 187, 193, 198, 236
Texas, 61–62
Thaler Abrams, May, xxi, *180*
Tikkun olam, 105–12
Tipograph, Doris Modell, *see* Modell
    Tipograph, Doris
Tipograph, Norman, xxi, *186*, *190*
Toledo, Ohio, 66–67
Tomashefsky, Boris, 85
Toubin, Leon, xxi, *61–62*, *156–57*, *187*
Tracy, Arthur, 20–21
Trains:
    food arriving by, 46
    riding, 19–22
Trayf, 74
Trenton, New Jersey, 65–66
Tzedaka, 31, 188
Tzitzit, 27

U

Union Temple, Brooklyn, 94–95, 96
United Jewish Appeal, 58

V

Vacations, 160
Values, 28
Vaudeville, 11

W

Walker, Jimmy, 155
Waterbury, Connecticut, 127–28, 129
Wechsler, Max, xxi, *1–2*, *96*, *126–27*, *182–83*
Weizmann, Chaim, 136–37, 140
West Virginia, 8, 9
Wilson, Mookie, 199
Winer, Joshua, xxi, *25–26*, *36–37*
Wise, Rabbi Stephen, 119, 164
Wolchok, Brenda Robinson, *see* Robinson
    Wolchok, Brenda
Wolsey, Rabbi Louis, 164
Workmen's Circle, 74, 190–91
World War II, 92, 108, 115–33, 189
    Holocaust, 108, 115–33, 135, 194
Wouk, Herman, 204

Y

Yaffee, Robert, xxi, *60–61*, *197*
Yahrtzeit glasses, 2
Yankee Jews, 25–39, 225
Yarmulke, 69, 190
Yeshivas, 93, 97–99, 232, 234
Yiddish language:
    glossary of Yiddish and Hebrew terms and
        abbreviations, 243–50
Yiddish language, 2, 66, 140, 228, 240
Yiddish stories, 191–92
Yiddish theater, 14, 74, 85–86, 202–3
Yizkor, 173–74, 241
Yom Kippur, *see* High Holy Days
Yom Kippur War, 144
Youth organizations, Jewish, 48
Yud, Nochum, 204
Yuntif, *see* Holidays

Z

Zametkin, Clara, 107
Zatz, Ludwig, 85
Zionism, 11, 66, 74, 136–37, 140–41, 142,
    164, 205, 233
    see also Israel